ASPECTS OF MODERN LANGUAGE TEACHING IN EUROPE

Language teachers and researchers into language teaching have come together from four European countries to pool their knowledge about major concerns confronting language teachers today. Four principal areas are covered: the classroom itself, its challenges and ways of confronting them; the teaching of grammar; the teaching and learning of vocabulary and idioms; and the use of modern innovative techniques and computer resources.

The first section covers language learning strategies and computer-assisted learning. The second section aims to answer questions facing all language teachers – how to encourage learners to learn, how to correct mistakes and how to bring a foreign country alive in the classroom. The third section attempts to demythologize grammar teaching, and examines the value of theoretical linguistics. The final section offers practical advice on vocabulary learning, explores how different varieties of dictionaries can make valuable contributions, and suggests ways of teaching and using idiomatic phrases.

Wolf Gewehr is Professor of Applied Linguistics at the University of Münster, Germany.

Contributors: Lothar Bunn; Georgia Catsimali; Pamela Faber; Wilhelm Grießhaber; Catalina Jiménez Hurtado; Manuel Jiménez Raya; Linus Jung; Terry Lamb; Carlos F. Márquez Linares; Antony J. Peck; Paul Seedhouse; Elke Stracke-Elbina; Sophia Zevgoli.

ASPECTS OF MODERN LANGUAGE TEACHING IN EUROPE

Edited by Wolf Gewehr
with
Georgia Catsimali, Pamela Faber
Manuel Jiménez Raya
and
Antony J. Peck
(Chief Consultant)

London and New York

First published 1998 by Routledge
11 New Fetter Lane, London EC4P 4EE

Simultaneously published in the USA and Canada
by Routledge
29 West 35th Street, New York, NY 10001

Typeset in Garamond by
Solidus (Bristol) Limited
Printed and bound in Great Britain by
TJ International Ltd, Padstow, Cornwall

British Library Cataloguing in Publication Data
A catalogue record for this book is available from the British Library

Library of Congress Cataloguing in Publication Data
Aspects of modern language teaching in Europe / edited by Wolf Gewehr.
p.   cm.
Based on the results of The German, Greek, English, Spanish
Teacher-Training Project which was conducted 1993–1996.
Includes bibliographical references and index.
1. Languages, Modern–Study and teaching–Europe. I. Gewehr,
Wolf. II. German, Greek, English, Spanish Teacher-Training Project.
PB38.E8A85   1998
418'.007'04–dc21   97-18038
                                    CIP

ISBN 0-415-17283-7 (hbk)
ISBN 0-415-17284-5 (pbk)

CONTENTS

CONTRIBUTORS

Lothar Bunn teaches German and philosophy at a German high school. He spent several years as a DAAD teacher at the University of Coimbra (Portugal) where he developed some innovative ideas for FL projects.

Georgia Catsimali lectures in theoretical and applied linguistics at the University of Crete in Rethymno (Greece). She was the representative of Greece, one of the four partners for the LINGUA project which is described in the Introduction.

Pamela Faber lectures at the translation faculty of the University of Granada in applied linguistics. She holds degrees from the University of North Carolina, the University of Granada and the University of Paris IV. She has taught English as a foreign language at the University of Granada, and is presently doing research in lexical semantics.

Wolf Gewehr lectures in applied linguistics at the University of Münster (Germany), and holds degrees from the University of Colorado, the University of Washington and the University of Münster. He is involved in language teacher education and also teaches German as a foreign language. He is one of the founders of the new Language Centre at the University of Münster.

Wilhelm Grießhaber lectures in applied linguistics and is head of the Language Centre at the University of Münster (Germany). His main research is in computer-assisted FL teaching with special emphasis on languages for special purposes (for example, law, economy, medicine, etc.).

Catalina Jiménez Hurtado lectures in German and translation at the translation faculty of the University of Granada (Spain). She is a graduate of the University of Granada, where she obtained her Ph.D. in pragmatics and lexical semantics. She is at present involved in dictionary research.

Manuel Jiménez Raya has many years of experience teaching English as a foreign language at secondary level. His principal research interests are in foreign language teaching and learner autonomy. He is a professor in the

English Department of the University of Granada (Spain) and at present lectures in language teaching methodology and applied linguistics.

Linus Jung holds degrees from the University of Granada and the University of Heidelberg. He teaches German language and Civilization in Granada and has collaborated with the University of Granada in research projects. He is at present working on his Ph.D. thesis.

Terry Lamb used to teach German as a foreign language at Belper High School in Nottingham (England) and is now a lecturer in the Department of Education at the University of Nottingham.

Carlos F. Márquez Linares holds a degree in English language and literature from the University of Granada and has an MA in lexicography from the University of Exeter. He is an assistant professor at the University of Córdoba (Spain) where he teaches uses and varieties of English.

Antony J. Peck used to be a senior lecturer and teacher trainer for French and German at the Language Teaching Centre at the University of York (England). He is well known not only for his book publications for language teachers, but also for his media work, especially a television series which was broadcast by the BBC.

Paul Seedhouse holds a doctorate from the University of York where he is a lecturer in English as a foreign language at the Norwegian Study Centre. His research interest is in the description of verbal interaction in TEFL.

Elke Stracke-Elbina teaches English and French in the Language Centre at the University of Münster (Germany). Her research concentrates on languages for special purposes and on language learners' autonomy by computer-assisted teaching strategies.

Sophia Zevgoli (MA) is a postgraduate at the University of Athens (Greece) and is at present studying for her Ph.D. at the University of Cambridge. Her main research interest is in teaching modern languages, especially English and German, in comparison with Modern Greek.

ACKNOWLEDGEMENTS

First of all, we would like to thank the Socrates and Youth Bureau and the European Commission for their cooperation and financial assistance that enabled us to carry out the research and seminars, the results of which are reflected in this book.

We also express our gratitude to Gillian Donmall (University of Derby) who was the initiator of this three-year LINGUA project and whose dedication and commitment brought the team together, and who, as President of the Association for Language Awareness, helped give the project its present orientation.

We thank especially Antony J. Peck for his work as chief adviser. His extensive experience in foreign language teacher training at the University of York is evident throughout the entire structure of this book.

We also thank all of the participants in the research seminars, whose work and ideas, although not directly reflected in this publication, were important to its success.

Last but not least, we thank our wives and husbands for the patience they have shown during the entire period of the work.

INTRODUCTION

General remarks

The importance of languages for effective communication between peoples has been accorded increased recognition recently in view of the changes currently taking place within the European Union (EU). As national boundaries vanish, language barriers are slowly disappearing as European citizens are being encouraged to acquire bilingual (or trilingual) competence. Governments are giving higher priority than ever before to languages in the school curriculum. Nevertheless, few would dispute that the teaching and learning of second (and third) languages is capable of improvement. In view of the increased facility for gaining employment in an EU country, the time is ripe to prepare teachers of a given language to teach that language successfully in the context of any EU country. However, this can only come about when foreign language (FL) teachers from different countries have the opportunity to exchange ideas and share classroom experiences.

As foreign language teachers in a European context, we not only teach students to communicate; we also help them to find the key which will enable them to enter the cultural world of the foreign language they are in the process of learning. It is interesting to emphasize, however, that this new world, always within a European context, has both similarities with and differences from the one students are already familiar with through their mother tongue. In a sense, this is also true with regard to language teaching methodology. Although each of us FL teachers operates in a specific context, we also share a great deal because those contexts are similar in that they are pan-European.

Traditionally, developments in FL methodology have originated under the auspices of the teaching of English as a foreign/second language, but we have found that interesting experiences have also taken place in relation to the teaching of other languages. Through this cross-fertilization of ideas and experience of both theoreticians and practitioners, much can be learned.

This book is based on the results of The German, Greek, English, Spanish Teacher-Training Project, a LINGUA project in which FL teachers from four countries participated over a period of three years. It is in part a reflection of our efforts to surmount language barriers and at the same time stimulate European awareness.

The German, Greek, English, Spanish Teacher Training Project

In coming together to share our experiences within the framework of this project, one of our principal aims was to examine approaches to FL teaching in our respective countries, and in this way compare to what extent they coincided. It was our wish ultimately to produce something new for the wider European forum in the area of pilot training courses for secondary school FL teachers in Europe.

The main objectives of this project were as follows:

1   to design programmes and develop courses for the in-service training of secondary school FL teachers of German, Spanish, English and Modern Greek;
2   to promote the exchange of teachers and staff on courses, and to establish frameworks for further cooperative ventures between teachers and learners of all four countries;
3   to promote cross-cultural knowledge and awareness within Europe and to promote positive attitudes towards language teaching and learning.

The participating countries (Germany, Spain, England and Greece) each had a team consisting of a project manager, assistants, advisers, academic colleagues, and secondary school teachers of each of the four languages involved. In the three years of the project's duration, the activity and interaction of the national groups was intense, both on a European and a national scale.

Given that there were so many people involved, the organization had to be carefully planned and activities monitored. From 1993 to 1996, research was carried out in each country, materials were exchanged, and workshops were held in Crete, Derby and Münster where findings were disseminated. In Crete and Derby, this was done strictly among the members of the national groups within the project, and then in Münster, the context was widened and FL teachers from all the countries involved were invited to a workshop.

History

In the initial months of the project, we found that the first thing to be done was simply for us to find out about each other. The task of each group was thus to draw up documentation which included a detailed description of the following items in each country:

1   educational system
2   role of FL teachers
3   specific teaching goals
4   syllabi
5   materials used
6   assessment and examinations
7   current practice concerning in-service training courses, as well as course content and methodology.

Insofar as differences went, there were two kinds: first, differences specific to the particular language being taught, and second, differences specific to the country in which each of us was teaching.

We found that the combination of two languages which have received extensive treatment, together with two which have not benefited to the same degree, formed a useful working basis. Some established practices related to English and German were usefully questioned, while Greek and Spanish profited from the work already carried out on the other two languages involved. Moreover, we were all anxious to promote the teaching and learning of Greek and Spanish.

Despite manifest differences between languages and countries, we nevertheless found that there were also many similarities. Specific problems were discussed which seemed to arise for us all, such as overly large classes, unmotivated students, insufficient classroom time, and inappropriate materials not well adapted to a European context. We also came to the conclusion that many of these difficulties could be overcome by adopting a more learner-centred approach to FL teaching; in other words, by concentrating more on the process of learning than on its product. From this type of perspective, education would be identified with the promotion of the development of learners. The role of the teacher would be ultimately to control their own learning processes, and even to continue to do so once the schooling period had finished.

Furthermore, all the language teachers participating in the workshop shared an intense interest in transmitting culture through language teaching because knowledge of any foreign language ought to be more than having a certain familiarity with its grammar. The capacity to communicate in a language necessarily implies knowing about the way of life and the cultural traditions of the people who speak it. For this reason, the study of culture should be fully integrated into the study of a foreign language. Learning about the FL culture has the advantage of making students more aware of their own, as they compare the two language cultures. It was agreed that the most effective way to make similarities and differences between cultures meaningful was to present them from a European perspective.

We also discussed the need to produce European-oriented teaching materials not just for English and German (where such materials already exist), but also for other languages, such as Spanish and Modern Greek. The fact was mentioned that as European citizens become increasingly multi-lingual, there is the danger that linguistic dexterity may not be associated with adequate knowledge and sensivity to associated cultures. For this reason, we decided that it was vitally necessary for this project to place emphasis on cultures as well as on languages so as to ensure harmonious accommodation of citizens of one cultural community in another.

Once we had found out about each other and the educational system in each country, we carried out a needs analysis for each second language via a questionnaire. Pupils were asked about their needs with reference to teachers and subject matter. Teachers were also asked about their needs with regard to training. This was of great help because it confirmed the validity of a pedagogical approach directed at communicative performance in a wide range of normal life circumstances in accordance with goals widely subscribed to by learners as well as the teaching profession.

With this in mind, we began to record what we considered to be instances of successful practice in teaching. This was carried out through reports, combined with video recordings of lessons, as well as cassette recordings of interviews. The findings of each team were presented in a summer workshop in Crete. Areas of disagreement and uncertainty were noted as well as those of agreement.

The ultimate result of all this work was the design, elaboration and subsequent implementation of an international pilot in-set course for FL teachers. This course, called 'Innovative Aspects of Modern Language Teaching in Europe', which drew the attention of the media, was held in Münster from 9–22 July 1995. Foreign language teachers from Germany, England, Spain and Greece all attended lectures, workshops, discussions, demonstrations and cultural events over a two-week period, participating in a truly European language experience.

For the first time, teachers of English, German, Spanish or Modern Greek, working in one of the four countries of the project, and in conjunction with the national teams, came together to listen to each other's classroom experiences, ideas and methodological perspectives, with the objective of working together to share knowledge and find common ground as modern language teachers in Europe.

Overview

We are conscious of the wide range of topics currently at issue in the area of language teaching methodology as a result of the interdisciplinary nature of the field, enriched by advances in, for instance, psycholinguistics and sociolinguistics and cognitive psychology. Our decision to restrict ourselves to the topics mentioned in this book is a deliberate one. In the discussion of our pan-European workshop in Münster, these were the areas we found to be of greatest interest to us as communicative language teachers, and in which the participants had sufficient expertise to make a significant contribution.

In this volume, we have brought together a rich sample of resources that educators may use to meet the everyday challenge of the classroom. They are of different kinds, ranging from theoretical developments in different aspects of language teaching methodology and learning to valuable classroom experiences.

Focus on language learner autonomy

Part I, 'Focus on language learner autonomy', is that which to a certain extent gives the background for those that follow. As we have said, our scenario is the communicative FL classroom in which the students learn how to cooperate and interact with others often in simulation of real-life situations. In this way they assimilate the new knowledge acquired, integrating it into that which they already possess.

The emphasis here is on how students learn, since obviously this must be the focal point for any sort of unified approach to language teaching in a European context. One of the most important outcomes of educational research in the last two decades has been the enhancement of the learner's role in the language learning process as well as a growing awareness of the need to develop his/her ability to learn autonomously. In a learner-centred approach to FL teaching, there should be no differences either between languages or countries because what is basically under examination is the way in which learners acquire new knowledge. To this end, theoretical as well as the application of theory to practical experience is discussed both generally and in specific contexts.

In Part I, FL teaching is viewed from the perspective of new technologies, which will become increasingly important in the future. Computer programs incorporating Multimedia will, in all likelihood, have a major role in language classrooms of the future, where the learner, by means of the computer screen, will be able to take part in a wide range of different activities that will facilitate language acquisition in imaginative ways.

Although no machine will ever be able to replace an enthusiastic and competent FL teacher, the presence of computers in the language classroom has the advantage of greatly contributing to learner autonomy, something in direct connection with the educational goals of the project. Students are in control and can proceed at their own pace. A multiplicity of interactive possibilities enables effective programs to have a wide applicability at different levels of attainment and ability, and to develop the learner's state of mind from one passive observation to intense application of productive skills. It is true that at the moment, computer-assisted language learning is not widely used, but there is no doubt that it will be so in the future, and the FL teacher and learner will have to learn how to exploit computer technology to the full.

Focus on the classroom

FL literature is a valuable source of cultural information as well as different types of contexts. Within our project, we found that the role of literature in FL teaching varies considerably from country to country as well as from language to language. The most significant factor seems to be whether the level of the language being taught was elementary or advanced. However, everyone was motivated to read when it was pointed out that the text belonged to the literary tradition of the foreign language.

Notwithstanding, the emphasis here is neither on the skill of reading nor *knowing about* literature, but rather on *doing things* with literary texts. In this respect, we wish to put the emphasis on creativity. This is important because it teaches students to produce and create meaning on their own, instead of passively listening to the teacher and limiting themselves to reproduce what they hear.

The type of exercise described here is useful because it can be used with virtually any literary text, even simplified ones. Students enter the cultural world of the text and acquire a deeper understanding of it because they are obliged to re-create it visually, first in their minds and then on paper. Such exercises of meaning construction foster learner autonomy because there are no 'right answers'. Students are participating in an activity in which they must cooperate with others and work together to agree on a 'translation' of the text into a visual medium.

In reality, we feel that the true goal of education should be to empower learners, giving them the tools necessary to function in a world of rapid and constant change where they will be obliged continuously to process new information which the traditional school curriculum cannot include. What schools can do, however, is to equip learners with the skills, strategies and habits which will enable learners to operate effectively in a world of modern information technology, teaching them how to solve problems on their own. Consequently, countries interested in the development of the European project must work together in a common effort to adapt education to the new individual, political, cultural and productive space, and to the rapid changes our societies are experiencing.

Part II, 'Focus on the classroom', also contains an innovative piece about the way teachers and learners talk to each other in the foreign language classroom. Going well beyond what has hitherto been considered to be the typical teacher–learner exchange pattern, the contribution demonstrates the complexities of foreign language learning and teaching talk using conversation analysis techniques for this purpose. Unlike much of the work done so far in this area, this contribution draws on a substantial number of recorded lessons from various European countries.

Grammar

Part III is about grammar. As we are all aware, grammar has long been an important component in the language syllabus. In fact, it had its heyday in the days of the grammar-translation method when it predominated over all the others. This ended with the creation of the communicative syllabus which foregrounded other lesson components, the result of which was that grammar was, in a manner of speaking, pushed out of the spotlight.

It is obvious, however, that grammar cannot be ignored, if only because of the importance given to knowledge of structures in national exams. Many teachers also seem to feel that grammar instruction is essential for the mastery of the FL because their own training has basically been linguistic. None the less, new perspectives on how to deal with grammar in the classroom are gradually being incorporated. The concept of grammar as presented in this book is not that of previous decades. This is reflected in the corporation of sociolinguistic/cultural information in the concept of grammar. The issue at hand is exactly what place grammar should occupy in the syllabus, and how it can be integrated into a learner-based communicative approach to FL teaching.

It is our conviction that structures should be taught in connection with the functions they fundamentally convey, since grammatical structure should not be taught as an end in itself.

It is also interesting to explore the extent to which contemporary linguistic theory can help teachers better understand how they carry out their work. For example, theoretical principles can possibly help them to understand why certain activities, lesson plans and organization of content are more effective than others. If we decide that this is not a chance occurrence, then perhaps there is a way to account for similarities across languages.

Vocabulary

Part IV deals with vocabulary in FL teaching. Vocabulary has often not been given the importance it deserves. We have found that among the FL teachers in our project, there was great interest in this component for a number of reasons:

1   words codify cultural information and values;
2   understanding words and the contexts in which they occur is basic to communication;
3   multi-word units in the form of idiomatic phrases foment cultural awareness.

Another important consideration is the importance that learners them-selves give to vocabulary acquisition. Words as tangible linguistic material are the substance of language. This leads FL learners to conclude that knowing a language is synonymous with knowing its vocabulary. This belief is hardly as naive as it may appear if we consider what *knowing* a word entails:

1   knowledge of the frequency of the word in the language, i.e. how likely you are to encounter the word in speech or print;
2   knowledge of the register of a word, or the limitations imposed on the use of the word according to variations of function and situation;
3   knowledge of collocation, both semantic and syntactic, i.e. the syntactic behaviour associated with the word along with its network of associations with other words in the language;
4   knowledge of semantics, i.e. knowing what a word means or 'denotes' as well as is connotation or associative meaning;
5   knowledge of polysemy, i.e. the different meanings that a word has.

By learning words in meaningful contexts, a great deal of information can be acquired by the learner at all levels of language. When we know a word, we are also familiar with the world it creates.

If we are not a native speaker of the language or do not live in the country where the language is spoken, our first acquaintance with the world within words is often through dictionaries. For this reason, dictionary knowledge is vitally necessary for a learner-based approach to lexical competence. This means being aware of the types of lexical information contained in dictionary entries, as well as the different types of dictionary on the market.

In order for learners to be equipped with dictionary skills, they must first know which dictionaries to use and for what tasks. If a student chooses the wrong type of dictionary, at the very least he will become frustrated at not being able to find the information he needs, but often an inappropriate choice of dictionary can lead to serious errors in language production. For these reasons, it is important that students learn about dictionaries in order to become more successful and effective learners.

However, vocabulary is not restricted to single words. Learners should also consider multi-word units which have become fixed in language over time. Such expressions show students to what extent words can combine with others and acquire new meaning. Here the meaning of the whole is far from being the sum of the meaning of its parts. Even more important, idiomatic phrases when used as a basis for language comparison can be a source of interesting classroom discussion and can build intercultural awareness, as they transmit idiosyncratic aspects of a language culture.

Summary

As FL teachers, we are all united in our principal objective: to teach students to communicate in a foreign language in the same way as they do in their mother tongue. Each of us has different ideas about the best way to go about achieving this goal, partly because of our backgrounds. This is one of the logical consequences derived from the differences in teacher training from country to country. As a result, we found that our individual circumstances and contexts often led us to emphasize certain areas and activities to the possible detriment of others.

Nevertheless, we found that when we placed greater emphasis on *learning* and less on *teaching*, our differences were considerably reduced. For this reason, one of the conclusions we reached was that language activities which lead students to discover the FL on their own are the best means of attaining any objectives proposed. The teacher's role should be one of guidance, and not that of an authoritarian purveyor of knowledge.

This will be even more important in the future because the rapid change of different knowledge areas logically demands a basic education that is more flexible, more versatile, and capable of adapting to new situations as well as meeting the needs of each individual member of the community. Within Europe, this can only be achieved if education instils in learners the ability to learn.

It is a truism that one of the most valuable gifts an FL teacher can give to his/her students is the awareness, the certainty that being able to speak, write and generally function in another language is much more than just having an adequate command of a specific inventory of expressions and structures. In a sense, it is like opening a window on to another world, a window through which students can view and participate in the daily life and culture of another country. This new window takes on increased significance when it is placed within the context of the whole house, Europe.

Part I

FOCUS ON LANGUAGE
LEARNER AUTONOMY

Today, educators, educational researchers, developmental psychologists and cognitive scientists are engaged in the design of school programmes and conducting investigations on learning strategies, study skills and abilities to learn. In Part I, two chapters pay particular attention to how conditions that foster them might be built into the materials, methodologies and environments for learning and schooling.

From the chapters in Part I, we can deduce that there is good reason to try to improve the characteristics of individual students as learners and to improve instructional techniques. In summary, the chapters share a special concern with the empowering of learners which also means a concern with empowering teachers to present alternative teaching strategies aimed at the individualization of instruction, caring for differentiation in the classroom through the enhancement of learning strategies that enable students to become independent and responsible learners.

The first two chapters complement each other and are concerned with the higher goals of learning; namely, learning how to learn and autonomy. Based on his experience, Manuel Jiménez Raya's chapter is an attempt to present a comprehensive conceptualization of learning how to learn; namely, as a complex of factors comprising learning strategies, reflection, metacognition, attitudes and the planning of learning. It is generally agreed that success in acquiring new knowledge or in using knowledge to solve problems must depend on the appropriate use of very fundamental mental abilities or processes. It is also agreed that the development of learning expertise is a complex and lifelong process which has received relatively little attention from research in second language learning and teaching.

The author maintains that, ideally, any training programme should include practice in specific task-appropriate strategies, direct instruction in the orchestration, overseeing and monitoring of these skills, and information concerning the significance of those activities, an issue also accepted by Lamb (chapter 2). Jiménez Raya also presents some clear methodological considerations, within which we can highlight a reflective approach based on the learner's own approaches to learning.

Lamb describes in detail an interesting and successful approach to the treatment of differentiation in a British secondary school. He examines the reasons for a focus on learning rather than teaching in the language classroom, drawing on theory, research, practical experience and national education policy in Britain. The implications of such a shift and an example of how it may relate to practice are then examined by means of a detailed study describing the approach in the classroom: classroom management and organization, materials and objectives.

Grießhaber and Stracke-Elbina (chapters 3 and 4) deal with the use of computers in the classroom and describe ways in which computer-assisted learning can be made more effective. Although new technologies do not solve basic problems of method or approach, they are a rich motivational resource. Although they will never take the place of the teacher, they are valuable aids in the classroom because they are more conducive to a learner-centred approach. Students become actively engaged in productive processes, becoming 'tuned-in' both to themselves and to others. This is largely due to the fact that the computer offers an enriched type of input, both in quality and quantity. Classroom interaction is thus facilitated both individually and in groups.

1

TRAINING LANGUAGE LEARNERS TO LEARN

Manuel Jiménez Raya

Introduction

Over the past decade, cognitive strategy instruction has emerged as an important issue in educational psychology and second language acquisition research and methodology. However, this does not mean that it has been incorporated into the language curriculum on a large scale. In my opinion, this is largely due to the fact that cognitive instruction is not easy to implement and, what is more, the results are only perceptible in the long run, because cognitive instruction consists of showing learners procedures that take some time to master. Nevertheless, they are essential because they reflect the processes used by people who are successful in learning a foreign language.

Popular beliefs about the innate nature of learning capabilities are also another factor contributing to this apparent reluctance to apply insights from cognitive psychology or cognitive (information-processing) accounts of second language acquisition and instruction. In fact, when language teachers are asked about the factors determining academic success, language learning strategies (if mentioned at all) receive considerably lower priority in comparison to other learning factors. This is due to a number of things, among which I would highlight a lack of information regarding what *cognitive instruction*, or *learning how to learn*, entails, and also a lack of information regarding methodological considerations about how to incorporate it into language learning instruction. The contribution of a cognitive perspective to foreign language instruction is its added focus on the thinking process, and the relationship between mental processes and performance, all of which help learners to become increasingly empowered. At this point, it is important to remember that learning depends entirely upon the mental activities of the learner. What the teacher does is relevant insofar as it affects the student's mental actions.

Learning how to learn

Learning how to learn represents a substantial shift away from rigid study methods towards more experiential and reflective activities which try to involve learners in their own learning and developing process. By implementing learner training, teachers give learners the opportunity to reflect and gather their thoughts with regard to the language learning process, something which normally results in improvements in learning efficiency and in higher degrees of motivation for learning.

Different terms are currently used to refer to the same phenomenon, the most common ones being 'cognitive instruction', 'learner training' and 'strategy instruction'. Personally, I prefer the first two terms because they are more comprehensive. Strategy instruction is a more restrictive term that can mislead teachers by conveying only a partial understanding of learning how to learn or process competence. The first two terms can help teachers and researchers to understand that learning how to learn is a complex phenomenon that entails different constructs and aspects, most of which are subject to modification by instruction. Strategy instruction[1] can at first sight give the impression of being something that is only concerned with one facet of the development of learning expertise, namely strategies. As is well known, there is more to learning how to learn than just developing learning strategies. Strategies, of course, occupy a central role in any current model of good thinking (Baron, 1985; Sternberg, 1985), but there are other aspects that are also central to the models previously mentioned, such as metacognition (knowledge about and regulation of cognition), motivation and positive attitudes towards learning, all of which operate in close interaction in the development of learning expertise.

We can now define learning how to learn as the procedure by which learners obtain insights about the learning process and about themselves, effective learning strategies, and develop positive attitudes towards language and language learning. This process is generally acknowledged to lead to improved cognitive activity and a greater degree of control on the part of the learner (O'Malley and Chamot, 1990; Oxford, 1990a; Pressley et al., 1990). No educational objective is more important for students than learning how to learn, and how to function as independent, autonomous learners. Besides providing the information and knowledge students will need in their professional lives, it is just as important for the school to give learners the opportunity to go on learning once the schooling period has finished.

It is now necessary to clarify what is normally understood by all the aspects and elements involved in the definition of learning how to learn, because, if we succeed in the task, it will facilitate its incorporation into the teaching practice of most language teachers on a large scale and thus learners will become more successful. We are convinced that success in language learning depends to a large extent on a successful orchestration of cognitive capacities.

In some respects, learning is no different from other skills. In other words, it is possible to develop expertise in learning by paying attention to the technical know-how by developing skills and knowledge.

Jiménez Raya (1993) has identified the following components in the development of learning expertise:

1 Reflective awareness, as the form of obtaining knowledge about oneself and others as learners and the learning process. It is also the means for evaluating the effectiveness of individual learning strategies.
2 The planning of learning (Dickinson, 1986).
3 Learning strategies or the steps, thoughts and operations involved in facilitating the acquisition, storage and retrieval of knowledge.
4 Metacognition, or knowledge about cognition.
5 Attitudes or some aspects of an individual's response to an object or class of objects (Lett, 1979, quoted in van Els, 1984: 116).

According to recent models of thinking, the important features of thinking include strategies for accomplishing learning goals, knowledge about those strategies and about one's own thinking processes, knowledge about the world in general, motivational beliefs, and overall cognitive style. A good thinker carries out a series of processes directed at the identification of a goal and the choice of the means necessary to accomplish that goal from different possibilities grounded in an impartial analysis of evidence.

Reflection in learning how to learn

There is a general consensus among contemporary educationalists that recognition should be given to the perspectives of teachers and learners, the ones who are principally and directly engaged in classroom interaction. What both parties do is directed by what they think (Wittrock, 1986, 1987). It is important, therefore, to clarify their thoughts and beliefs, and because they are normally the only witnesses to their own beliefs, attitudes and conceptions, it is essential that it is done in their own terms. It is generally believed that we learn by interpreting new materials in terms of previous knowledge. We will learn more effectively when the contents of our learning (in this case strategies, attitudes, metacognitive knowledge) are guided by and in consonance with our own personal constructs.

It is reflectivity that allows the teacher the possibility of incorporating insights such as the ones mentioned above. We can thus maintain that reflection is the basis for decision making, planning and action in learning.

Through the use of reflection it is possible to bring to the forefront relevant aspects of the learning process, thus making students aware of effective and ineffective habits and strategies. Reflection about learning processes thus contributes to making the implicit explicit. It also helps to develop a deeper understanding of the different aspects and factors involved in the process of learning a foreign language.

Learners usually have their own ideas about how 'best' to tackle learning as well as about the role of the teacher and their own role among others. These ideas can often make learning more difficult rather than facilitating it. Through constructive reflection, learners can recapture a given experience, examine their own understanding of it and contrast it with others. In this sense, learning to learn does not mean merely following the teacher's instructions, but rather exploring and discovering new perspectives and possibilities, using one's own conceptions as a starting point.

This approach to learner training is based on a strong belief that the only effective learning is that which is self-discovered. Awareness is essential in any activity we undertake, but it is even more relevant in learner training, because of the enormous complexity in the development of learning potential. A certain amount of training is implicit in any activity undertaken in the classroom. In fact, each activity is selected because we are convinced that that is the way learning takes place.

Learning strategies are present whenever we attempt to learn anything, but unfortunately not all learners gain insights about these strategies and capture them. For this reason, awareness is essential to the learner, who should be made aware that good performance depends on appropriate strategies rather than luck or special ability. However, the teacher's role should not be solely limited to awareness-raising. On the contrary, he/she should guide the students towards models of good thinking and the acquisition of qualities shown by successful learners, always within the context of the learners' own strategies. It is only when learners consciously reflect on their cognitive activity that they benefit from failure. According to Nisbet and Shucksmith (1986: 47), it is the capacity to examine situations, tasks and problems that determines the difference between a successful learning experience and an unsuccessful one.

However, we must bear in mind that learners ought to take as a starting point their own interpretations and conceptions about the nature of language and language learning, because the only learning which significantly modifies behaviour is self-discovered and self-appropriated learning.

Reflection involves a process of questioning how and why things are as they seem to be. If, as is generally believed, the most successful approach to learner training is one in which we can raise students' awareness by helping them to question their own conceptions of the learning process and informing them of different possibilities, it is vital that the students develop the capacity to pay attention to how they go about learning. Understanding of cognitive processes is more likely to occur when we are required to consider and explain, or to elaborate our position to ourselves or to others. The need to put into words what we know or think we know is the driving force which makes us evaluate, integrate and elaborate knowledge about cognition in new ways.

Donato and McCormick (1994) suggest that the goal of strategy training is not just training in the use of specific strategies. Rather, they argue, it is a question of encouraging in learners a more strategic conception of learning, while some authors go even further and question the possibility of teaching a strategy directly.

Planning learning

Planning learning means involving learners in the determination of aims and objectives, as well as learner participation in decisions concerning materials, methods and evaluation. However, this does not imply that teachers should abdicate their traditional classroom responsibilities, but rather they should share them as learners become ready for them. None the less, it does advocate a commitment on the part of the teacher to make learners increasingly responsible through a gradual process of negotiation and transfer of certain duties. In this process, it is essential that teachers foster and approve of learners' assumption of increased responsibility.

It is up to teachers to decide the degree of responsibility they are prepared to pass on to learners and also the amount which their learners are ready to accept. The idea that the responsibility for learning belongs to the learner is becoming increasingly popular among educational researchers and teachers (Holec, 1979; Weinstein and Mayer, 1986; Wenden, 1991). In fact, some of them identify the development of learner autonomy with helping learners learn how to learn.[2]

Learning strategies

The role of the learner as an active processor of information is currently emphasized, both through teaching/learning models in general (Weinstein and Mayer, 1986) and through academic study models in particular (Thomas and Rohwer, 1986). A strategy is currently defined as the set of procedures used for achieving a plan, goal or objective. In learning, a strategy is the sequence of procedures used to facilitate learning. We use strategies every time there is an attempt to learn something new, such as vocabulary words, or to extract meaning from oral or written texts. Strategies are also used to control the direction and amount of attention a given task requires, as well as to motivate ourselves. For example, a strategic listener may make use of the strategies given below to extract meaning from an oral text.

The learners will try to understand the task requirements (*self-management*); next they will decide about what aspects or information they will need to understand (*planning learning*); they will *direct their attention* to the task and ignore possible distractions; they will also try to anticipate some of the information they will encounter (*prediction*); when listening, they will focus on relevant information, excluding that which is irrelevant and redundant (*selective attention*). They will probably *monitor* comprehension, *infer* meaning of unknown words from context, and, after the task has been completed, they will provide themselves with some kind of reward or personal motivation (*self-reinforcement*).

This is by no means an exhaustive account of the strategic activity learners may engage in. Nevertheless, it illustrates the number and importance of strategies in any learning activity. Strategies will vary in accordance with the subject involved and the task at hand. Strategy use will also vary according to a variety of different factors, such as methodology, teacher demands, preference, learning style, nature of the task, prior learning experience, context, age and stage of learning, and cultural background (Oxford, 1990b; Politzer and McGroarty, 1985).

Learning strategies are thus generally acknowledged as enhancing the learning process when used appropriately, paving the way for independent and self-directed learning. They are relevant for education because, as research has shown (Cohen, 1990; O'Malley and Chamot, 1990), there are differences in the frequency of use and variety of learning strategies used by successful and unsuccessful learners. Oxford *et al.* (1990: 199) write: 'Though all language students use some kind of strategies, the more effective students use them more consciously, more purposefully, more appropriately, and more frequently than do less able students.'

Despite the existence of problems in the area of learning strategies, especially regarding issues of concept and classification, there is general agreement on the following premises:

1   The use of adequate strategies enhances learning.
2   Strategies can be learned and taught.
3   Strategies are specific learner characteristics.
4   Strategies are not always directly observable.
5   The use of strategies is determined by the learner's cognitive style.
6   Strategies are responsible for the assimilation of new information.
7   Strategies facilitate retrieval of information.

None the less, we have to be very cautious when applying insights from research because, as Galloway and Labarca suggest, most research in the field of second language acquisition is done in an attempt to predict success: 'Predictors of success have no place in education when they explain away the learner. Absolute classifications have no value when applied to humans who embody scores of other traits, all of which interact' (Galloway and Labarca, 1990: 127).

As we have indicated above, most research efforts have concentrated principally on the identification of those strategies used by 'effective' language learners in different contexts, and under different conditions of exposure and performance of different kinds of tasks. They have also explored whether these strategies may be taught and learned. Thus, taxonomies of learning strategies are varied and often differ in the terminology used and in their definition. None the less, most researchers classify them into three categories:[3]

1 Metacognitive strategies for directing the learning process. These are higher order executive skills that may entail planning, monitoring or evaluating the success of a learning activity. Also included as meta-cognitive strategies are selective attention and directed attention. These help students to regulate their cognitive activity throughout the schooling period by engaging in active planning, checking, testing, monitoring, revising and thinking about their performance.

2 Cognitive strategies for manipulating information to be learned. They operate directly on incoming information, manipulating it in ways that enhance learning. In this category we find strategies such as elaboration, translation, inference, induction, deduction, grouping vocabulary items, creation of mental images to facilitate retention of information, and transfer. These strategies contribute to deep processing of learning material and to the establishment of meaningful mental linkages.

3 Social/affective strategies for controlling emotional reactions and cooper-ating with others. They represent a broad grouping that involves either interaction with another person or ideational control over emotion and affect; they are used for self-motivation and encouragement, to reduce anxiety, to promote interaction opportunities and cooperation with others. Strategies included under this category are cooperation, self-talk, questioning for clarification and self-reinforcement.

Research on learning strategies represents an effort to understand how we can help learners to improve their learning, retrieval and thinking potential. For this reason, we advocate their inclusion in learning programmes because they have a positive influence on learning outcomes. However, we have to be cautious in taking their effectiveness for granted. We must remember that no strategy is universally effective. This is the reason why we have suggested that the approach to learner training should be one of information, reflection and questioning to guarantee that no strategy is imposed upon the learners.

Metacognition

O'Malley *et al.* (1985: 24) indicate that learners without metacognitive approaches are essentially learners without direction and ability to review progress, accomplishments and future learning directions.

The learner has to construct his/her own knowledge about strategies and learning in general. This personal construction of knowledge is connected with active and conscious reflection about when and why a given strategy is useful as well as about the demands of a given task. The use of strategies, and learning, requires a system that constantly controls the cognitive activity.

Metacognition is usually conceived of as a complex of related aspects having to do with knowledge about cognition (metacognitive knowledge) and its regulation, i.e. how students direct, plan and monitor their cognitive activity. From an information-processing perspective, metacognition is the basis of intelligent activity because it underlies an efficient use of learning strategies.

Metacognitive knowledge refers to the beliefs individuals hold about themselves as learners, the requirements of the different tasks, and about the learning process. This knowledge about knowledge, these thoughts about thoughts, can exert a positive or negative influence on the way a given student approaches language learning. In fact, effective deployment of strategies depends on students being equipped with knowledge about when strategies should be used. Explicit attention to metacognitive knowledge about strategies in these models contrasts with the great bulk of strategy instruction (McCormick et al., 1989) in which there has been little or no attention to information about why, when and where to use the strategies that are being taught.

The inclusion of metacognition in teaching learning how to learn is justified on the basis of perceptions that do not always correspond with what we actually do. As Galloway and Labarca write: 'we are unaware of what idiosyncratic and distorted notions learners have of what language is and how these underlie and feed their efforts to perform' (Galloway and Labarca, 1990: 149).

Enhancing metacognition provides new insights into foreign language cognitive abilities and adds new information about the differences between successful and less successful learners. Metacognitive variables have proved to be the best predictors of success in both young and adult learners. In fact, in order to orchestrate cognitive and social-affective strategies, students need to observe and guide their own thinking to guarantee maximum effectiveness.

Of the two dimensions of metacognition, we shall concentrate on the first, because the second (regulation of cognition) is achieved through metacognitive strategies, discussed above.

In relation to metacognitive knowledge, Flavell (1979) distinguishes between metacognitive knowledge and metacognitive experience. The first has already been defined, while the second refers to conscious experiences about cognitive endeavour or activity. Flavell also identified different interactive categories of metacognitive knowledge:

1 *Person knowledge*. This category includes all the acquired knowledge and beliefs related to what human beings are like regarding cognitive aspects.
2 *Task knowledge*. The individual has ideas about task demands and whether an activity calls for deliberate learning.

3 *Strategy knowledge.* We also learn about cognitive strategies or procedures. Successful learners know when and where to use the strategies they know, the benefits associated with their use and the effort needed in their use. This metacognitive knowledge, as well as the two other types, helps the learner to recognize when particular strategies are appropriate.

Attitudes

The study of attitudes is central to explaining individual differences. They are inextricably linked to the teaching–learning process, because the attitudes of learners towards the teacher, the language or school are factors that bear a substantial influence on the learning process. Depending on the nature of these attitudes, language learning effectiveness will vary accordingly. Attitudes, as a predisposition to respond in a pre-established way to the situations one encounters, have three components: cognitive, affective and conative or behavioural. This inevitably implies the acceptance of the following:

1 The active role of attitudes in the language learning process, such as curiosity, interest in finding out new information, and active involvement in the learning task. These are all factors that contribute positively to learning.
2 The contribution of affective and emotional factors to the process of learning. It would seem contradictory to conceive that cognition can work independently of emotion and affection.
3 A positive attitude manifests itself in accordance with that character. A positive evaluation of the learning atmosphere will increase learners' interest in the subject and in participating actively in lessons.

There is also agreement that attitudes are learned and therefore capable of modification by further learning. From our perspective, it is important to know our learners' attitudes towards learning because the teaching of the most effective strategies will not produce any benefits if students continue to show negative attitudes towards the learning process in general, or towards any of its components in particular. Attitudes guide perception and cognitive processes, and for this reason attitudes towards learning must form part of our teaching aims. Consequently, we can redirect negative attitudes that have the actual power to block learning and therefore become an obstacle to the student.

Methodological considerations

Teaching learning how to learn is not always easy for teachers to understand and to implement, and when they do, they have the task of convincing the learner that it is worth the effort needed to improve learning efficiency. For this reason, teaching learners how to learn must be perceived as a long-term endeavour because the mastery of attitudes, metacognitive knowledge and strategies takes time.

There are different methodological decisions connected with teaching learning, the first of which has to do with the kind of treatment it is going to receive and whether we are going to integrate it with language instruction, or, on the contrary, if we are going to assign a specific time for it. Wenden (1986) advocates an integrated and informed approach, in which language instruction and the development of learning expertise take place at the same time because learning in context is generally agreed to be more effective. We say *informed* because the learner has to be conscious from the very first moment of the benefits it will yield; this approach tells learners why a given strategy is useful. Although students also need to know *why*, *when* and *where* to use strategies, this in itself is not enough. A reflective approach is the most appropriate because as Gibbs (1981) suggests, instructions or advice provided by the teacher are not normally acted upon, but ignored. Reasons for this are the following:

1 Advice is inappropriate for the learner because it does not reflect an understanding of the process of student learning.
2 Advice is impossible to follow because what is described is impossible.
3 Advice involves a threatening attack on the existing ways that students have of doing things.

For these reasons, a reflective approach in which students actually think about how they learn is more suitable. The teacher must create situations which allow this to happen and take advantage of learner formulations which will lead to class discussion about the learning process, attitudes, metacognitive knowledge and learning strategies.

Concerning learning strategies, it is convenient to select and concentrate on one strategy by giving suggestions for its use and by asking students to evaluate its effectiveness and on the basis of this evaluation to adopt or reject it.

Strategies are difficult to learn and even more difficult to transfer to new situations. To make the most of the learning strategies taught, learners must fall into the habit of using them and applying them to new situations. This can only happen once strategies become firmly established. To this end, there is general agreement that in order to guarantee more effective learning teachers should do the following:

1 Promote learners' confidence in their capacity to become better learners.
2 Motivate students to adopt new strategies and attitudes.
3 Concentrate on one strategy or attitude at a time, do not attempt to teach more than one strategy at a time.

4   Model and explain the new strategies.
5   Explain to the learner why, when and where to use the strategies.
6   Provide extensive opportunities for practice.
7   Remember that learning how to learn involves a complex of factors and that all must be included in cognitive instruction.
8   Encourage monitoring of new strategies, so that students can gain control.
9   Promote a reflective approach to learning how to learn.

From experience, I have found that new ideas often frighten teachers, many of whom are discouraged by the complexity of new concepts or by the difficulty in finding the right materials. Others say they simply do not have enough time in an already overcrowded curriculum. For this reason, if I were asked by a practising teacher what is the easiest way to implement strategy training, I would recommend that he/she concentrate on the strategies implicit in the materials currently being used, make these strategies explicit and foster reflection about learning. Every task in our textbook has been designed to parallel the mental activity learners may engage on cognitively when learning. Despite this fact, it is easy to forget about it (the how of learning) and concentrate solely on content and its transmission. Furthermore, not all learners understand the strategies built into the materials; this justifies the explicit information we are advocating in this chapter. As practical advice, I would recommend teachers to prepare a table in which they can write the activity, the strategy(ies) contained in it and some tips about training; that is, the information they will give to learners about when, why and how to use the strategy or strategies. This table can be completed when planning lessons.

The learner diary in learner training

Of special value in learning how to learn is the learner diary, an instrument that complies with all the requirements for successful self-development as a learner. It is valuable on its own, but its value is much higher if it is complemented with learner training activities. Learner training is time-consuming; the significance of this fact can be minimized if learners elaborate their reflections and perceptions about learner training in the diary.

Learning how to learn can be implemented in several ways. Among the different approaches we can distinguish the following:

1   those relying on the design of specific activities;
2   those based on an explanation of the strategies in the language training activities;
3   those based on learner self-reflection and the development of awareness of one's mental activities and resources.

23

It is the latter approach that we will concentrate on here. Some authors have argued that the so-called poor language learners have at their disposal a wide range of strategies that they do not know how to use, and that learner training should be cautious in its attempts to foster in them the behaviours observed in good language learners (Porte, 1988). Having a strategy is not enough; one must understand it and be ready to apply it.

My experience with the use of learner diaries goes back to 1989 when I started teaching in Instituto de Bachillerato 'Padre Poveda', a secondary school in Guadix (Spain). There I became involved in an experiment aiming at developing learner autonomy. The implementation of an autonomous programme requires the existence of a framework that enables the learner to work autonomously exercising responsibilities. The methodological framework used for the promotion of learner autonomy consisted of different activities that allowed learners to exercise their responsibility in language learning.

Learner training was essential in the preparation of students to work autonomously. In fact, as has previously been mentioned, it is identified by some authors with the development of autonomy. In my opinion, learning how to learn is a necessary condition for learner autonomy, although there is more to autonomy than this.

Learner training is necessary for many different reasons, the most outstanding of which is that it leads to improved performance and greater effectiveness by involving learners in experiential and reflective activities. According to Kohonen (1989), good learners do not just come about, they must be educated. I found that it was also necessary as a way of helping learners to become more conscious about what learning a language entails. Within learner training one of the key activities was the writing of a learner diary.

Originally, learners had to answer four questions:[4]

1 What have you learned today?
2 Who have you learned it from?
3 How have you learned it?
4 How did you feel?

As these were open-ended questions, it was believed they would guide and encourage learners to examine the process and content of learning and that they would obtain benefit from answering the questions. However, after a few entries it became a routine activity from which no benefit was gained whatsoever. Its purpose was far from being even remotely achieved. The entries in the diaries were monotonous and repetitive as students found a kind of model answer to the different questions, which they reproduced on almost all entries. I particularly remember the diary of a girl who would include the same answer to the fourth question: 'I felt very well and contented today.'

Obviously, that was not the purpose for which students were asked to write a diary. In general, entries contained in the diaries were of no interest either to the teacher or to students themselves, and there was no improvement as they supposedly gained experience in its writing. Furthermore, there was no reflection involved, just routine answers to the four questions.

Suggestions indicating my worries about the diaries were made individually and to the class as a whole with no positive effects on the entries of the diaries. The purpose for which the diary was intended was far from being even modestly achieved. I asked learners about their opinion as to the usefulness of keeping a diary. I immediately discovered that they were also disappointed and considered the writing of the diary to be a waste of time. However, they continued to keep them because it was a course requirement. Unfortunately this type of diary is becoming widespread. In my participation in teacher training activities, I have found out that many teachers who use such diaries have no clear idea about the reasons for asking students to write a diary. They do so because it is an in-vogue activity in language teaching methodology.

The diary had originally been conceived as a learner development instrument. As an instrument to help learners to become more effective by contributing to the development of a conscious awareness of their cognitive abilities, it would also help them to obtain insights into the process of language learning and develop their personal strategic behaviour and metacognition. In other words, it was the tool that would help them to achieve a higher degree of autonomy, as it would facilitate the planning of their actions, the identification of their problems and the evaluation of their learning. The keeping of the diary would help learners learn how to learn and progress in the acquisition of autonomy.

After the discussion, we decided that the diary would become a free composition on learning, in which the four questions would help learners as an indication of what kind of information to include, but without any obligation to answer them. It was then up to the students as to what kind of information to include and reflect upon. This way the writing of the diary was a complementary activity in learning how to learn that did not include guided discussion, thus avoiding the tendency shown by students to model examples provided rather than generate their own strategies.

After the new format was introduced, the diary started to fulfil the purpose for which it was conceived. The learners involved were encouraged to reflect and consider their reasons for learning English as a foreign language, their learning experience, the strategies they used and their usefulness, as well as their beliefs and reactions to language learning in the classroom and outside. This can be seen in the following extracts from actual diaries:

> I usually study all the vocabulary in a very curious way, because I don't really study them. When I'm copying the words from the reader, and I look them up in a dictionary its meaning, and in other

dictionary its pronunciation, after doing this work, the words with its pronunciation and translations have remained in my mind: For it, only a few days before the exam I only must have a review of it.

(Alejandro)

[W]hen I find these words (or expressions, sometimes), first, before looking it up in the dictionary, I try to guess the meaning; it's useful specially when I try to guess the meaning of a set phrase or a word that is composed with two other words, for instance 'fingernail'. So I can keep it in my memory more easily. When you discover the meaning of something guessing it, you feel happy and stop to think: What a great imagination I have, and that way, it's easier to keep in your memory.

(David)

It is possible to assert that writing encourages students to adopt a questioning and analytical attitude towards their own learning strategies, beliefs and the teaching methodology. This questioning and reflective approach to learner training originated in the writing of the diary contrasts with more teacher-centred ones, in which teachers give advice and train students in specific techniques whereby students remain dependent on further inputs from experts to bring about change.

In my experience with learner diaries I can say, with the benefit of hindsight, that it became an instrument which heightened learners' awareness of their own learning and helped them to gain control over it. The diary helped the teacher to get to know the different individual learners and to identify their specific problems. Moreover, the diary became a direct form of communication between learners and teacher as it promoted genuine dialogue and understanding between both parties.

The diary was conceived as a learner development instrument (Jiménez Raya, 1993). It is an instrument which helps learners to become more effective by contributing to the development of a conscious awareness of their cognitive abilities, to the obtaining of insights into the process of language learning and to the development of their personal strategic behaviour and metacognition.

The diary is thus a kind of critical and reflective autobiography of a subject as a learner that allows them to record their thoughts, feelings, achievements, hunches, problems and attitudes, as well as their impressions about different elements and aspects that are part of learning a foreign language such as methodology, materials, teacher, etc. In the writing of the diary the individual learner conceptualizes his/her own learning processes and beliefs about learning, focusing on what he/she does to tackle a learning task and how he/she feels. Thus, the learner is elevated to the position of explorer, who uses writing to discover how to go about learning English, considers reasons for learning English as a foreign language, the strategies to use and their usefulness, the strategies used by other students and those suggested by the teacher, as well as their beliefs and reactions to language learning in the classroom and outside. It is an instrument that heightens learners' awareness of their own learning and helps them to gain control over their learning.

One key aspect in the use of learner diaries is whether or not they should be read by the teacher. There are different positions regarding this issue; my personal opinion is that learner diaries should be seen by the teacher on a regular basis if they are to serve the purpose we are discussing. If the teacher has access to the learners' diaries he/she can obtain feedback on methodology used in the classroom and information on difficulties experienced by the different individuals. It would also give the teacher the opportunity to help the learner improve the entries in the diary, suggesting new areas of reflection, tasks the learner should undertake to become more effective at language learning, and new strategies that the learner could try.

The aim of diary writing, then, is to make the development of learners' awareness possible by enabling them to identify areas of potential difficulty, conflict or success, and by making explicit their own personal constructs, thus gradually assuming conscious control of the process. It cannot be overstressed that it is only when the learners know what they are actually doing that they can become autonomous and learning can take place.

Conclusion

Recent developments in cognitive psychology suggest that students should be taught effective strategies which are well-matched to the actual tasks that are used in the language classrooms. Current models of cognitive instruction favour teaching only a few strategies at a time, making sure that students also learn when and where to use strategies. We have advocated an approach to learner training which includes not only the teaching of learning strategies, but also aspects such as beliefs about learning, attitudes and the ability to plan one's own actions. Learners can benefit greatly in the long run if a portion of formal lesson time is devoted to helping them become more independent and effective learners. Learning how to learn is as important as what is learned. It is the task of the teacher to help learners to develop learning strategies, attitudes, skills and procedures that will help them progress in the acquisition of communicative competence and process competence.

Notes

1   Strategy instruction is nowadays acknowledged by some researchers as including a complex interaction of factors such as motivational beliefs, knowledge of how and when to use strategies (Pressley *et al.*, 1990).

2   Cf. Terry Lamb, 'Autonomy in language learning', chapter 2, this volume.

3   The present division is based on O'Malley and Chamot's and their research group's different classifications. These researchers have proposed different taxonomies all grouped under the three categories. The difference among the several taxonomies lies in the strategies identified in the different research projects.

4   The diaries were written in English. It may be argued that writing the diary in the foreign language can constrain the amount of information included because of students' limited proficiency in the target language. I agree that thoughts in the mother tongue can be more elaborate, but we must remember that our task as foreign language teachers is to encourage the use of the foreign language as much as possible.

References

Baron, J. (1985) *Rationality and Intelligence*, Cambridge: Cambridge University Press.

Cohen, A. (1990) *Language Learning. Insights for Learners, Teachers and Researchers*, New York: Newbury House.

Dickinson, L. (1986) *Self-instruction in Language Learning*, Cambridge: Cambridge University Press.

Donato, R. and McCormick, D. (1994) 'A Sociocultural Perspective on Language Learning Strategies: The Role of Mediation', in *The Modern Language Journal* 78/4: 453–464.

van Els, T., Bongaerts, T., Extra, G., van Os, Ch. and Jansen-van Dieten, A. (1984) *Applied Linguistics and the Learning and Teaching of Foreign Languages*, London: Edward Arnold.

Flavell, J. H. (1979) 'Metacognition and Cognitive Monitoring: A New Area of Cognitive-Developmental Inquiry', in *American Psychologist* 34/10: 906–911.

Galloway, V. and Labarca, A. (1990) 'From Student to Learner: Style, Process, and Strategy', in D. Birckbichler (ed.) *New Perspectives and New Directions in Foreign Language Education*, Lincolnwood: National Textbook Company.

Gibbs, G. (1981) *Teaching Students to Learn: A Student Centred Approach*, Milton Keynes: Open University Press.

Holec, H. (1979) *Autonomy and Foreign Language Learning*, Oxford: Pergamon Press.

Jiménez Raya, M. (1993) 'El diario del aprendiz como instrumento de entrenamiento cognitivo en la adquisición del inglés', Universidad de Granada. Unpublished Ph.D. thesis.

Jiménez Raya, M. (forthcoming) 'The Use of Learning Autobiographies in Language Learning'.

Kohonen, V. (1989) 'Experiential Language Learning – towards Second Language Learning as Learner Education', in *Bilingual Research Group Working Papers*, Santa Cruz: University of California.

McCormick, Ch. B., Miller, G. and Pressley, M. (1989) *Cognitive Strategy Research*, New York: Springer-Verlag.

Nisbet, J. and Shucksmith, J. (1987) *Estrategias de aprendizaje*, Madrid: Santillana.

O'Malley, J. M. and Chamot, A. U. (1990) *Learning Strategies in Second Language Acquisition*, Cambridge: Cambridge University Press.

O'Malley, J. M., Chamot, A. U., Stewner-Manzanares, G., Russo, R. P. and Küpper, L. (1985) 'Learning Strategies Used by Beginning and Intermediate ESL Students', in *Language Learning* 35/1: 21–46.

Oxford, R. L. (1990a) *Language Learning Strategies: What Every Teacher Should Know*, New York: Newbury House.

Oxford, R. L. (1990b) 'Missing Link: Evidence from Research on Language Learning Styles and

Strategies', in J. Alatis (ed.) *Georgetown University Round Table on Languages and Linguistics 1990*, 438–458, Washington, DC: Georgetown University Press.

Oxford, R. L., Crookall, D., Cohen, A., Lavine, R., Nyikos, M. and Sutter, W. (1990) 'Strategy Training for Language Learners: Six Situational Case Studies and a Training Model', in *Foreign Language Annals* 22/3: 197–216.

Politzer, R. L. and McGroarty, M. (1985) 'An Exploratory Study of Learning Behaviors and their Relationship to Gains in Linguistic and Communicative Competence', in *TESOL Quarterly* 19/1: 103–123.

Porte, G. (1988) 'Poor Language Learners and their Strategies for Dealing with New Vocabulary', in *ELT Journal* 42/3: 167–172.

Pressley, M. & Associates (1990) *Cognitive Strategy Instruction*, Cambridge, MA: Brookline Books.

Sternberg, R. J. (1985) *Beyond IQ: A Triarchic Theory of Human Intelligence*, London and New York: Cambridge University Press.

Thomas, J. W. and Rohwer, W. D. (1986) 'Academic Studying: The Role of Learning Strategies', in *Educational Psychologist* 21/1 and 2: 19–41.

Weinstein, C. E. and Mayer, R. E. (1986) 'The Teaching of Learning Strategies', in M. C. Wittrock (ed.) *Handbook of Research on Teaching*, New York: Macmillan.

Wenden, A. (1986) 'Incorporating Learner Training in the Classroom', in *System* 14/3: 315–325.

Wenden, A. (1991) *Learner Strategies for Learner Autonomy*, New York: Prentice Hall.

Wittrock, M. C. (1986) 'Students' Thought Processes', in M. C. Wittrock (ed.) *Handbook of Research on Teaching* (3rd edn), New York: Macmillan.

Wittrock, M. C. (1987) 'Teaching and Student Thinking', in *Journal of Teacher Education* 38: 30–33.

2

NOW YOU ARE ON YOUR OWN!

Developing independent language learning strategies

Terry Lamb

This chapter begins with a brief examination of the educational and pedagogical theory which supports the development of greater learner autonomy in the languages curriculum. This is followed by a case study of one school in England which has made considerable progress in the implementation of the theory as a means of delivering the new Modern Foreign Language National Curriculum for England and Wales.

Focus on learning

In his book *The Nature of Learning*, Cullingford (1990: 1) makes the statement that 'what children learn depends on how they learn'. At first glance this claim may appear self-evident to the reader. Further consideration, however, will stimulate reflection on many of the teaching and learning processes which are often taken for granted in the day-to-day planning of language lessons.

The first point to note is the focus given to learning as opposed to teaching. One commonly held view is that a child's education is determined solely by the direct intervention of the teacher 'delivering' the curriculum: learning is a direct outcome of teaching, since anything taught will automatically be learned, provided it has been taught thoroughly enough. A result of this viewpoint is the teacher-centred classroom in which the teacher is busily performing while the pupils 'listen' with varying degrees of involvement. For language teachers, who are all too often the only source of the target language in the classroom, the pressure to be teaching actively all the time is felt particularly acutely, with the result that they typically work far harder than their pupils, tending to feel guilty if they are not personally being active in the classroom. In this situation pupils may only be involved superficially, resulting in loss of concentration and a resultant deterioration in behaviour. The conscientious teacher, determined to maintain control of the situation, will often become even more active, frantically conducting the class like an orchestra, until eventually he/she will run out of energy and give the pupils some written work to do. Unfortunately, however, unless this work is appropriate for all the pupils, the situation will not be helped in the long term, and teacher–pupil relationships will possibly break down. Cullingford's focus on pupils' learning serves as a timely reminder that the aim of the teacher must be to encourage learning, and therefore the teacher must constantly reappraise what pupils are doing in order to enable them to learn.

Focus on how pupils learn

Having returned to the very core of what the relationship is between teaching and learning, the reader can then turn his/her attention to the second element in Cullingford's statement, namely the concern with *how* pupils learn. This can be examined in two different ways: first, it raises the question of the vast range of individual differences represented in the average classroom; second, it can relate to the notion of learning strategies, both cognitive and metacognitive.

There have been many studies undertaken relating to individual differences and the ways in which these affect the learning situation. It is beyond the scope of this chapter to review in any detail the range of abilities and personalities with which the classroom teacher is faced. Nevertheless, it must be stated that differences in ability, both general cognitive and specific linguistic, combined with a broad spectrum of personality types, represent an enormous challenge to the teacher who must find resources which are differentiated and varied activities which are appropriate to the aims and objectives of the lesson and then organize the classroom so that these resources and activities can have maximum effect.

This variety is further complicated by the issue of learning styles which are only partly related to cognitive and personality differences. Studies in the field of the psychology of learning provide us with many definitions and taxonomies which address the question of how individuals learn. An impression of the variety of learning styles can be gained by a brief examination of one way of broadly categorizing them, namely into 'deep' and 'surface' learning. 'Deep' learning is characterized by a search for meaning in an area of study. Such learners typically attempt to probe beneath the surface, looking for patterns which will facilitate further learning, interpretation and summary. These are the learners who will often organize the material to be learned into diagrams and charts in an attempt to make sense of it. 'Surface' learning on the other hand is typified by the individual who simply accepts knowledge as a series of unrelated facts which must be understood in the order in which they are presented. Such learners may approach revision, for example, by starting at the beginning of the material and memorizing it detail by detail. It must be added, however, that this dichotomy is not as simple as it may appear, as some learners will approach different areas of learning in different ways. Furthermore, no judgement is being made as to the relative success of the different learning styles, since other factors, such as memory, also need to be taken into consideration. It is simply intended to impart a flavour of the variety of learning styles present in any language classroom, with some pupils looking for patterns, some collecting individual linguistic items, lexical or functional, some learning from experiential, practical activities, some learning most effectively from the written word, and indeed some for whom the written word is an interference to the learning process. If classroom practices are to be differentiated in order that each individual child may achieve his/her potential, this must also be taken into consideration.

The second issue raised by the focus on how children learn is that of learner strategies. These can be broadly divided into two areas, cognitive and metacognitive. The first area relates to the mental processes which a learner brings into play when learning a language. Much research has been carried out in this field, mainly by psycholinguists specializing in English as a foreign language who have studied the ways in which individuals (mainly adults) comprehend new language, remember it, and then access it (see, for example, O'Malley *et al.*, 1985; Rubin, 1989). More narrowly definable than broader learning styles, these strategies can lead to more efficient language acquisition and use. Metacognitive strategies, on the other hand, relate to the way in which learning is organized, including, for example, the planning, monitoring and evaluation of learning activities.

Recent research into language learning has revealed the importance not only of the teacher understanding the ways in which individuals learn languages, but also the learners themselves (Wenden and Rubin, 1987; Oxford, 1990; Wenden, 1991). Greater understanding of the learning process, both in terms of cognitive and metacognitive strategies, leads to improvement both in achievement and motivation, since learners are thus empowered to take control of their own linguistic development. From this, the idea of learner training emerges, with learners being asked to reflect on how they have understood, retained or recalled language, to evaluate its effectiveness, and to use this increased awareness to plan future learning, be it in terms of new learning objectives or more effective resources and activities.

Developing learner autonomy in the modern languages curriculum

Many language teachers are beginning to re-examine the processes of teaching and learning, focusing increasingly on the learner. As has already been noted, this brings with it an increased awareness of the need to differentiate in order to cater for the wide range of learner differences and needs, and this has enormous implications for resources and classroom organization.

Furthermore, such learner-centredness is leading to developments in the area of learning strategies and learner training. Such teachers are reappraising the aims of the languages curriculum in order to encompass the notion of learner autonomy, and are looking to experience gained in flexible learning situations.

The aims of flexible language learning methods

1 To meet individual needs more effectively by allowing for total differentiation, which can involve individualized learning if learners are to be engaged in tasks which are appropriate and at which they can experience success.

2 To create a learning environment where the necessary variety of resources and learning routes can be effectively managed.

3 To achieve this by the development of the learners' sense of responsibility for their own learning, enabling them to exercise some control over what they do, when and with whom. The establishment of the notion of a teacher–learner partnership is thereby encouraged, where genuine negotiation can take place. Current research is attempting to establish the effects of this on learner motivation.

4 To develop the metacognitive skills of target setting, monitoring and evaluation, in order to enable learners to diagnose their future language learning needs.

5 To enable the teacher's time to be used more effectively in order to target specific learning needs in the lesson and to monitor individual progress for summative and formative purposes. By releasing the teacher from his/her whole-class teaching role for a greater proportion of the lesson time, he/she can direct attention where it is most needed and is free to support and reinforce learning, to extend where appropriate, to monitor and assess, and to encourage the development of cognitive and metacognitive strategies in order to encourage even greater learner autonomy.

6 To improve standards of achievement in language learning. There is a strong indication, again the subject of current research, that the targeting of individual needs with appropriate resources in a supportive and well-organized learning environment, does encourage greater success. Furthermore, research has already indicated that learning is enhanced when the learner is active and when learning is at least partly self-initiated.

7 To help learners in schools to develop skills which can be more generally applied across the curriculum, for example, planning, problem solving, self-assessment, in order to discourage the compartmentalization of learning.

8 To enhance social learning by encouraging learners to work not only as individuals or as part of a whole class, but also in more flexible groupings as appropriate to the activity. Such collaborative learning has been

endorsed by considerable amounts of research which have not only addressed the socializing aspects but also the implications for learning of peer group support (Cullingford, 1990: 197).

9   To develop autonomous language learning skills in order to enable learners to take advantage of self-access facilities which are increasingly to be found in commerce, industry and further and higher education.

10   Related to the previous aim is the aim of encouraging positive attitudes towards foreign language learning so that learners will feel ready and confident to study any language they may need later in life, for personal, leisure or vocational purposes.

The Modern Foreign Languages National Curriculum for England and Wales

It is inappropriate to the nature of this chapter to describe in detail the Modern Foreign Languages National Curriculum for England and Wales. Nevertheless, three important aspects need to be addressed in order to provide the context for languages curriculum development. These are related to differentiation, language learning opportunities and assessment.

Differentiation

Differentiation is defined in the non-statutory guidance which accompanies the National Curriculum document as 'the process by which curriculum objectives, teaching methods, assessment methods, resources and learning activities are planned to cater for the needs of individual pupils' (NCC, 1991). As has been indicated earlier in this chapter, this issue is highly complex, placing great demands not only on the teacher's ability to plan, create resources, use existing materials and organize the classroom but also to identify the individual needs in the first place and then to monitor progress. The picture is further complicated by the reminder from the Modern Foreign Language Working Group, which was established to make recommendations on the nature of the National Curriculum, that 'language acquisition is a continuous but uneven process ... pupils will progress at different rates or may even at times regress' (DES, 1990: 11). Advice is offered by means of examples of differentiated work and a consideration of classroom organization to facilitate both group and independent work, with the important point being made that pupils will bring with them from their primary schools experience in learning in this way. The suggestion by OFSTED (the Office for Standards in Education), the government body set up to inspect all schools in the country, that '(schools) should create opportunities for pupils, working as a class, in smaller groups and independently, to practise their language skills and to apply them in authentic situations' (OFSTED, 1993: Inspection Schedule – Guidance) obviously reinforces this requirement, as does the statement 'where teaching is good . . . the lessons . . . cater appropriately for the learning of pupils with differing abilities and interests, and ensure the full participation of all' (OFSTED, 1993: Quality of Teaching – Guidance).

Opportunities for learning

In the Programme of Study (Part One), the National Curriculum sets out forty opportunities for learning and using the target language which pupils must be offered. Included in this is the opportunity to develop their independence in language learning and use, which can mean both working on their own or with others, and the opportunity to develop language learning skills and knowledge of language. These are now statutory requirements. This is reinforced by OFSTED who state that 'where learning is good, pupils adjust well to the demands of working in different contexts, selecting appropriate methods and organising effectively the resources they need. They evaluate their work and come to realistic judgements about it' (OFSTED, 1993: Quality of Learning – Guidance).

Assessment

The requirements of the teacher to 'assess pupils' progress continuously, determining each individual's level of attainment and shaping the future work so as to ensure progression' (OFSTED, 1993: Inspection Schedule – Guidance) are equally demanding. Initial attempts to realize this led to extremely complex, time-consuming and not particularly beneficial systems being introduced in many schools. The document *Teacher Assessment at KS3* (SEAC, 1992) highlighted the complexities of integrated assessment, but further complicated the situation by making the educationally sound statement that

> Pupils need to be active in their own learning. . . . This will involve pupils in planning, understanding learning objectives, making action plans to achieve individual goals, organising tasks and understanding the criteria for assessment. Pupils should be aware of how and why they are being assessed. . . . Opportunities for pupils to review their work should be built into normal classroom activities in order to check that goals are being achieved and ensure that information gained through assessment is used to set further goals and help pupils to progress.
>
> (SEAC, 1992: 3)

Learners' needs: the LINGUA project's findings

Central to the original brief of the LINGUA project was an analysis of teacher needs in relation to modern foreign languages within the school curriculum.

Members of the teams in each country collaborated in order to produce a questionnaire for language learners from which to extract data.

The pupil questionnaires revealed that motivation to learn is not only stimulated by the social context, but is also market-led insofar as learners see an ability to communicate in the foreign language as enhancing their career prospects, both at home and abroad. A foreign language is seen as a potentially valuable tool in local work, but also as the key to overseas jobs markets.

In answer to the question 'What are the things you want to be able to do with this language as a result of learning it?', using a 1–5 scale where 1 = very little indeed and 5 = a great deal, popular answers were as follows:

I want to be able to speak this language and hold a conversation with native speakers	3.7
I want to be able to write in the language whenever it would be useful	3.5
I want to be able to read this language whenever it would be useful	3.7
I want to be able to understand people speaking in this language, e.g. on television, radio or in films	3.6
I want to be able to evaluate how I am getting on myself	3.0
I want to be able to learn independently	3.1
I want to be able to acquire skills of learning any foreign language so I can learn other languages too	3.5

Learning a foreign language is not only an advantage for the present day, but also an enjoyable and valuable transferable skill for the future, as independent and involved learners who are motivated to learn one language are thus acquiring the confidence and skills to study any language later in life, for whatever purposes.

The questionnaires also show that there is a real desire to be able to manipulate the language, and that learners are keen to be competent to use language for a variety of purposes. Furthermore, they wish to have control over their learning by being in a position to evaluate diagnostically their own progress in order to advance competence. It is clear that a variety of activities is necessary in order to address the diversity of needs. Flexible learning strategies help to fulfil these requirements.

In response to the question 'What helps you learn in the classroom?' (1 = hardly helps at all, 5 = helps a great deal), popular answers were:

If I am clear what I have to do	4.3
If the teacher makes the meaning of new words clear	4.3
If the teacher makes clear in English how the language functions	4.0
If the teacher speaks the language all the time making sure I understand all the important points	3.5
If the teacher makes clear how grammar and using the language go together	3.6

If the teacher encourages me	3.8
If I can see the progress I am making	3.8
If I keep being successful	4.0
If the teacher marks my work promptly and thoroughly	3.7

Learner autonomy requires learners' awareness of learning strategies. Flexible learning methods are overt and learners are trained in the skills of target setting and self-assessment. Learners themselves here cite the importance of being responsible for their own progress via clarity of purpose and awareness of learning methods. An ability to assess one's own progress is an important advantage for learners; it helps them to have control over their learning and increased involvement would seem to increase motivation. It is interesting to note the desire for prompt feedback. One response to this within the differentiated learning environment is for students to be able to assess a proportion of their work themselves providing immediate feedback. Furthermore, as the teacher moves away from centre stage and devolves responsibility for learning, he/she is released to support, monitor and assess on a more individualized basis. All learners wish to be valued and to be given the opportunity to achieve, otherwise motivation could be affected.

Autonomy in practice: a case study

The context

This particular case study relates to a mixed comprehensive school in a small town in Derbyshire in the Midlands. The school is non-selective and contains pupils of all abilities from a broad socio-economic background. All pupils in the school must study at least one modern foreign language from entering the school in Year 7 (age 11) until Year 11 when GCSE examinations are taken, the insistence on languages for all pupils in Years 10 and 11 being a new requirement.

Pupils are taught in completely all-ability classes throughout the entire five years of language learning. The term 'all-ability' is one used in Derbyshire to distinguish it from the mixed-ability situation and, as the term implies, it ensures that pupils with special educational needs are fully integrated into the mainstream classroom. Language teachers in the school thus found themselves in a context in which the various factors were conducive to change. The factors were as follows:

1   They were faced for the first time with a situation in which all pupils had to continue to study a modern foreign language. Though they did welcome this new requirement, they recognized that it would bring with it new challenges.

2   Pupils would continue to be taught in all-ability classes and this meant that the policy on differentiation would have to be extended to ensure individual progress and motivation.

3   The National Curriculum was about to be introduced, necessitating a complete review of the way in which languages were taught to ensure differentiation, coverage of the programmes of study (including the opportunities for independent work which must be offered to all pupils) and the fulfilment of assessment requirements.

4   The language teachers had for some time been exploring ways of differentiating more effectively in all skill areas, i.e. in speaking and listening activities as well as in reading and writing tasks, and of addressing the classroom management implications of this.

The result of the curriculum review was a renewed commitment to extending the notion of differentiation to ensure that all of the pupils' needs were being met and that National Curriculum requirements were being fulfilled. It was recognized that some amount of individualized provision was implied by this, and that the issue of classroom management therefore needed to be addressed as a matter of urgency. The key to this seemed to be the development of pupil autonomy, with pupils being encouraged to play a more active part in the management of their own learning. This implied that the scheme of work would need to address not only the linguistic content but also the framework for learning.

With the development of pupil autonomy as the driving force, it was decided that the following principles would underlie the scheme of work:

1   Pupils would need to have full access to the scheme of work, with learning objectives being made quite explicit.

2   Pupils would be involved in decision making and would have the power to negotiate when targets are being set, giving them greater control over their own learning. They would thus also be encouraged to reflect on why they are doing a particular activity in terms of its relationship to the target, and to evaluate its effectiveness as a learning task.

3   Related to this is the inclusion of a system of self-assessment which would facilitate self-diagnosis and make feedback more immediate and manageable.

4   An appropriately wide choice of learning resources and activities would need to be made available to the pupils so that their individual needs, whether relating to ability, learning style or motivation, could be addressed.

5   Pupils would need to be involved in the management of these resources and activities in order that they might have access to whatever was deemed appropriate, and to remove some of the burden from the teacher who would otherwise be unable to offer such a wide range at any one time.

6   The learning system would need to be 'user-friendly' so that pupils and teachers would feel confident about how it works. It was considered very important that, despite the complex demands of the aims and principles underlining the scheme of work, the framework for learning must underpin and facilitate learning rather than dominate it.

The learning process: the presentation stage

It is important to recognize at this point that the teachers in question were not looking to a full-blown flexible learning scheme along the lines of those often used in industry or higher education, where individuals are able to determine the objectives of their learning, being largely left to pursue their studies alone as and when appropriate. In contrast to many of those schemes, the teacher would still have a role to play in determining and presenting the topic. This would involve the usual techniques of presentation familiar to practitioners of communicative methodology and include the early stage pre-communicative activities such as imitation (requiring an immediate response), repetition (with more demand being made on memory), and low-level questioning. These would be largely teacher-centred and teacher-led.

The learning process: the semi-autonomous stage

Following the initial presentation, pupils would take part in highly structured and for the most part still pre-communicative activities which would reinforce the core language. These would still be teacher-led or at least teacher-directed, but would increasingly involve the pupils in pair- or group-work. As such they can be regarded as semi-autonomous activities, providing a training ground for more independent work.

At an early stage of language learning, this stage would also need to include an introduction to the resources available to support learning. Pupils would need to learn how to operate the cassette players, access the cassettes, use the computer and the language-master, and find any of the resources that they may need to use. The way in which the learning system operates would also need to be introduced in a clear, appropriate and differentiated way.

The learning process: autonomous learning

What happens next in the learning process was considered by the language teachers in the case study school as crucial to the fulfilment of the aims and principles they had set themselves. This was to be the stage where real learning would take place with individuals being given the opportunity to internalize the language, to practise it as much as is necessary, to extend the knowledge and enhance the skills to appropriate levels, and to use it for the purposes of real communication. Learners would now be able to identify their own needs and take some responsibility for satisfying them.

The Profile

The Profile is a document developed by the teachers in the school in question with the aim of empowering the pupils in their language learning. It is the key which provides access to the two main elements of the scheme of work, namely the objectives of the syllabus and the resources available to support achievement of those objectives. As the syllabus has been designed around units of work, each containing functional and structural elements within a topic area, a Profile has been produced for each unit.

The language learning objectives

These are made explicit in the Profile in two ways:

1   The overall goal of the unit appears on the front cover. For example, Unit One of the German course, aimed at 11-year-old beginners is introduced as follows: 'In this unit I am aiming to talk about myself and write a letter to a penfriend.'
2   More precise objectives then follow, appearing as a series of numbered 'I can ...' statements, divided into the skill areas of listening, speaking, reading and writing (Table 2.1).

Resources and activities

Following the presentation of the language and some semi-autonomous practice, pupils are then enabled to target their own very specific needs by having access to a whole range of resources and learning activities. These will enable learners to work at their own level, in the skill needing attention, and in the style which suits them best at the time. Learners will be able to work alone, or to negotiate pair work or group work.

As has already been stated, the variety of resources implied by the commitment to such a level of differentiation is enormous. At any one time

Table 2.1 'I can ...' statements

Sprechen
1   Ask and talk about families.
2   Ask and talk about pets and reply.
3   Ask and say when someone's birthday is.
4   Say dates.

pupils may need access to the following:

- worksheets (to practise any of the four language skills)
- textbooks (a variety)
- reference books (e.g. atlases and dictionaries)
- authentic materials (e.g. brochures, magazines and newspapers)
- listening equipment (including cassettes)
- games
- talk cards
- computers and other interactive hardware
- videos
- answer sheets
- assessment work

Pupils therefore need to be able to find the appropriate tasks for themselves.

With this in mind, the language teachers also include a study guide in the Profile, designed to link specific resources and activities to the various learning objectives (Table 2.2).

Materials can be located by means of two simple devices:

1) The number on the left corresponds to the learning objective, i.e. 1 refers to the statement 'I can ask and talk about families' (Table 2.1). This means that the pupil can identify the tasks which will enable him/her to work on this particular area, the tasks being identified by a code such as C3 (referring to a task sheet or envelope containing a game, talk cards, etc.), LM (referring to Language Master cards), or EK1 (a textbook, in this case *Einfach Klasse 1*).

2) These tasks are organized according to level, be it level of language or level of complexity of task, which is represented by stars (one-star, two-star or three-star tasks). Having thus narrowed down the choice, pupils can then look at the tasks and decide which they wish to do. Obviously pupils will also need to work in the context of certain ground rules to ensure that, for example, all four skills are being practised. Nevertheless, there will still be considerable freedom of choice. Furthermore, the negotiation which will of necessity take place, both with the teacher and fellow pupils will bring social

Table 2.2 Study guide

	*	**	***
1	C3 C4 LM11–15	C8 EK1 S.32 C9	C17(2) C21
2	D6 LM26–35 D14	D11(1) EK1 S.120	D11(2) D44
3	E20 LM16–20	E21 E30	E31(1)
4	E4 E5 LM21–25	E14 E25	E26 EK1 S.38

benefits. Pupils quickly see the advantages in, for example, doing listening activities with the cassette player in much smaller groups, having more control over the number of times a passage is repeated, and will learn to accept the implications of this for cooperation with their peers.

Monitoring and recording work

Pupils are expected to check their work as soon as a task has been completed. This offers several advantages:

1   Pupils receive instant feedback on their work.
2   Pupils are forced to examine their work closely rather than simply looking at the final mark.
3   The identification of errors by the pupils themselves encourages greater reflection on the reasons for those errors.
4   Teachers are spared much of the less valuable marking (such as the marking of pre-communicative drills, or comprehensions where answers may be provided in English if the task is an interpreting one or in the form of a table or multiple-choice responses). They can then concentrate on marking tasks which the pupils are unable to mark themselves, such as many writing or speaking activities, and the nature of the classroom organization will in fact enable this to be carried out alongside the pupil in the classroom.
5   Pupils will be able to use the information gained from the marking to make decisions regarding subsequent activities.

In order to help pupils to manage the choice of activities and the recording of information, the Profile also contains a work plan (Figure 2.1).

Pupils are expected to fill in the work plan for each task, and this enables both pupil and teacher to monitor the tasks done, in terms of number and level of task achieved as well as breadth of skills being practised. The pupil also enters which work has been done as homework, since this is also differentiated in the same way as classwork, with pupils themselves deciding on appropriate and achievable tasks.

Metacognitive skills

The Profile offers pupils access to the scheme of work and also a framework for organizing their learning. In order to help them to evaluate their success at this and to reflect on ways to improve their learning skills, the Profile also contains a checklist of metacognitive skills such as the one in Figure 2.2. (This list is only one example, since the skills to be highlighted in this way may vary as the pupil progresses.)

Date	Activity	Level	Skill	Class/home	Mark	Teacher signature

Figure 2.1 Work plan.

Assessment

Following discussion of the assessment issues related to the aims of the school's approach to language teaching and learning, the teachers agreed that the following principles were vital:

- it should be non-threatening to the pupil
- it should be part of the learning process
- it should be differentiated
- it should be manageable

It was decided that the concept of end-of-unit tests did not fit in with these principles, and that ways of integrating assessment must consequently be explored. Obviously the framework for learning already contained a major contribution to this in the way of self-assessment and formative teacher assessment. It was felt, however, that more rigorous assessment would need to be introduced, in which conditions could be more carefully controlled.

The result was the introduction of the concept of essential tasks which have the following characteristics:

- They reflect the work being done by pupils both in format and content.
- They assess achievement according to National Curriculum criteria and levels.
- They are tackled by individual pupils whenever they feel adequately prepared for an assessment at that level.

	Done well	To improve
Organisation of work/notes		
Using time well		
Record keeping (Workplan)		
Understand National Curriculum levels		
Working at the right level		
Homework		
Presentation		
Bringing equipment		
Finding out new words for myself		
Collect information about country		
Working in pairs/groups		
Volunteering answers		
Using the language to the teacher		
Using the language with others		
Thinking about my accent		

Figure 2.2 Checklist of metacognitive skills.

- Though not done in formal examination conditions, i.e. with the whole class working in silence, they are completed in a special area of the classroom designated for that purpose, with the expectation that other pupils will not disturb them.
- Where it is appropriate to use references, this will be allowed. Occasionally, however, it will be necessary to assess how much language has been assimilated.

Learners' responses to flexible learning

Initial questionnaires completed by language learners within the school who, at the age of 11 or 12 had experienced a full year of the methods outlined above, revealed that for every one child who best enjoyed lessons when all students were working together with the teacher, three children preferred to work independently. Furthermore, they highly rated group work, using the Language Master, playing language games and using reference books, particularly dictionaries.

These findings are supported by research carried out in a second Derbyshire school which has embraced the concept of learner autonomy. Here the following points emerged:

- learners enjoy setting their own pace
- learners enjoy making informed choices about their needs according to their ability, being able to work on what they want, when they want
- learners feel they work as well or even better when they have responsibility for their own learning
- learners' organizational skills improve once they become accustomed to working in this manner
- learners are able to draw on skills from other curriculum areas
- learners develop skills of self-assessment: 'I can mark my own work and see for myself where I went wrong'
- learners are motivated to seek help if unsure, thus increasing the efficiency of their work in relation to progress achieved.

Conclusion

This chapter has examined a particular response to the needs of the modern languages learner within a specific context. Though responding to the context, namely the demands of a National Curriculum and the specific concerns within a school influenced by its own locality, intake and priorities, the response is grounded in theories of education and learning which inform the overall aims, and as such it is more than merely a convenient solution to a problem.

At the heart of both the theoretical and practical aspects of this work lies a commitment to learning. The focus on learning rather than teaching, which requires a focus on the individual rather than the group, and the implications of this for differentiation of content and learning process as well as for the development of learning skills, was presented as the central principle which would inform the languages curriculum in the case study school.

The conclusion drawn by the language teachers in the school was that this central principle implies, indeed necessitates, a commitment to learner autonomy for both ideological and pragmatic reasons. Fortunately they found that many of their aims and principles were shared by those educationalists involved in the development of flexible learning programmes, so there was already existing experience on which to draw. The emerging Modern Foreign Languages National Curriculum, particularly in its concern for differentiation, for varied learning opportunities which would include independent and collaborative work, and for methods of assessment which would facilitate careful continuous monitoring, by both teacher and pupil, of individual progress and achievement, was also making demands which seemed to the languages department to require an increase in pupil autonomy.

The resulting framework for learning has been briefly outlined. The effects on achievement and motivation are being monitored, but research already indicates considerable improvement. In all year groups pupils are able to work at their own level: able pupils are successfully attempting higher level tasks to which previously they would not have had access, since it would have been impossible to organize activities on an individual basis to the same extent; similarly, less able pupils are able to work at their level with a large variety of resources and learning activities. GCSE examination results have also improved drastically for those pupils who have been encouraged to learn more autonomously. Pupil questionnaires and recorded interviews indicate very positive attitudes towards this way of working, and motivation appears to have increased. Obviously it would be unwise to ignore other factors which may have contributed to this improvement, such as the positive effects of teachers being able to operate in a style to which they are personally and professionally committed, increased general awareness of the importance of learning languages in the European context, or the improved status of languages in the school curriculum since they became a compulsory subject. Nevertheless, the evidence of its success combined with an appreciation of the principles which underpin it indicate that such methodology is worthy of further consideration. Research into learner autonomy in relation to foreign language learners in secondary schools is still at a very early stage, particularly in the field of metacognitive skills and their relationship to motivation and achievement. If, however, we accept Cullingford's view on the correlation between learning and the learning process, as quoted in the introduction to this chapter, we must continue to explore possibilities for its realization.

References

Cullingford, C. (1990) *The Nature of Learning*, London: Cassell Educational Ltd.

Department for Education (1995) *Modern Foreign Languages in the National Curriculum*, London: HMSO.

Department of Education and Science (DES) (1990) *Modern Foreign Languages for Ages 11 to 16. Proposals for the Secretary of State for Education and Science and the Secretary of State for Wales*, London: DES/WO.

National Curriculum Council (NCC) (1991) *Science and Pupils with Special Educational Needs*, London: HMSO.

National Curriculum Council (NCC) (1992) *Modern Foreign Languages in the National Curriculum*, London: HMSO.

OFSTED (1993) *Guidance on the Inspection of Secondary Schools*, London: HMSO.

O'Malley, J. M., Chamont, A. U., Stewner-Manzanares, G., Russo, R. P. and Kupper, L. (1985) 'Learning Strategy Applications with Students of English as a Second Language', in *TESOL Quarterly* 19: 557–584.

Oxford, R. (1990) *Language Learning Strategies: What Every Teacher Should Know*, New York: Newbury House.

Rubin, J. (1989) 'How Learner Strategies can Inform Language Teaching', in V. Bickley (ed.) *Proceedings of LULTAC, Sponsored by the Institute of Language in Education*, Hong Kong: Department of Education.

SEAC (1992) *Teacher Assessment at KS3*, London: HMSO.

Wenden, A. (1991) *Learner Strategies for Learner Autonomy*, Cambridge, MA: Prentice Hall.

Wenden, A. and Rubin, J. (1987) *Learner Strategies in Language Learning*, Cambridge, MA: Prentice Hall.

3

MULTIMEDIA IN COMPUTER-ASSISTED LANGUAGE LEARNING

Wilhelm Grießhaber

Computer-assisted language learning is currently experiencing a come-back. Many schools are setting up computer laboratories for language teaching purposes and not only for technical subjects, and attractive multimedia programs with sound and video clips are competing on the market. Nevertheless, there seems to be little discussion of relevant language teaching methodology. After their debates in the 1980s, proponents and opponents of this new medium seem to have lost their appetite for argument.

In this chapter, I will discuss first the technical prerequisites of the computers and, briefly, the corresponding programs. The effect which the arrangement of computers in the classroom has on possible social forms of foreign language teaching will then be discussed. Several programs and their use are introduced in the main part of the chapter, where it becomes apparent that different programs can be suitable depending on the learner's age and competence level. Special emphasis is laid on authoring tools with which teachers and learners can employ the computer as a tool in order to investigate the language and to use it for the purpose of communicating. In this context, the linking of learners through the pedagogical network and the so-called 'electronic blackboard' play an important part in the realization of new forms of group work.

Technical prerequisites and didactic concepts

There is hardly a medium that seems as high-tech as a computer. The information appears virtually on the screen, it cannot be handled (apart from on paper printouts) and it disappears again when the computer is switched off. People who are not computer literate frequently ask where a certain piece of information is actually stored, as the information on a disc is not accessible without technological aids. The lack of concreteness which characterizes computer-assisted information processing seems also to have led to computers being attributed with intelligence, an image that has found its way into everyday language in the form of expressions such as 'the computer is calculating/searching/printing'. When the use of computers for language teaching began, it was heavily determined by algorithmic concepts of information processing (see Figure 3.1a), which in turn determined programming itself. The program contains a command for the manipulation of data, a given variable in the example is to be increased by ten, and it then checks whether a certain figure or value has been reached or indeed surpassed. If the figure has not been reached, the procedure is repeated; in the other case the next step is initiated. This operational pattern also forms the basis of programmed instruction, which is mainly linked with Skinner and his teaching machines. Information is presented to the learner, who is then tested on it. If the learner gives the correct answer, the system presents the next unit of information; if he or she does not, the former unit of information is repeated in a slightly different way (see Figure 3.1b).

According to this concept, computers are used on the one hand to relieve teachers of the monotonous task of rule familiarization and on the other hand to offer learners the possibility of processing strings of linguistic signs and learning the rules for the formation of correct utterances at their own speed and in their own time (see Figure 3.1b). It was believed that – in contrast to human language instructors – such tutoring programs would offer the exact language level to suit the student and would not, even in the case of repeated mistakes, diminish the learner's motivation through impatience (see, e.g. Langenscheidt-Redaktion, 1985).

It was not until the 1980s that computers became more powerful and could process pictures, sound and even films in addition to numbers and letters. At the same time, due to improved user guides the programs did not become more complicated but the introduction of icons actually made them more user-friendly than the old systems, even for users with little knowledge of computers. Both developments, the multimedia capabilities and the user-

Figure 3.1a Algorithm   *Figure 3.1b* Programmed instruction

friendliness, predestine the computer as a tool in foreign language learning (see Grießhaber, 1992). With the help of this technology, language can be presented not only as a system of lexical items and corresponding combinatory rules, but also as a means of interactive communication. Quick and direct access to even the smallest communication units enables the learner to study units of language used in communication independently. Employing computers for this purpose is fundamentally different from the early approaches to the replacement of human instructors through teaching machines for the presentation and familiarization of rules. The new and fascinating possibilities do not only make possible new methodological approaches to foreign language teaching, but necessitate them.

Didactic concepts for the teaching of communication skills depend to a large extent on the way the classroom is laid out. In a class which aims at enabling the learners to communicate, the students must first of all be given the possibility of communicating during class. For this purpose, a circular seating arrangement, in which all participants can see and talk to each other, is the best set-up. However, this communicative ideal can come into conflict with the teacher's didactic task of drawing the attention of all the learners to a 'blackboard' from time to time. Most importantly, such a circular arrangement of desks and computers for the learners takes up a large amount of space, which is usually not available. Thus, more economical layouts (see Figure 3.2) predominate, with differing emphasis regarding the number of computers (and learners), the role of the teacher in the language teaching process and the communicative skills aimed at.

The most usual seating arrangement is probably in parallel rows (see Figure 3.2a): the learners face forwards – and look at their monitors, the teacher and the board. In such a setting, which is typical for teacher-centred classes, the instructor can easily supervise each student, whereas communication between the learners is made difficult. The students in the back row can

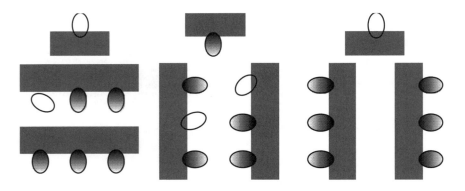

Figure 3.2a Parallel   *Figure 3.2b* Centrifugal   *Figure 3.2c* Centripetal

only see the backs of the students in front, who have to turn round for group work. The teacher, on the other hand, has no direct visual access to the learners' computer screens. Here the centrifugal arrangement of the desks along the sides of the room and facing the wall, which is also fairly widespread, can help (Figure 3.2b). The teacher can quickly assess the learner activities and assist from behind. However, it is difficult to focus the learners' attention towards a central point. As in Figure 3.2a, communication between the learners is very limited. A U-shaped centripetal arrangement of the desks (Figure 3.2c), however, encourages communication in class: teacher and students can see each other over their screens, can talk to each other and can look at a board. However, this arrangement does not allow the teacher direct access to the students' screens.

Traditional suppliers of language laboratory systems achieve central control of the individual student computers through proprietary network solutions, by which the screen content of the teacher's computer can simultaneously be transferred to the students' computers. As a result, the learners are made to focus on their own screens and are mentally disassociated from the group they form with the other learners. It is precisely this central aspect of traditional language laboratory methods which makes truly communicative FLT more difficult, if not impossible. For this reason, solutions such as those given in figures 3.2a or 3.2b, which disconnect learners from group communication and place them in a synchronized learning process performed individually, are to be considered obsolete in the light of foreign language teaching methodology. As an alternative, modern network communication programs offer the integrated solution of an electronic blackboard for the integration of the learners. The screen of the teacher's computer can be shown to the class with the help of an LCD-panel and overhead projector or beamer. Screen-sharing programs make new forms of group work possible, as the teacher can call up every students' screen on his/her own computer. Thus the teacher has permanent access to the activities of the learners and can even help them directly via keyboard and mouse when they encounter problems. As a result of this centralized projection solution, the learners' attention is directed towards a focal point of perception, in contrast to the synchronized individual work. This solution opens up completely new dimensions of group work (see below).

Only for individual self-tutoring studies does a setting as in Figure 3.1a make sense in terms of economy of space. However, experience with self-access materials at the Applied Languages Centre at Münster University has shown that the individual computers should be isolated acoustically through partitions, as otherwise the students feel too inhibited to practise speaking aloud.

The popularity of the uncommunicative layouts of figures 3.2a and 3.2b is hard to explain. Language instructors seemingly have a strong desire for direct control of the learners' activities. They wish to be able continuously to observe and control the learner utterances and other activities (for example, on the computer screen). The didactic concept on which this procedure is based aims at complete control of the learning process with the intention of allowing virtually only correct foreign language utterances during the acquisition process. This rule-based concept runs contrary to insights gained into the foreign language learning process: language is acquired through usage with meaningful content.

For use in group work, computers for the teacher and student work stations should have multimedia capabilities, i.e. they should have a powerful processor, a CD-ROM drive, a high-resolution colour screen as well as headphones and microphone. Furthermore, the teacher's computer should be equipped with loudspeakers or powered speakers and an LCD-panel with overhead projector or beamer. If it is additionally connected to an audio cassette recorder and video recorder, other data of a topical nature can also be used in class. A modem that allows access to the Internet should definitely be an integrated feature. All computers should be integrated into a network and be able to exchange data with the help of a screen-sharing program (for further information see Grießhaber, 1995).

Commercial programs for language presentation

Multimedia programs are impressive due to their phenomenal capacity for the presentation of data. They can present videos with textual inserts more precisely than any other medium. In contrast, the elaborate presentation equipment used in audio-visual teaching now seems virtually archaic. Multimedia computers can start an hour-long film at any place absolutely precisely with virtually no time-lag and can replay a selected passage. This program-based 'intelligent' control mechanism makes possible non-linear branching, which would be impossible using a video recorder. Thus, these programs offer the best prerequisites for the presentation of language in interactive communication situations for didactic purposes. The visible actions are an aid to language intake, they appeal to different senses and present the learner with a basis for networked information acquisition and processing. In the following, these functions, which so far have been discussed in a fairly abstract way, will be illustrated through examples. After the presentation of two programs in the first section for children starting to learn a language, the second section will deal with three advanced multimedia programs for adolescents or adult learners.

Programs for beginners

Beginners have very restricted access to the language they are learning and therefore need special teaching and learning materials which take this fact into account. As FLT in schools usually concerns children, the following discussion concerns programs for children learning a foreign language. For adolescent or adult language beginners, programs other than the ones presented here should be considered (see Stracke-Elbina, 1995, 1996).

Investigating stories with Just Grandma and Me

A large number of interesting electronic books is now available for children learning a foreign language, of which *Just Grandma and Me* from the series 'Living Books' by Brøderbund is presented here as an example (Figure 3.3). The program, which is available on CD-ROM, 'narrates' the adventures of a small boy when he goes to the beach with his grandmother. In the 'Play' mode a young proficient speaker reads short scenes written from the boy's perspective, the words highlighted as they are being read. In this way, the user can see exactly which word is being read aloud at any given moment. The story being narrated is depicted as a cartoon, which helps the child to understand the meaning of the foreign language text without taking recourse to its mother tongue. In the 'Explore' mode the viewer controls the tempo and can initiate a wealth of actions and activities through clicking at objects, which provide the motivation for many different kinds of speech acts and in the course of which the main characters also use direct speech. The program is available in the languages American English, Spanish and Japanese.

Figure 3.3 Just Grandma and Me. © 1992 Living Books® All rights reserved. Used by permission.

'Reading' this book is literally child's play so that the operating of the program in no way interferes with its use.

The stories correspond to a child's world and feature language material that expresses what a child may already have experienced or will experience in the future. The most important thing, however, is that they are very exciting, full of surprises and make you want to read on. Thus they fulfil one of Leont'ev's main requirements for good texts for use in FLT:

> The language teaching text should ideally be structured like a literary text that (depending on how good it is) offers the reader the chance to empathize with the 'hero'. As part of the teaching process the unit should underline these characteristics as much as possible, i.e. should present the learner with the task of carrying out this speech activity 'together with' or 'on behalf of' the hero.
>
> (translation based on Leont'ev, 1971: 126)

These 'books' contain many methodological possibilities. From the central computer, the teacher can first of all show the whole class the book and explain how it works on the electronic blackboard. Then the pupils can 'read' the book on their own or with a partner on their own computers, after which the whole class discusses how they liked it and what to do next. Working in pairs, the pupils can tell each other the story or a variation of it and then progress to beach adventures they have had themselves. In addition, the pictures also offer many opportunities for vocabulary work in large or small groups. In short self-tutoring periods the children can also do exercises in which they repeat what has been said in order to acquire the correct pronunciation, just as in a language laboratory. Audio-visual purists' only criticism might be that the written text is presented at the same time as the narrated text.

With materials of this type it is important that the teacher develops the systematic aspects of the language and includes them in the teaching process. The 'books' contain neither an index nor a vocabulary list, nor are they written with grammatical progression in mind. This is where traditional foreign language teachers voice their scepticism: how can past tense, with its many irregular forms, already be used at the beginning? Though the different episodes are written at children's level, they consist of syntactically quite complex language. They cannot be used to go through in order to discuss and explain all the grammatical phenomena they contain. While speaking and exploring the episodes, the children learn to use syntactic units correctly for communication purposes that have not been broken down and to filter out the basic, easy structures suitable for their own level of competence by subconsciously dissecting structures (see, for example, the results of Wong-Fillmore, 1979). During this process they will certainly make many mistakes – just like children learning their mother tongue. Through asking questions about the content and repeating utterances correctly, the teacher can unobtrusively present and introduce the correct form.

Vocabulary work with Community Exploration

Vocabulary work is one of the most important, though not highly popular tasks connected with learning a language. Though all relevant didactic guidelines propagate learning new vocabulary monolingually in context, learners nevertheless still compile vocabulary lists in the two languages, whether on index cards or in special vocabulary notebooks. *Community Exploration* provides a countermeasure to this inclination. The program's opening screen shows a bird's eye view of a small (American) town. Through clicking on a complex you enter the school, the fire station, the supermarket, a housing estate, and so on. Within the buildings you can walk through the rooms by clicking on doors and objects, you can watch people carrying out tasks in short animated sequences and hear the name of an object by clicking on it, thereby highlighting it. Learners can thus explore this unknown world and at the same time acquire thematically structured basic vocabulary. An electronic cassette recorder on the screen indicates that learners can check their pronunciation by listening to the model pronunciation, recording their

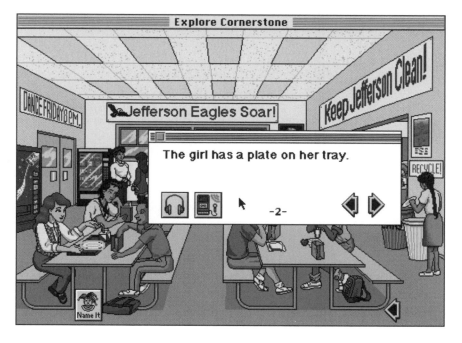

Figure 3.4 Community Exploration. (Used by permission of Jostens Learning Corporation.)

own and then comparing the two. In a practice or test mode learners can check on what they know. A log-book can be activated that allows the teacher to analyse the different learning routes taken, so that particular difficulties or marked improvement of learners are noticed and can be acted upon.

In a similar way to *Just Grandma and Me*, the program can be used in phases involving the whole class and for short self-study periods or for in-depth studying outside of class. It is important for the exploitation of the program's didactic potential that the learners become interested in the program and are given specific tasks, in order that their explorations result in meaningful speech acts. Only then can a network of connecting mental tracks leading to the words be built up. The learners might write short stories about their exploratory travels, for example, and present them to their fellow pupils.

Programs for advanced learners

Multimedia programs offer many opportunities of language presentation for advanced learners, too. In schools, FLT curricula for advanced learners are frequently dominated by literary topics, which are to provide an introduction into the culture of the country in question. As a result, written texts, about which the learners talk and write, are mainly used, with additional information given in the form of pictures or film versions of literary works. In this case, there is little sense in simply presenting these texts on a screen instead of on paper. On the one hand, printed books are easier and more pleasant to read than computer screens due to their higher resolution and, on the other hand, they are still easier to carry and transport than a computer. Finally, it is obviously easier to underline and annotate texts on paper than as electronic documents. Nevertheless, the computer also possesses out-standing qualities for the presentation of language in advanced foreign language teaching. It has the edge whenever film versions of a literary work exist, as is often the case with plays, screen plays or other film versions of literary works. In the case of historical documentations such as that of Bill Clinton's election campaign in 1992, the computer also comes into its own.

Textual work with Macbeth

Plays, whose written form merely provides a basis for their realization in an actual performance, are particularly suited for the presentation on a computer that integrates several media. 'Electronic Play Books' are capable of showing the text as well as extracts of film versions of different performances. *Macbeth* can be used to show the potential such publications have. It contains the text of the play with its acts and scenes, a comprehensive index with quote references, extensive commentary on individual passages, an introduction into the age of Shakespeare and contemporary theatre life, including a map of the City of London as well as annotated film clips of different film versions of the play.

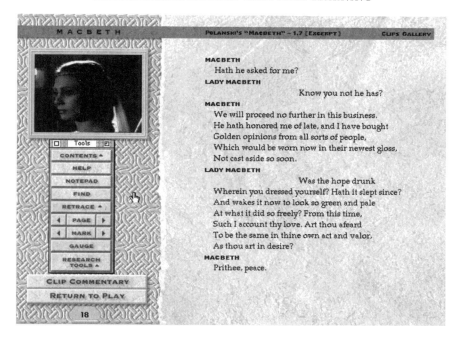

Figure 3.5 Macbeth (with permission, The Voyager Company)

This play book can either be used when working with the whole class or for decentralized work in small groups or individually. The electronic concordance makes the program ideal for analysing content and language. In the blink of an eye different passages can be linked and compared. Instead of looking up an unknown word straightaway, learners can thus try to guess its meaning by studying the different passages in which it occurs, before looking it up in a dictionary merely to check whether the assumption was correct. These steps are particularly useful for periods of individual work. The students can work on their own or in small groups while the teacher takes note of their procedures. When interesting aspects come up, the teacher can make one group's work the topic for the whole class, either at once or at a later stage.

Poetry in Motion

Like plays, poetry, too, is specifically intended to be recited and – as is the case with modern American poetry – can be linked to music. Thus poetry is also ideally suited to being presented via multimedia computers. The program *Poetry in Motion* contains video recordings of poetry readings given by contemporary American authors. As an option, the published text or the

57

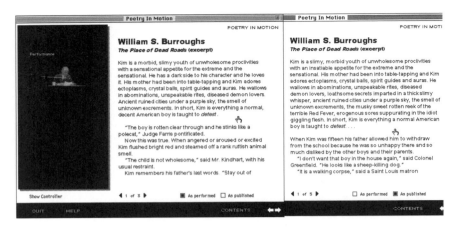

Figure 3.6 Poetry in Motion (left) the recited text, (right) the published version (with permission, The Voyager Company)

recited text can be called up on to the screen at the same time. Videotaped interviews with some of the poets are also included.

The visual presence of the poets gives the poems a new dimension, which cannot be achieved by audio recording or written text alone. As the program also contains a user-friendly concordance function, comparisons of the language used can easily be undertaken. Indeed, the main task of the teacher, when using programs such as these, should be to help the students undertake independent language research.

Contemporary history at your fingertips: Clinton – Portrait of Victory

In our fast-moving television world, topical events are temporarily (and often excessively) presented on all television channels simultaneously. However, background information tends only to be given in magazines broadcast at less popular viewing times or in the printed media, so that they are noticed less. Thus originally highly spectacular events tend to fade from people's memories after only a few months. One example of this phenomenon is probably the Gulf War of 1991. Multimedia programs – such as *Desert Storm*, for example – offer a rich source of information on such events for classroom projects. *Clinton – Portrait of Victory*, a program about Bill Clinton's election campaign of 1992, shall serve as illustration.

The program contains background information on Bill Clinton as a person and his election campaign, includes a photo album with commentary and videotaped extracts of his speeches as well as interviews with various people involved in the campaign. The program is user-friendly, though the somewhat overpowering presentation may weary less emotionally inclined European users.

Figure 3.7 Clinton – Portrait of Victory (with permission, Epicenter Communications)

The program is suitable for adolescent learners who have only vague preconceptions of the colourful American election campaigns and thus will receive an interesting insight into the campaign machinery, the rhetoric of the candidates and also contemporary spoken American English. Using the program in class necessitates giving the students specific research tasks, to be carried out on their own or in small groups. Though the individual programs date quite quickly, new programs on topical events are published all the time, so that there is always suitable new material available.

Authoring tools for developing own programs

As even complex programs have become increasingly user-friendly, even people who are not computer experts can put together quite ambitious multimedia presentations relatively easily. Teachers therefore do not have to rely solely on 'canned' products but can also enjoy 'homegrown fresh fruits' of their own. Nowadays, programs are so simple that even adolescents or teachers wary of computers can produce sophisticated results in the FL classroom.

The authoring tools mentioned in the following all have the development of receptive and productive skills as their aim. Dominating among the

59

receptive aspects is the function of language presentation with specific features offered by the program for the exploration of language. Teachers and students can compile customized materials which suit the teaching method and the interests of the participants. However, the productive tools cover the widest areas of usage. In accordance with task-oriented FLT methodology, they enable the learner to produce foreign language utterances with relevance for communication purposes.

Expanded Book Toolkit

The above-mentioned program *Poetry in Motion* was compiled with an authoring tool which the publishers also sell as a program for producing one's own electronic books. In a short space of time, quite ambitious programs can thus be created. All the user has to do is to create a text in a word processing program, format it attractively, save it chapter by chapter in RFT, a neutral format for exchanging formatted documents between different word processing programs, and import it in the *Expanded Book Toolkit*. The program then interactively requests one chapter at a time and bit by bit produces the electronic book. Using the appropriate tools, the layout of the text can be perfected further so that there are no isolated lines at the beginning or end of a page. And voilà – you have made a virtual book!

If desired, pictures, sound or even digitalized films can be incorporated – just like in the programs available commercially. In the example given in Figure 3.8 the Wolf asks Little Red Ridinghood where she is going in direct speech, for which all you have to do is to digitalize the sound, which is no more difficult than inputting text. While the book is being produced, you then click on the loudspeaker symbol and choose digitalized sound in the dialogue and that's it! When the 'reader' uses the mouse to click on the loudspeaker symbol in the finished version, he/she will hear the sound. This function is useful if you wish to include tongue twisters, for example, or words that are often pronounced wrongly. It is equally easy to incorporate digitalized video clips, which appeal to even more senses (see below for simple video production).

Of central importance for the reading process is a further feature which tends to be overlooked initially. Normal text in word processing programs is shown as a scrolling text, i.e. a long text is viewed through a window which always shows a changing extract. This goes against ingrained reading habits, where the reader expects – like with a printed text – that every page has a characteristic appearance which is easy to remember. These invariable orientation markers are lacking in the case of scrolling text, with the result that the reader loses his/her feel for the structure of the text. While the text is being imported, the authoring tool divides up the text so that it appears in fixed, unchanging positions – as if printed – on the pages, thus achieving the spatial orientation that the reader is used to from printed books. This is the reason why texts produced with the tool have an enhanced receptive quality compared to simple scrolling texts.

From a didactic point of view, the essential feature of these 'home-made' books does not lie in their attractive design, but in the reading function which the authoring tool automatically compiles, i.e. the range of tools for exploring the book (below left in Figure 3.8). Using 'Page'/'Chapter', it is possible to open a book of several hundred pages at a certain page or chapter; the 'Find' command locates specific passages in the text. Using 'Mark' you can highlight single pages and add brief annotations, so that passages scattered throughout the text can be easily collated and compared. With the command 'Retrace' it is possible to retrace the 'reading path' one has taken through the book, if one wants to examine a certain passage more closely, for example. P/B/U are used to change passages to bold type, underline them or to reverse such a command. Finally, readers can insert annotations to the left of the text or turn down the top right-hand corner of a page, just like in a proper book.

A further function which is of importance for foreign language learning is the compilation of concordance lists (see below right in Figure 3.8). The program locates all occurrences of a specific word in the text and presents a complete list containing the following information: the search word ('Wolf'), the number of occurrences ('13') and a list of the sources with page number.

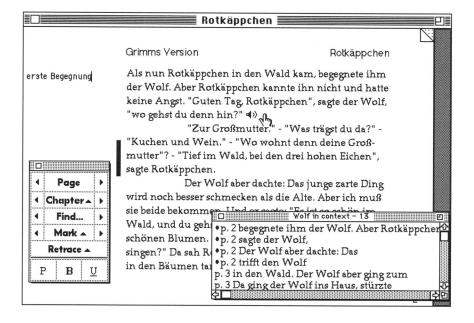

Figure 3.8 Rotkäppchen, a 'book' produced with *Expanded Book Toolkit*

By clicking on a line in the list you automatically go to the passage in the text where the word was found and can study the expression in context. These lists can be saved and can also be printed out using a word processing program, so that preparation for lessons is made much easier by being able to assess precisely the distribution of certain expressions in the text.

With the help of these search functions the learners are able to gain explorative access to complex language. They can study the distribution of certain expressions themselves and come up with well-founded hypotheses on the usage of certain linguistic items. The size of text corpus necessary for such projects can be acquired in the form of electronic books such as *Jurassic Park*, or smaller pilot studies can be carried out. These are tasks that are suited for self-study work outside the classroom or can be integrated into lessons as short work phases.

Creating your own multimedia presentations: Billboard

Is there anything that motivates language learners more than to experience being able to use the new medium effectively in communication? Unfortunately, such an experience is rare in the normal foreign language classroom. Utterances in the foreign language – even if spoken to a classmate – are really directed at the teacher, who assesses their correctness and grades them accordingly. True transfer of information rarely plays a role in these proceedings. Butzkamm (1993) describes the problems and makes suggestions for the transition from exercises aiming at formal correctness to speaking with actual content in the teacher-centred classroom. A further possibility lies in strengthening product-oriented studies. Ritter (1995) develops the methodological foundation of action-oriented use of computers in foreign language teaching and reports in detail on experiences of their implementation in 'proper' teaching. Pupils of an eighth grade grammar school class wrote books, in which they introduced themselves in English. The books were compiled by the students on their own during several sessions with a very high degree of motivation and afterwards shown to each other as well as to family and friends. In a case such as this, the foreign language utterances fulfil a real communicative function.

Such projects can of course also be carried out without a computer. However, the traditional method using typewriter, Tipp-ex, scissors and glue is more arduous and becomes frustrating more quickly than computer-aided word processing, with which expressions can be tried out tentatively and altered slightly until they fulfil the intended communicative aim satisfactorily. Finally, it must be added that the books produced with the computer are more attractive, even when printed with cheap ink-jet printers, than the books produced painstakingly by hand. After all, the aesthetic quality of products created in the foreign language classroom also influences the learning process.

Whereas normal text production and even multi-columned layouts with illustrations and charts can nowadays be achieved with simple integrated software packages, there are not as many user-friendly multimedia authoring tools, even though they are much more interesting than products on paper for the purposes of foreign language teaching due to the integration of text, picture and sound or video. However, they require not only powerful multimedia computers but also an integrated didactic network (see above). Without any great organizational effort, work can either be done separately or integrated. Something that has been prepared on one computer can immediately be presented to the entire class, realizing the system's communicative potential. An example of an authoring tool of this kind is the program *Billboard*, which has been developed at the Applied Languages Centre in Münster.

Billboard is reduced to essential functions and consists of a 'drawing space', a space for text to be inputted and control features (see Figure 3.9). Pictures can be inserted into the 'drawing space', be they pictures which the students have drawn themselves, comic-strips, illustrations taken from graphics CD-ROMs or 'home-made' Photo-CDs or pictures from a digital camera. It is possible to browse through the pages manually, print them out or use them as a 'slide-show'. The most interesting feature is the simple integration of audio data to create multimedia presentations.

The easiest way to make pictures for explorative project work is to use a

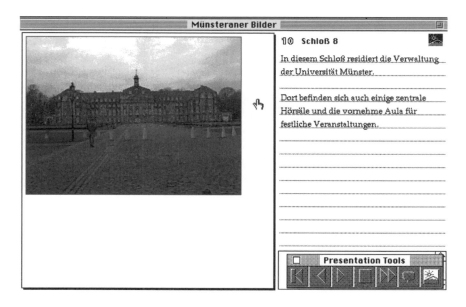

Figure 3.9 Billboard

digital camera, as the photos can be transferred directly into the computer and altered there without the need for costly additional photochemical development. A simple black-and-white camera like the QuickCam (Connectix), which can be operated directly from the serial port of a computer, is sufficient. At the same time, the QuickCam can also be used as a simple video camera, with which basic videos can be produced in the vicinity of the computer. Simple digital colour cameras with a higher resolution, such as the QuickTake (Apple), operate independently from the computer and thus make it possible to take pictures outside the classroom or indeed the building during project work or excursions.

Sound recordings can be made directly in *Billboard* via a microphone or an attached cassette recorder. The students can thus record their written texts or dialogues themselves. In the same way that word processing with the computer is much easier than the traditional method of producing texts, digital sound processing is also much easier than analogue sound processing with tapes or cassettes, so that the program facilitates the revision of recorded utterances. In this way, language awareness is trained without the diminishment of enjoyment that can result from being corrected by the teacher. The presentation of a multimedia show they have put together themselves makes the learners create texts in the foreign language with communicative use for other people.

Outlook

The future of multimedia in foreign language learning has only just begun. Established publishers of teaching materials are only slowly venturing to bring programs with sound and video on to the market. In Germany, the consideration of the computers installed in schools, which for the most part are not computers with multimedia capabilities, has led to the (over-) cautious development of programs whose hardware requirements fall below the computing power necessary for multimedia use. The gap thus created through the technical possibilities was used by producers from outside the established educational publishers with new ideas who, however, might still profit from the didactic know-how of the established producers. However, many programs developed without a didactic aim have proved their suitability as teaching and learning materials in FLT.

The programs discussed above prove without a doubt that they fulfil one important didactic function better than established media: the attractive presentation of the subject to be learned – the foreign language. At the same time, the technical possibilities of this medium open up new ways of shaping the learning process. Phases of individual work and periods of group work can alternate within the lesson without a change of location or rearrangement of chairs being necessary. On the whole, the role and qualifications of the instructor will change: teachers will have to include new teaching and learning materials in their preparation and will have to incorporate learning contexts from outside the classroom to a greater extent. On the one hand, the learners will have to be given more independence in shaping their individual learning processes, and on the other hand new forms of instruction for explorative learning.

Finally, it has to be pointed out that authentic communication with native speakers of the target language will play a greater role in connection with the Internet. To the extent to which schools actually have access to the Internet and its resources, learning groups will form across continents and work on joint projects. While such communication has mainly occurred via text-based e-mail systems up to now (see Eck *et al.*, 1995), it will increasingly be supplanted by multimedia communications systems. Today it is already possible to hold video conferences with only minimal effort (the above-mentioned QuickCam together with special video conferencing software would already suffice). Pictures and digitalized sound for the joint production of 'books' according to the file transfer protocol (ftp) can already be sent via the Internet or as annotations to e-mails. Thus the possibilities already exist; they merely have to be put into practice by teachers in the classrooms as there are not fully developed 'learning programs' as yet but only communication tools.

Foreign language teaching methodology will therefore have to concern itself with the question of how the direct exchange with native speakers of the target language can be initiated as early as possible without the risk of learners feeling overtaxed and breaking off the contact.

References

Books and journals

Butzkamm, W. (1983) 'Der kritische Moment: zwischen formbezogenem Üben und inhaltsbe-zogenem Sprechen', in M. Heid und Referat für Medientechnologie des Goethe-Instituts München (eds) *Kommunikation im Klassenzimmer und Fremdsprachenlernen*, München: Goethe Institut.

Eck, A., Legenhausen, L. and Wolff, D. (1995) *Telekommunikation und Fremdsprachenunterricht: Informationen, Projekte, Ergebnisse*, Bochum: AKS-Verlag.

Grießhaber, W. (1992) 'Fremdsprachenlernen mit Maus und Mikro', *Bildungsarbeit in der Zweitsprache Deutsch* 3: 107–113.

Grießhaber, W. (1995) 'Mit Maus und Mikro fremde Sprachen lernen. Beispiele und Konzepte computerunterstützten Fremdsprachenunterrichts', in *Handbuch Hochschullehre*, Bonn: Raabe, GS A 3.2.

Langenscheidt-Redaktion (ed.) (1985) *Computergestützter Fremdsprachenunterricht. Ein Handbuch*, Berlin u.a.: Langenscheidt.

Leont'ev, A. A. (1971) *Sprache – Sprechen – Sprechtätigkeit*, Stuttgart: Kohlhammer.

Ritter, M. (1995) *Computer und handlungsorientierter Unterricht. Zur allgemeinen und fremd-sprachendidaktischen Reichweite eines neuen Mediums*, Donauwörth: Auer.

Stracke-Elbina, E. (1995) 'Work in Progress: Think and Talk French. Ein Französischkurs für Anfänger mit Computerunterstützung', in *Fremdsprachen und Hochschule* 44: 73–82.

Stracke-Elbina, E. (1996) 'Aus der Lernerperspektive: Möglichkeiten und Grenzen des Selbstlernens in einem Computerlernstudio', Vortrag gehalten auf der AKS-Tagung 1996, Bayreuth.

Wong-Fillmore, L. (1979) 'Individual Differences in Second Language Acquisition', in Fillmore, L., Kempler, D. and Wang, W. S.-Y. (eds) *Individual Differences in Language Ability and Language Behavior*, New York: Academic Press.

Programs

Billboard (1995) Grießhaber, Münster: Sprachenzentrum der WWU.

Clinton – Portrait of Victory (1993) Burbank, CA: Warner New Media.

Community Exploration (1994) San Diego, CA: Contér.

Expanded Book Toolkit v. 1.5 (1992) Irvington, NY: Voyager.

Jurassic Park (1991) Santa Monica, CA: Voyager.

Just Grandma and Me (1992) Novat, CA: Brøderbund.

Macbeth (1994) New York: Voyager.

Poetry in Motion (1992) Santa Monica, CA: Voyager.

Reasoning Skills (1993) Fairfield, CT: QUEUE.

4

FRENCH FOR BEGINNERS

Computer-assisted language instruction

Elke Stracke-Elbina

The aim of this chapter is to present some observations on the use of computer-assisted material for independent study made in connection with the multimedia beginners' course *Think and Talk French*. First of all, a short survey will give some information about the genesis and the structure of such a French class for beginners held at the Applied Languages Centre (ALC) at Münster University (Germany). The program *Think and Talk French* will then be described and discussed. Emphasis will be placed on the learners' perspective which is being uncovered through an empirical study in which data have been collected through questionnaires and interviews. In this context, the importance of the combination of self-study periods and accompanying group sessions will be emphasized by presenting a case study. The investigation sheds light on possible innovative forms of language learning and teaching, and the results ultimately point to the efficiency brought to the learning process by the combination of independent study in the computer laboratory and group instruction.

The genesis and the structure of this French class

Since the 1994 summer semester, experimental French courses for beginners have been held at the ALC. For the duration of two semesters, participants from all academic fields with no prior knowledge of the French language engage in a 'normal' language class (in a 'normal' classroom). These group sessions, which usually take place every two weeks, alternate with periods of independent study in the computer laboratory.

After receiving a short introduction to working with the multimedia program *Think and Talk French* at the first meeting, students then proceed to prepare the following group sessions on their own. They work independently in the computer laboratory at the ALC and prepare an average of three or four *scènes* for the following group session.

Students have been asked to fill out two questionnaires during the course.

In the following I will refer to these questionnaires as well as to other data collected in this ongoing project, namely the above-mentioned interviews.

The computer program *Think and Talk French*

This somewhat unusual French class for beginners works with the French version of the series Think and Talk published by Hyperglot, which constitutes the students' 'coursebook'. *Think and Talk French* consists of fifty *scènes*, which lead to a good grounding in the French language. Regarding the tenses, for example, the student learns *présent*, *futur proche*, *passé composé* and *futur simple* and is also introduced to *imparfait* and *conditionnel* – though quite late in the course of the program, i.e. in the very last *scène*. The contents of the fifty lessons correspond to those of other course books used in adult foreign language teaching with the one exception that tourist activities are rarely dealt with. Professional and social situations dominate. The learner encounters a group of people working in an office who are involved in all kinds of activities, of which the following list of selected *scènes* may give some idea: *Allô, Marie* (*scène* 3); *Qui êtes-vous?* (5); *Une discussion* (6); *Combien d'argent avez-vous?* (8); *Une conversation au bureau* (13); *Dialogue dans le corridor* (17); *'Cher Monsieur . . .'* (18); *Un week-end avec . . .* (22); *Aimez-vous travailler?* (24); *Le rendez-vous du samedi soir* (30); *Prenez note!* (*On téléphone de Belgique*) (33); *Une invitation à dîner* (34), etc.

Think and Talk French was developed for self-study purposes and employs the widely known Berlitz methodology. One important aspect of this methodology is the fact that absolute monolingualism is adhered to, so that the learner receives all new information as well as virtually all instructions in French. As the students at the ALC are mostly German, this is of considerable importance. Since most computer programs are developed in the English-speaking world for native speakers of English, German students who wish to learn French often complain about bilingual, English-French programs, such as *Learn to speak French*, or the *French Vocabulary Builder*. Even if the students' knowledge of English is good, they would rather concentrate on one foreign language, i.e. the one to be learned.

The program *Think and Talk French* comes on several CDs and with a short User's Guide, which is written in English, however. Here the student learns how to use the program successfully when working independently at the computer. At the ALC the students learn all they need to know about the handling of the program in the very first session of the course. The teacher demonstrates and explains the program in detail, so that the learner feels confident and comfortable when working on his/her own for the first time. Even students with no previous experience with computers are thus able to work on their own very quickly.

It is worth mentioning in this context that there is always a student assistant in charge of the computer laboratory, who can help whenever there is a problem. The presence and, if necessary, assistance of this student assistant has proved to be of great importance for learners who regularly work in the computer laboratory. It seems as if the presence of such a person in charge, even if one does not need their help very often, is an important psychological factor in the learning process.

The learner is supposed to work through each *scène* of *Think and Talk French* in four steps which emphasize one of the four basic skills respectively. In the first step, 'Listen and Understand!', the learner listens to the text of the *scène*. This acoustic presentation of the text involves music as well as other sounds, for example, the ticking of a clock, the clattering of a typewriter or the noise of an approaching car. In addition to this, simple drawings serve to help the learner understand the text (see Figure 4.1).

By listening to the text as often as he[1] wishes and by repeating (often 'murmuring') the new sounds forming the unknown words, the learner thus develops a basic understanding of the text autonomously, i.e. without the help of a teacher or any other person.

In the second step, 'Read!', the learner then reads the text that so far he has only heard and not seen. The possibilities of computer technology allow the learner to go precisely to the desired passage in the text and to listen to it again or as often as he wishes. There is none of the slipping that learners and teachers know from working with tape recorders. Simply by clicking on the desired passage in the text, the learner can hear it (see Figure 4.2).

After practising listening and reading, the third step of *Think and Talk*

Figure 4.1 Step 1: 'Listen and Understand!' (with permission, The Learning Company, Inc.)

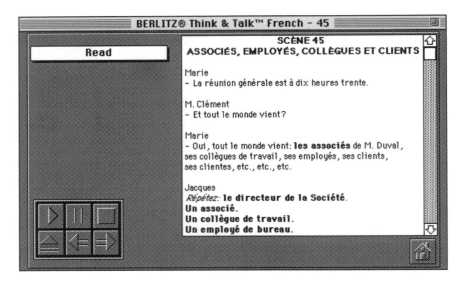

Figure 4.2 Step 2: 'Read!' (with permission, The Learning Company, Inc.)

French introduces the learner to writing in the foreign language. In the third step, 'Write!', the program dictates short, randomly chosen passages to the learner. The learner may listen to the sentence as often as he wishes before trying to write down what he has heard. By clicking on the appropriate icon, he can compare his own version with the correct one (see Figure 4.3).

The fourth step, perhaps somewhat optimistically called 'Think and Talk!' by the program developers, is meant to make the learners not only repeat precise passages from the text, but also to answer built-in questions. In contrast to Step 1, the learner now records his own voice, listens to it and compares it to the model. Furthermore, he is invited to talk spontaneously and say whatever comes to his mind (see Figure 4.4).

This step reminds us of the type of exercises students can do in the traditional audio laboratory, but there are two notable differences. First, the acoustically presented text can be complemented by the written text any time. Second, the learner does not have to work through the text in a linear order, but can move through it freely and concentrate on what he considers to be important. The invitation to talk freely and say whatever comes to one's mind has not been followed by the learners who were observed in the last two years.

These four steps of listening, reading, writing and speaking, which the learner goes through in each *scène*, are complemented in some of the *scènes* by grammar tables and/or exercises which the learner works through on his own as well (see Figure 4.5).

Figure 4.3 Step 3: 'Write!' (with permission, The Learning Company, Inc.)

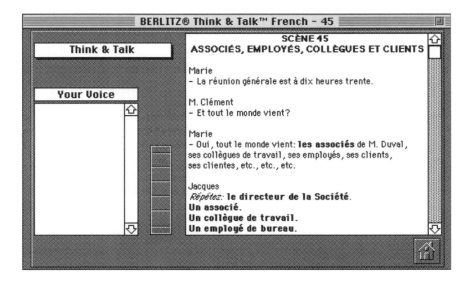

Figure 4.4 Step 4: 'Think and Talk!' (with permission, The Learning Company, Inc.)

Furthermore, the learner can look up words which he does not understand at all in an incorporated French-English dictionary (see Figure 4.6).

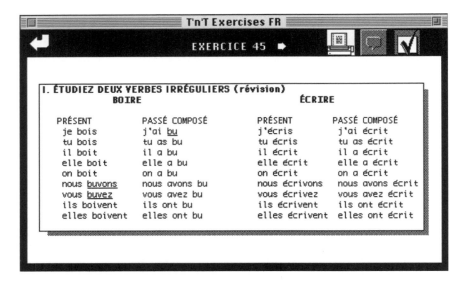

Figure 4.5 Exercises

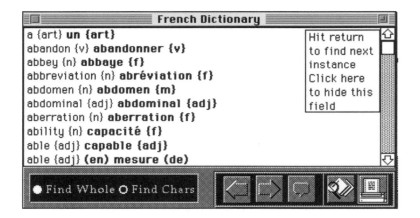

Figure 4.6 Dictionary

The questionnaires revealed very quickly that the students could not work with this dictionary in a satisfying way. The students express very clearly that they would prefer a built-in French-German dictionary. Furthermore, they often criticize the lack of contextualization of the words, which are only offered in an alphabetical list. That is why a French-German dictionary, developed at the ALC, was implemented into the program. The new dictionary was enthusiastically welcomed by the learners.

Having described the basic features of *Think and Talk French*, it is now time to underline some important aspects of the independent study work undertaken with this program in the computer laboratory. First of all, the actual work with the text of the *scène*, which, in the traditional language classroom, may be prepared by the teacher by introducing new vocabulary, by reading the text aloud, by parapharasing it, or by using other methods to help the learners understand it, is, in the experimental setting described, transferred entirely into the preparation time of the individual student and thus becomes that student's responsibility. Second, different learning channels are being used which is of course beneficial to all learners and types of learners. The learner can choose which channels he wants to use more often and which steps, i.e. which skills, he wants to deal with more intensively. Third, the analysis of the questionnaires reveals that the time spent in the computer laboratory differs considerably from student to student. The autonomous learner decides himself how much time he wants to spend on preparation. Thus, differences in the individual speed of the learning process can be balanced.

As the students who take the French class in question come from varying academic fields, the differences in foreign language learning habits are quite considerable. It seems likely that a fourth-year student of mathematics who has not learnt any foreign language for the last four or five years brings other prerequisites to the French language class than a first-year student of Spanish who has just entered university and has had foreign language teaching up to this level. The possibility of independent study in the computer laboratory takes these differences into account as the students can learn whenever they wish and for as long as they want. Autonomous language learning in the computer laboratory thus makes possible the individualization of learning.

The most important aspect of this kind of learning, however, may be that the students enjoy what they are doing. The learners work actively with the text by scrolling through it and clicking on those passages that are of special interest to them. Thus they can work very intensively with the text, which, in the 'normal' presentation in a course book might not have been that exciting. At the same time, the learner is dealing with pronunciation, vocabulary and grammar. Perhaps this new way of working with a text and also the nature of the first spelling and grammar exercises make the idea of foreign language learning less off-putting for the student.

The learner's perspective

The learners themselves recognize and appreciate this last aspect; the questionnaires demonstrate that many students enjoy this way of learning a foreign language that is new to each and everyone of them. They express their opinion in phrases like '*Es macht mehr Spaß und ist effektiver*' ('It is more fun and more effective'),[2] '*Es ist auf jeden Fall unterhaltsamer, abwechslungsreicher und innovativ'* ('It is, definitely, more entertaining, more varied and innova-tive'), *'Macht mehr Spaß!'* ('It's more fun!') and *'Arbeit am Computer bereitet mir aber viel Spaß'* ('Working at the computer I find a lot of fun'), which all emphasize the fun (*Spaß*) they have when working with the program.

Furthermore, many learners – and they were neither future foreign language teachers nor students of pedagogy or psychology, but in the main, students of economics or law – remark that they think the combination of listening, reading, writing and speaking is of advantage to their learning process. Some regard this as *the* big advantage of computer-assisted foreign language learning. To quote from the questionnaires: *'Vieles bleibt besser im Kopf; man gewöhnt sich gleich an die Aussprache, das selber Sprechen, alles wird gleichmäßig aufgebaut, Lesen, Schreiben, Hören, Reden'* ('A lot can be remembered much better; you get used to the pronunciation straight away, to speaking, everything is developed equally, reading, writing, listening, speaking'), *'Eigentlich ziemlich gut, u.a. durch die Möglichkeit über das Hören zu lernen'* ('Actually quite good, among other things due to the possibility of learning by listening'), *'Vom Hören, Sprechen und Verstehen her sehr vorteilhaft. Was fehlt, ist die grammatische Aufarbeitung'* ('Very positive as to listening, speaking and understanding. What is missing is the subsequent grammar work'). The quotations underline the positive effect of combining the different skills. Listening is of particular importance to the students who enjoy this step which they seem to miss in traditional language classes where, quite often, the teacher is the main source of spoken language, even if he/she brings tapes and videos to the classroom.

Most students have a very critical attitude towards the grammar presentation and the exercise section in *Think and Talk French*. Grammar is often presented in an unsystematic and thus unsatisfying way, and the infrequent exercises do not correspond to the grammatical structures discussed.

The group sessions

It is in this context that the group sessions play a decisive role in the whole setting. As was foreseen by the teacher and confirmed by the students, the grammar presentation and the exercises offered in the computer program *Think and Talk French* proved to be insufficient. Without the complementary group sessions, the advantages of the program might easily have been outweighed by its disadvantages, since the students still had many questions after having worked through the allotted task of three or four *scènes*. But thus the group sessions – initially every two weeks, later, on behalf of some weaker students, every week – turned into real working sessions, where problems and questions which the students themselves brought into the classroom were discussed. The teacher prepared additional material, such as grammar tables and exercises, and also stimulated communicative exercises, which were much enjoyed by the students in tandem and group work. Thus perhaps the greatest advantage of independent studies, i.e. allowing the learner to be active, to develop his/her own hypotheses about the unknown language, is combined with effective instruction which concentrates on the problematic aspects; that is, on those times in the learning process when the learner needs help. It goes without saying, however, that communicative competence can only be developed in the classroom – and not in the computer laboratory where the students work on their own.

A case study

Up to now all references to the learners' perspective have drawn on the questionnaires which allowed a first approach to the learners' point of view and their evaluation of the course. I would now like to refer to the previously mentioned interviews, twelve of which have so far been recorded and transcribed. These data underline the importance of the combination of independent studies with group instruction and ultimately point to the efficiency of this combination.

In the following, I want to present a case study by analysing some extracts from an interview with a student, Else. Else is a third-year student of Visual Communication and has never learnt French before. The interview was led by a research assistant instead of the teacher in order to avoid any psychological inhibition on the learner's side.

First of all, Else not only enjoyed both self-study work and group instruction, but explicitly welcomes the combination:

(8) *Else*: Und, ja eben gerade auch dieses beidseitige, eben den Kurs und das alleine am Computer was zu machen, also diese Kombination fand ich eigentlich gerade ganz gut.

[(8) *Else*: And, yes, exactly this two-fold, exactly the class and to do something at the computer on one's own, well, this combination is actually what I found quite good.]

The computer itself constituted a motivating factor for Else when choosing this language course. This important aspect tends to be forgotten among language teachers who, on the whole, have a much more reserved attitude towards the computer as a medium in foreign language learning and teaching. When asked in more detail about her opinion on the independent study work in the computer laboratory, Else emphasizes several positive aspects:

(35) *Else*: Ja, also einmal, daß man – muß ich jetzt mal kurz überlegen – daß ich da ziemlich konzentriert dann dran arbeiten kann, wenn ich einmal hingefahren bin und mich hingesetzt hab.
[Beide lachen]

75

(36) *Else*: Dann hab ich auch, zumindest in den meisten Fällen, so eine Stunde oder sowas eingeplant.

(37) *Else*: Und dadurch, daß da nichts anderes Ablenkendes da war, nur dies, das hat irgendwie mir geholfen, mich mehr darauf zu konzentrieren als bei anderen Sachen.

(38) *Else*: Und ich fand das auch, das Programm, auch ganz lustig gemacht mit diesen Personen, die man dann so nach und nach kennenlernt und die sich verändern.

(39) *Else*: Das fand ich irgendwie unterhaltsam.

(40) *Else*: Und ich find auch die Möglichkeiten, die da geboten sind, eben mit dem Nachsprechen und Hören . . .

(41) *Else*: Dann hab ich mir manchmal auch so nach Stimmung ausgesucht was, worauf ich am meisten Lust hatte. . . . Und hab dann ja auch eigentlich immer, wenn ich dann so was nachgegeben habe, immer was davon gehabt, auch wenn ich dann. . . .

(42) *Int.*: Ja, hmhm.

(43) *Else*: Ach, heute lese ich nur oder so.

(44) *Int.*: Ja, und du hast schon dann, und du hast dir dann immer so was rausgesucht, weil du bist so eigentlich so mit. . . .

(45) *Else*: Ich hab immer schon was gefunden, was ich da machen wollte gerne.

[(35) *Else*: . . . yes, well first of all that you – I have to think about this for a second – that I can work in a quite concentrated way there, once I have gone there and have sat down.
[Both laugh]

(36) *Else*: And then I have, at least usually, planned on one hour or so.

(37) *Else*: And because there was nothing else that could distract me, only this, that has somehow helped me to concentrate more on it than with other things.

(38) *Else*: And I also found that the program was done in quite a funny way with these persons one gets to know little by little and who change.

(39) *Else*: I somehow found this entertaining.

(40) *Else*: And, I also find the possibilities, which are being offered, specifically the repeating and listening. . . .

(41) *Else*: I have sometimes chosen something according to my mood, something I felt like doing most. . . . And then I actually always, when I yielded to such a feeling, I always profited from it, even when I. . . .

(42) *Int.*: Yes, hmhm.

(43) *Else*: Well, today, only reading or something like that.

(44) *Int.*: Yes, and then you have, you have always picked something, because you are actually. . . .

(45) *Else*: I have always found something I wanted to do.]

Working at the computer allows Else to concentrate closely upon what she is doing. At the same time, Else enjoys the program, which she finds entertaining and amusing. Again, the importance of enjoying the learning process is underlined as well as the importance of listening and speaking. Else appreciates her independence when working in the computer laboratory, as she can choose the steps according to her mood, so that she always finds something to work on, something she enjoys doing. But, as she says clearly later on in the interview, she would not have gone on with the computer work without the accompanying group sessions.

(87) *Else*: Dadurch, daß der andere Teil des Kurses. . . . Also ich könnte nie diese Computersachen alleine machen.
(88) *Else*: Also ich glaub, wenn nicht beides zusammenkäme, der Kurs mit so echten Gesprä/ also mit richtig Leuten und so und Antworten und so, dann hätte ich das nicht länger, also nicht so durchziehen können, glaub ich.

[(87) *Else*: Because the other half of the course. . . . Well, I could never do this computer stuff alone.
(88) *Else*: Well, I think, if there hadn't been both, the class with real conver/ I mean with real people and, and answers and, I wouldn't have been able to, well continue, any longer like that, I think.]

Else explicitly states her need for 'real people' as well as real answers and immediate reactions to questions and problems.

It should be clear by now that it is by no means recommended merely to furnish learners with a program like *Think and Talk French* and then leave them alone. Simple proof is the fact that the computer laboratory at the ALC is attended far more regularly by students who have accompanying group sessions than by those who work completely on their own — though there are certain types of learners who work quite successfully on a completely autonomous basis. After the first successful course of *Think and Talk French*, the computer laboratory now offers a similar class for Spanish. The class works with the Spanish version of *Think and Talk*, which, by the way, offers an Italian and German version as well. Again, the accompanying group sessions play a very important role in the learning process, even if the group instruction, just like in the *Think and Talk French* class, is of minor importance if you consider it from a quantitative point of view, i.e. if you measure the time the student spends in the computer laboratory and in the 'normal' classroom for group instruction, which is far less.

Innovative forms of learning and teaching and the efficiency of the learning process

Modern computer laboratories build on the fact that computers form an increasingly large part of students' daily lives; this makes possible new learning experiences which can be described as highly motivating. These new experiences may result in traditional ideas about teaching perhaps being at least partly substituted by new forms of language teaching. The independent learner is placed in the centre of the learning process and exerts considerable influence on his learning process and learning speed, but he is always assisted by the teacher. The role of the teacher may change, as he or she is no longer the only and supreme source of knowledge – which becomes even more evident when students have access to the Internet, for example, and thus have the possibility of authentic communication in the classroom via e-mail. Some aspects of teaching, for example, offering the right pronunciation of a certain word, often become unnecessary when students work with a computer program such as *Think and Talk French*. However, the teacher still has to explain certain phenomena, rules and exceptions. The time gained, however, may be spent much more effectively on more communicative phases in the classroom. The group sessions in the experimental *Think and Talk* class usually open with a questions-and-answers session, but here it is the student who asks the questions. These questions are authentic, as they are the result of the autonomous learning process and shed light on those instances where the learner has encountered certain problems which he can now resolve with the help of his teacher. The teacher is his partner in the learning process; the teacher explains things, gives advice and directs the learning process only insofar as he or she supports the learner in the organization of his learning. Of course, the individual need of the teacher's assistance varies from student to student. The interviews clearly reveal that there are types of learners who need a lot of feedback and encouragement from the teacher, and some even want to be told in great detail what to do. They still need a lot of teaching during the process of learning how to learn. Others, however, enjoy the freedom of their learning process and appreciate this new way of learning, especially in contrast to traditional language classes at high school level.

As for the efficiency of the learning process, a first positive estimation can be made. The aim of this beginners' class is to enable students to get a grounding in the French language so that they can continue their studies in intermediate and advanced French classes. Students who wish to take part in intermediate and advanced courses at the ALC have to achieve a certain score in a placement test in order to gain a place in the well-attended language classes. The first group of students who worked with *Think and Talk French* completed the test moderately successfully.

They all achieved the necessary result and were able to continue their study of the French language in the regular French classes. In the questionnaires, as well as in the interviews, the students expressed their satisfaction with the results they obtained and said they were highly motivated to continue.

The computer program *Think and Talk French* for beginners offers possibilities of integrating a computer-assisted self-study program into the course program offered at an Applied Languages Centre such as the one at Münster University. Such multimedia programs take into consideration daily experience with computer technology and offer opportunities for developing them for foreign language learning. One of the tasks of the language teacher is to make these new experiences fruitful and productive for the process of learning and teaching foreign languages.

Notes

1   When 'he' is used with reference to a learner or student, it is, of course, being used as a neutral pronoun and can refer to both male and female students.

2   I have translated these quotations from the learner questionnaires as literally as possible into English. This may be helpful for those readers who have only a basic knowledge of the German language to understand the original text a little better.

References

Books and journals

Eck, A., Legenhausen, L. and Wolff, D. (1995) *Telekommunikation und Fremdsprachenunterricht: Informationen, Projekte, Ergebnisse*, Bochum: AKS-Verlag.

Fechner, J. (ed.) (1994) *Neue Wege im computergestützten Fremdsprachenunterricht*, Fremdsprachenunterricht in Theorie und Praxis, Langenscheidt: Berlin.

Grießhaber, W. (1992) 'Fremdsprachenlernen mit Maus und Mikro', in *Bildungsarbeit in der Zweitsprache Deutsch* 3/92: 107–113.

Grießhaber, W. (1995) 'Mit Maus und Mikro fremde Sprachen lernen. Beispiele und Konzepte computerunterstützten Fremdsprachenunterrichts', in *Handbuch Hochschullehre*, Bonn: Raabe: GS A 3.2.

Langenscheidt-Redaktion (ed.) (1985) *Computergestützter Fremdsprachenunterricht. Ein Handbuch*, Langenscheidt: Berlin.

Rüschoff, B. (1988) *Fremdsprachenunterricht mit computergestützten Materialien: Didaktische Überlegungen und Beispiele*, München: Hueber.

Stracke-Elbina, E. (1995) 'Work in Progress: Think and Talk French. Ein Französischkurs für Anfänger mit Computerunterstützung', in *Fremdsprachen und Hochschule* 44/95: 73–82.

Stracke-Elbina, E. (1997) 'Aus der Lernerperspektive. Möglichkeiten und Grenzen des Selbstlernens in einem Computerstudio', in R. C. McGeoch and U. O. H. Jung (eds) *Ende oder Wende, Universitäter Fremdsprachenunterricht an der Jahrtausendwende*, Bochum: AKS-Verlag.

Programs

Learn to Speak French v. 4.02 (1994) Knoxville, TN: Hyperglot.
Think and Talk French (1986 and 1991) Knoxville, TN: Hyperglot/Berlitz.
Think and Talk Spanish (1986 and 1991) Knoxville, TN: Hyperglot/Berlitz.
French Vocabulary Builder v. 1.0 (1995) Fremont, CA: Hyperglot.

Part II

FOCUS ON THE CLASSROOM

In Part II of this book, 'Focus on the Classroom', Faber (Chapter 5) draws our attention to some imaginative ways in which literary texts can be used for teaching. She points out that works of literature, and extracts from works of literature, as authentic examples of the language being studied, are a powerful motivating force. Such texts are, moreover, to be valued as examples of how the most gifted speakers of the language use it for the most telling purposes, and thereby give students access to the cultural values which stand behind the language. She goes on to draw on her practical teaching experience by showing how literary texts can be exploited in the classroom. She also describes how a number of exercise types can be sewn together to make a coherent teaching unit in which students have opportunities to use the language productively.

Faber lays great store by students penetrating behind the text itself to explore the cultural values of the society to which it gives expression. She shows how this objective is attained by the use of exercises which focus students' attention on cultural meanings. One of the techniques she uses and advocates requires students to move between meanings expressed sometimes in a textual form, and at other times in a visual form. In practical work such as this, the teacher's role changes subtly to become a participant in the learning process.

We sometimes think that the teaching and learning of foreign languages is restricted to primary and secondary school classrooms. However, languages are also learned and taught in universities. University teachers also face the problems common to teachers of other educational levels. Bunn (Chapter 6) presents an interesting example of peer teaching, of collaborative learning in the classroom. He grouped students in such a way that they would benefit from each other. Bunn describes his experience with mixed-ability learners of German at the University of Coimbra/Portugal. The paper exemplifies the extent to which students can learn language within a simulated real-life context. The title of the project, 'Living Together', is indicative of its main goal, the mastery of discourse strategies in the foreign language to deal with everyday situations which arise in the communal life of families and other groups in an apartment building. Different groupings were used so as to exploit all the methodological possibilities inherent in different social relations. Greater competence in the foreign language was fostered by the practice of language in real context.

It is the task of the teacher to help learners to develop learning strategies, attitudes, skills and procedures that will aid their progress in the acquisition of communicative competence and process competence. From this we can learn how important classroom management skills are for the successful learning of foreign languages.

The third chapter in Part II is contributed by Paul Seedhouse (Chapter 7). Drawing on work done for his doctoral thesis, he throws important new light on the way language teachers talk to their students. He demonstrates that the three-part interaction pattern (teacher initiation, followed by learner response, followed by teacher follow-up or evaluation), hitherto regarded as typical, is, in fact, a far more complicated process. Drawing on a rich corpus of foreign language lessons, video recorded for the purpose of pedagogical and linguistic analysis, Seedhouse illustrates the range of interaction patterns between teachers and students which characterize language teaching. He highlights the challenges faced by language teachers, of maintaining simultaneously a dual focus on both form and meaning, while repairing students' errors of phonology, grammar and discourse, and not allowing the flow of the lesson to disappear. The matter of turn-taking, and allocating turns, while safeguarding good relationships, is also dealt with.

Seedhouse adopts and justifies a conversation analysis approach to his work, and in the course of his contribution indicates that all teachers, both those in training and those in service, will benefit from a greater understanding of the complexities of classroom talk.

5

THROUGH THE CAMERA'S LENS

An innovative approach to analysing literature

Pamela Faber

Introduction

Despite the many reasons in favour of teaching literature in a language classroom, the truth is that if literature is taught at all, it is often relegated to the background. However, the importance of literature as a language source cannot be overstressed because, more than any other text type, it is capable of connecting the student to the culture and the world encoded in the language he/she is engaged in learning (Collie and Slater, 1987).

The secret of using literature in the foreign language classroom is to avoid traditional classroom teaching roles, and thus stimulate motivation by creating conditions under which language can be learned (Hill, 1986: 9). Using a more innovative approach, teachers can bring students into the world created in the text and cause them to become personally involved in it. In this chapter, I will show how a literary text can 'come alive' for students through meaningful tasks. Such activities first deconstruct the text into basic sequences of images, actions and dialogue related to basic units of structured information (frames/scenarios) already present in long-term memory storage. Second, this information will be used to construct another text, translating the extract into an audio-visual medium.

Reading literature

The process of reading is a process of meaning-creation. Precisely for this reason, reading can be said to include a wide variety of skills, interwoven with a range of cognitive procedures, perception, language, thinking and memory. Two of the most relevant cognitive skills are understanding conceptual meaning and the selective extraction of important points from a text. Both of these skills can be enhanced by reading literary texts, an activity which should begin as soon as the student has acquired a minimum competence in the foreign language he is learning.

From the very beginning, competent readers reject/ignore irrelevant elements in the text and centre their attention on those which are central to textual meaning. Although understanding may seem difficult at first, the decoding of a literary text (or any text, for that matter) is just a specialized case of standard information processing. Students also understand a text on the basis of what they bring to it. Understanding is achieved when they can recognize the information in the text as somehow connected with the daily life knowledge they already possess. In other words, they must pick out a specific piece of data, synthesize it, and then categorize it.

Categorization as a cognitive energy saver is immensely important in our daily lives. If we had to store everything we perceive as a unique entity, we would soon run out of memory space. Words represent categorizations of experience, and we will see that behind each of these categories is a kind of situation embedded in knowledge and experience.

Reading literature as a goal-directed activity

Even though students at secondary level may be more or less aware that knowing how to read in the foreign language is one of the most necessary skills, and one that they will be liable to use with the greatest frequency in the future, they must still be encouraged to view reading as a significant activity having both short-term as well as long-term goals. Insomuch as short-term goals are concerned, most students want to have something interesting to do. This is best achieved by asking them *to do things with the text*, things that they find interesting and relevant to themselves and their environment in some way, either in terms of similarity or contrast.

To this end, the teacher can supply students with interesting, short-term goals as a means of understanding the text better. In this type of class, learner responsibility is also encouraged through group activities involving meaning construction.

The text chosen is an extract from 'The Duchess and the Jeweller', a short story by Virginia Woolf (see Appendix). The meaning construction activities will first be the explication of cognitive domains implicit in the verbal lexicon to structure the principal frame/event present in the text. The second step will be the use of this information to image the text, and to construct a visual representation in which the language of film/television scripts allows us explicitly to direct focus.

Time sequence

When students read a text for the first time, they will understand it better if they have an activity to carry out which directs their attention to the basic cognitive axes of time and space. The following exercise will help to situate the text in time, and fix the basic sequence of events clearly in the students' minds. It will also help them to think about the text, and connect it to a specific type of event.

Exercise 1

Order the following notes in the sequence in which they appear in the text. Underneath each sentence write the sentence(s) of the text which corresponds to each.

Sequence in text:

_____ Oliver wonders if the pearl is a fake.

_____ The Duchess invites Oliver to her house.

_____ Oliver thinks about the coming weekend.

_____ Oliver decides to test the pearls.

_____ Oliver and the Duchess greet each other.

_____ Oliver escorts the Duchess to the door.

_____ Oliver realizes that the Duchess has lost money gambling again.

_____ Oliver hears his mother's voice warning him.

_____ Oliver decides to give the Duchess the money because of Diana.

_____ The Duchess begs Oliver not to tell her husband.

_____ Oliver asks the Duchess what she wants of him.

_____ The Duchess shows him what is in her bag.

_____ The Duchess repeats her invitation to Oliver.

Frame construction

After reading the text and ordering the events, the students should have an approximate idea of what is taking place. This means relating the events in the text to previous knowledge in long-term memory. Even if all the vocabulary is not familiar to them, they should have grasped the fact that the scene encoded in the text is a commercial transaction. This is the kind of event that everyone is familiar with, and this type of schema or *frame* should already exist as part of the knowledge the students bring to the text.

A *frame* is one of the ways information is stored in our mind. It can be defined as any system of concepts related in such a way that if one of the concepts in the system is understood, so all the others are as well (Fillmore, 1982: 11). For example, a cake with lighted candles on it is part of a birthday party frame and gives us a whole context of understood cultural knowledge of what happens at such an event (giving presents, eating cake, singing songs, playing games). In other words, the activation of one part, or a combination of parts of the frame, will activate the whole.

Frames are also implicit on a smaller scale. In fact, each verb in our language can be said to characterize a small abstract scene. To understand the semantic structure of the verb it is necessary to understand the properties of schematized scenes, implicit in the semantic roles of its arguments. A commercial event, such as the one in the text, contains the conceptual content of the verbs *Sell*, *Buy* and *Pay*.

The Duchess comes to Oliver's shop *to sell* ten pearls. She needs money for a gambling debt. Oliver decides *to buy* the pearls even though he suspects they are imitations, and finally *pays* twenty thousand pounds because he is in love with Diana, the daughter of the Duchess.

The scene is thus composed of the following participants:

1   A *Buyer* [Oliver]
2   A *Seller* [the Duchess] who wants to exchange something of value for money
3   *Goods* which the *Buyer* acquires [Ten fake pearls, and indirectly, an invitation to see Diana]
4   *Payment* or money [a cheque for twenty thousand pounds] given in exchange for the goods.

Each of these verbs within the semantic domain of *possession* focuses on certain semantic participants, thus putting the others in the background (Fillmore, 1982: 116). The action of *selling* (lines 1–20 in the text) focuses on the *seller* in respect of the *goods*. In this part of the extract the attention is centred on the Duchess as she shows Oliver the pearls.

The action of *buying* (lines 21–52) focuses on the *buyer* in respect of the *goods*. In this segment of the text, the Duchess is totally in the background. Oliver is focused while he tries to decide whether to buy the pearls or not.

The action of *paying* (lines 52–69) focuses on the *buyer* in respect of both the *money* and the *seller*. The pearls cease to be important, and the interaction between Oliver and the Duchess comes into the spotlight as he hands her the cheque for twenty thousand pounds.

Relationships between semantic participants: a sociogram

The semantic participants within these frames do not exist in a vacuum. Their interrelationships form a network which in itself makes the text cohere and situates them within the frame. The construction of a sociogram helps the students to understand relations between the characters by transcoding information to diagrammatic display. Such an exercise helps the students to visualize the main information they have found in the text (Grellet, 1981: 158–160).

Exercise 2

Join the characters with arrows and the letter marking their relationship in the text.

Characters: Oliver, the Duchess, Diana, Spencer and Marshall, Wicks and Hammond

P/C = parent/child
F = friendship
E = employment
A = affection
D = dislike

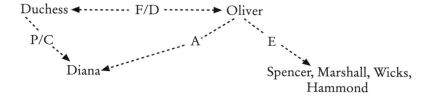

Visualizing the text

When the text is broken down into different types of actions within a frame and the relationships between different characters is made clear, it becomes much easier to understand. Even if all the words are not familiar, the students know what is happening because they possess access to the event type in which different types of information are ordered in chunks.

This type of analysis is a prerequisite to the next major activity, which is imaging the text. This involves translating it, but not in the prototypical sense of the term. The type of translation referred to is the translation of the text from a written to a visual medium. We cannot forget that students live immersed in a culture of screen images. A good exercise to make the students see the text in their minds is to try to convert it into a simplified film script.

As we have seen, when a scene is being described in a text, we are looking at it through language, language which codifies the author's point of view. In the text, characters and background are always described from a certain perspective to the extent that we only see the things that the author wishes us to. This becomes even more evident when we look at the text with a camera in our hands, and try to codify the author's perceptions by converting them into images.

Writing a film script

The task of the student film director is to rewrite the scene in the extract as a film script, describing the camera movements and focus. This is not as difficult as it may sound. Three types of camera shots and three types of camera movement are sufficient for our purposes:

Types of camera shots:

1 *Close shot*   a camera shot taken at a very short distance from the subject
2 *Medium shot* a camera shot in which the subject is in the middle distance, permitting some of the background to be seen
3 *Long shot*   a camera shot taken at a relatively great distance from the subject and permitting a broad view of a scene.

Types of camera movement:

1 *Pan*   to rotate a camera on its axis in order to keep a moving person/object in view or to film a panorama
2 *Dolly*   to move the whole camera in order to follow who/what is being filmed
3 *Zoom in/out* to bring a subject/scene into a close-up or to cause it to recede into a long shot.

Extracting the dialogue

The dialogue is first extracted from the text and written down separately, eliminating all other descriptive elements in the text:

'Good morning, Mr Bacon,' said the Duchess.
'And today, Duchess – what can I do for you today?' said Oliver, very softly.
'All that's left me, dear Mr Bacon,' she moaned.
''From the Appleby cincture,' she mourned.
'The last ... the last of them all. If the Duke knew...' she whispered.
'Dear Mr Bacon, a bit of bad luck. That villain! That sharper!' she hissed.
'Araminta, Daphne, Diana,' she moaned. 'It's for *them*.'
'You have all my secrets,' she leered.
'Old friend,' she murmured, 'old friend.'
'Old friend,' he repeated, 'old friend.'
'How much?' he queried.
'Twenty thousand,' she whispered.
'You will come down tomorrow?' she urged.
'The Prime Minister – His Royal Highness ...' She stopped. 'And Diana ...' she added.

'Twenty thousand' she moaned. 'My honour!'
'Twenty –' he wrote.
'Oliver!' the Duchess entreated. 'You'll come for a long weekend?'
'Thousand,' he wrote and signed it.
'Here you are,' he said.

Extracting the images

The second step is to make a list of the images in the text. This inventory will be the actions which the camera must film, if students decide to transmit all of the information within the text.

Dialogue and images

The final step is to mix the dialogue and the camera shots to create a film script. It goes without saying that in this sort of exercise there is no correct answer. However, there should be a certain justification for the decisions made. Possible answers are offered for the first two images.

Images

[Description of scene]

        'Good morning, Mr Bacon,' said the Duchess.

IMAGE 1:   The Duchess and Oliver shaking hands.
        FOCUS: *Oliver and the Duchess, part of the room in the background*
        SHOT: *Medium shot*
        'And today, Duchess – what can I do for you today?' said Oliver, very softly.

IMAGE 2:   The Duchess, her bag, the ten pearls.
        FOCUS: *The Duchess taking out and opening her bag*
        SHOT: *Begin with medium shot, zoom in on bag*
        'All that's left, dear Mr Bacon,' she moaned.
        'From the Appleby cincture,' she mourned.
        'The last . . . the last of them all.'

IMAGE 3:   One pearl in Oliver's hand. [*Specify focus and camera shot*]

IMAGE 4:   The Duchess, her finger held to her lips. [*Specify focus and camera shot*]
        'If the Duke knew . . .' she whispered. 'Dear Mr Bacon, a bit of bad luck. That villain! That sharper!' she hissed.
        'Araminta, Daphne, Diana,' she moaned. 'It's for *them*.'
        'You have all my secrets,' she leered.

IMAGE 5:   The Duchess's tears. [*Specify focus and camera shot*]
        'Old friend,' she murmured, 'old friend.'

'Old friend,' he repeated, 'old friend.'

'How much?' he queried.

IMAGE 6: Oliver's hand and the bell. [*Specify focus and camera shot*]

'Twenty thousand,' she whispered.

'You will come down tomorrow?' she urged.

'The Prime Minister – His Royal Highness . . .' She stopped.

'And Diana . . .' she added.

IMAGE 7: The Duchess covering the pearls with her hand.

IMAGE 8: Oliver's hand and the bell. [*Specify focus and camera shot*]

IMAGE 9: Oliver, the Prime Minister, Diana by the river. [*Specify focus and camera shot*]

'Twenty thousand' she moaned. 'My honour!'

IMAGE 10: Oliver's hand and the bell. [*Specify focus and camera shot*]

IMAGE 11: Oliver writing in his cheque-book. [*Specify focus and camera shot*]

'Twenty-' he wrote.

IMAGE 12: The picture of Oliver's mother. [*Specify focus and camera shot*]

'Oliver!' the Duchess entreated. 'You'll come for a long weekend?'

IMAGE 13: Oliver writing in his cheque-book. [*Specify focus and camera shot*]

'-Thousand,' he wrote and signed it.

IMAGE 14: Oliver giving the cheque to the Duchess. [*Specify focus and camera shot*]

'Here you are,' he said.

IMAGE 15: The Duchess leaving the shop. [*Specify focus and camera shot*]

The students must decide if they are going to include all the images in the script and what kind of shot and/or camera movement will be involved. This entails a choice of focus and perspective, as well as a grasp of what the characters are feeling. Long shots are more informative of context and surroundings, while close shots indicate strong emotions. The shots are also planned in conjunction with the plotline, and a decision must be made if the representation of events is to be chronological, or if there are any flashbacks or flash-forwards. For example, Image 9 is a flash-forward where Oliver imagines himself with the Prime Minister and Diana.

In this activity, the students are extracting elements from one text to construct another. To this end, it is necessary to make a selection of features to be incorporated in the setting. At times, this might even mean writing implicit information. For example, since the script cannot open with dialogue, the students must write in the first scene when the Duchess enters the shop. Since this is for contextual information it would be a long shot, with the camera either panning or dollying to follow her movements.

Conclusion

Approaching literature through this type of project work is an ideal way for the students to be able to visualize what the author is trying to convey. The students are asked to use cognitive processing skills they already possess to understand textual meaning, and then to construct another text based on the meaning relations they have established through previous discussion and exercises. In this way, they are given the key to enter the world of the text through meaning construction.

Appendix

Extract from 'The Duchess and the Jeweller' by Virginia Woolf (1944/1982)

Contextual information

After a childhood of poverty, Oliver Bacon has become the richest jeweller in all of England. Though he should be satisfied with his wealth, he is not, and still seeks something beyond his grasp. The Duchess of Lambourne, an old acquaintance, has come to his shop to see him on business.

'Good morning, Mr Bacon,' said the Duchess. And she held out her hand which came through the slit of her white glove. And Oliver bent low as he shook it. And as their hands touched the link was forged between them once more. They were friends, yet enemies; he was master, she was mistress; each cheated the other, each needed the other, each feared the other, each felt this and knew this every time they touched hands thus in the little back room with the white light outside, and the tree with its six leaves, and the sound of the street in the distance and behind them the safes.

'And today, Duchess – what can I do for you today?' said Oliver, very softly. The Duchess opened her heart, her private heart, gaped wide. And with a sigh but no words she took from her bag a long washleather pouch – it looked like a lean yellow ferret. And from a slit in the ferret's belly she dropped pearls – one, two, three, four – like the eggs of some heavenly bird.

'All that's left me, dear Mr Bacon,' she moaned. Five, six, seven – down they rolled, down the slopes of the vast mountain sides that fell between her knees into the one narrow valley – the eighth, the ninth, and the tenth. There they lay in the glow of the peach-blossom taffeta. Ten pearls.

'From the Appleby cincture,' she mourned. 'The last ... the last of them all.' Oliver stretched out and took one of the pearls between finger and thumb. It was round, it was lustrous. But real was it, or false? Was she lying again? Did she dare?

She laid a plump padded finger across her lips. 'If the Duke knew ...' she whispered. 'Dear Mr Bacon, a bit of bad luck ...'

Been gambling again, had she?

'That villain! That sharper!' she hissed.

The man with the chipped cheek bone? A bad 'un. And the Duke was straight as a poker; with side whiskers; would cut her off, shut her up down there if he knew – what I know, thought Oliver, and glanced at the safe.

'Araminta, Daphne, Diana,' she moaned. 'It's for *them*.'

The ladies Araminta, Daphne, Diana – her daughters. He knew them; adored them. But it was Diana he loved.

91

'You have all my secrets,' she leered. Tears slid; tears fell; tears like diamonds, collecting powder in the ruts of her cherry blossom cheeks.

'Old friend,' she murmured, 'old friend.'

'Old friend,' he repeated, 'old friend,' as if he licked the words.

'How much?' he queried.

She covered the pearls with her hand. 'Twenty thousand,' she whispered.

But was it real or false, the one he held in his hand? The Appleby cincture – hadn't she sold it already? He would ring Spencer or Hammond. 'Take it and test it,' he would say. He stretched to the bell.

'You will come down tomorrow?' she urged, she interrupted. 'The Prime Minister – His Royal Highness . . .' She stopped. 'And Diana . . .' she added.

Oliver took his hand off the bell.

He looked past her, at the backs of the houses in Bond Street. But he saw, not the houses in Bond Street, but a dimpling river; and trout rising and salmon; and the Prime Minister; and himself too, in white waistcoat; and then, Diana. He looked down at the pearl in his hand. But how could he test it, in the light of the river, in the light of the eyes of Diana? But the eyes of the Duchess were on him.

'Twenty thousand' she moaned. 'My honour!'

The honour of the mother of Diana! He drew his cheque-book towards him; he took out his pen.

'Twenty –' he wrote. Then he stopped writing. The eyes of the old woman in the picture were on him – of the old woman his mother.

'Oliver!' she warned him. 'Have sense! Don't be a fool!'

'Oliver!' the Duchess entreated – it was 'Oliver' now, not 'Mr Bacon.' 'You'll come for a long weekend?'

Alone in the woods with Diana! Riding alone in the woods with Diana!

'Thousand,' he wrote and signed it.

'Here you are,' he said.

And there opened all the flounces of the parasol, all the plumes of the peacock, the radiance of the wave, the swords and spears of Agincourt, as she rose from her chair. And the two old men and the two young men, Spencer and Marshall, Wicks and Hammond, flattened themselves behind the counter envying him as he led her through the shop to the door. And he waggled his yellow glove in their faces, and she held her honour – a cheque for twenty thousand pounds with his signature – quite firmly in her hands.

References

Collie, J. and Slater, S. (1987) *Literature in the Language Classroom*, Cambridge: Cambridge University Press.

Fillmore, C. (1982) 'Frame Semantics', in The Linguistic Society of Korea (ed.) *Linguistics in the Morning Calm*, Seoul: Hanshin Publishing Co.

Grellet, F. (1981) *Developing Reading Skills*, Cambridge: Cambridge University Press.

Hill, J. (1986) *Using Literature in Language Teaching*, London: Macmillan.

Woolf, V. (1944/1982) 'The Duchess and the Jeweller', in *A Haunted House and Other Short Stories*, London: Triad Grafton.

6

SIMULATED LIVING ABROAD

A new way of modern language acquisition

Lothar Bunn

Introduction

The demand that foreign language curricula should be kept open to revision is not a new one.[1] It takes into account that not only changes of parameters in FLT research but also changes in the anthropogenic and socio-cultural background of learners as well as in their individual learner biographies necessitate new concepts of foreign language teaching.[2] The increasing role which foreign language contacts are playing for many people in their work has in the German-speaking countries increased the call for the teaching of languages for specific purposes. A consequence for both LSP and general language teaching has been that learners need more skills-oriented language instruction.[3] With respect to oral skills, the teacher is called upon to provide situations for oral communication and possibilities for autonomous learning.

Against this background, this chapter presents a classroom project which helps the learners to cope with the communicative requirements of situations from everyday life. The learners are confronted with a real-life situation: they are living together in a high-rise block of flats and have to communicate with their flat-mates and neighbours. The main focus of this chapter is to show how learners can be helped to cope with the language requirements of these situations, and one particular feature of the classroom project will be emphasized – the systematic alternation of different types of interactive classroom activities.

Following a general description of the project, I will thus first of all describe the classroom interaction forms that determined this language course and explain the methodological concept. The alternation of classroom interaction forms involving the variation of the learning and studying activities will then be presented. Finally, the topics dealt with will be introduced in order to illustrate the aspect of course content.

Description of the project

Participants in this classroom project were Portuguese students of German in their first year at the University of Coimbra/Portugal. The course extended over one semester and met for six hours a week. The participants were given the following simulation instructions:

You (i.e. the participants in this language course) are uncomfortable in your present living situation. Consequently, you are going to move out. While looking for a new flat, you come across the following advertisement in a newspaper:

München-Haidhausen, vier Zimmer, Küche, Bad
in Hochhaus zu vermieten. 82 m2. Erstbezug.
Einbauküche, Balkon, Garage. 1400 DM
Kaltmiete. Bezug ab sofort. Tel. 089/2253436.

(München Haidhausen: four-room flats in high-rise for rent;
82 sq.m., first occupancy, fitted kitchen, balcony, garage.
DM 1400 w/o utilities. Imm. avail. Tel. 089/2253436.)

You form a family or communal living group with your brothers and sisters, parents, children or friends and put in an application for a flat with the manager. In groups of four you move into the flats. This course will consist of 5 families or flat-sharing groups. The flats will become your living space during the course, in which you will live with a family or flat-mates. You will simulate the living space in our classroom and furnish and decorate your flat, get to know the neighbours, establish house rules, put on a house party, argue, gossip, help each other out, complain, in short: you are living in a block of flats and must master everyday situations in the foreign language.

The course was organized in such a way that exactly half of the students were advanced speakers of German (ADV) and the other half were beginners with a much lower level of competence (BEG). This lack of homogeneousness concerning language competence thus led to a division in the course. In this particular case, Portuguese remigrants with an excellent knowledge of German shared a German class with students whose knowledge of German could be classed as lower intermediate level.[4]

Social organization and grouping of students

The aim of the course was to make the learners willing to and capable of dealing linguistically with situations on their own. In order that this aim might be achieved, learning environments were created, in which practising such situations under the guidance of the course instructor was made possible.

Two students, an ADV and a BEG respectively, worked together in tandem for the duration of the course. Two tandems either formed a 'family', or a flat-sharing group (FSG), called *Wohngemeinschaft* ('*WG*') in German, who then moved into a flat together. The course consisted of twenty students, ten tandems or five flat-sharing groups (Figure 6.1).[5]

Plenary ········▶ **Tandem** ········▶ **FSG** ···········▶ **Plenary**

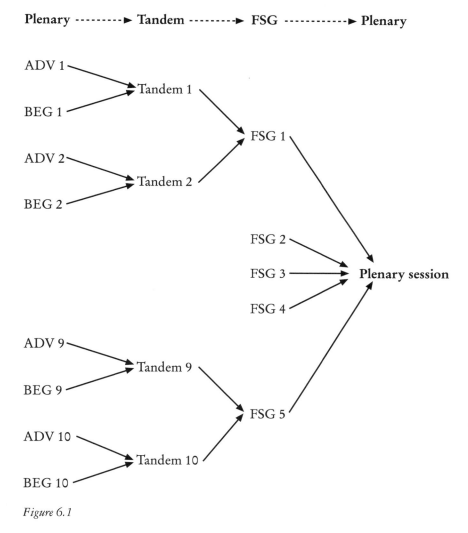

Figure 6.1

The different phases of a teaching sequence

The course may be divided into sequences on different topics, such as 'Establishing a set of house rules'. Every topic consisted of four phases, which

I would like to illustrate using the topic 'Furnishing a flat' as an example. The following illustration should first of all serve as an overview.

The teaching sequence 'Furnishing a flat' (*c.* 8 hours) is as follows:

Phase 1:   *Plenary*
- grammar
- useful phrases
- model dialogues

Phase 2:   *Tandem*
- grammar and vocabulary exercises
- writing a dialogue
- simulation practice

Phase 3:   *FSG* (Flat-sharing group)
- simulation

Phase 4:   *Plenary*
- simulation by an FSG in front of the plenary
- plenary of BEG

The topic 'Furnishing a flat' was introduced to the whole class. Useful phrases for the following purposes were collected:[6]

- making suggestions
- expressing opinions
- contradicting/rejecting
- agreeing
- challenging
- consenting

For example, useful phrases for *making a suggestion* are:

- *ich schlage vor* (I would suggest)
- *wie wär's, wenn . . .* (how about . . .)
- *sollten wir nicht* (shouldn't we . . .)
- *laß uns doch . . .* (why don't we . . .)

Or useful phrases for *consenting* are:

- *also gut* (OK)
- *meinetwegen* (it's fine with me)
- *von mir aus* (as far as I'm concerned)

The teacher explains the use of 'two-way' prepositions:[7]

> Den Tisch *stellen* wir am besten *an die* Wand.
> Der Tisch *steht an der* Wand ungünstig.
> (We had best put the table against the wall./
> Against the wall is not a very good place for the table.)

As homework, the advanced students are given the task of practising how to explain the use of these two-way prepositions clearly and simply and to write some relevant exercises with the help of grammar textbooks. The students then began working in tandem, each pair also receiving additional exercise material[8] from the teacher. The advanced students were told to explain the grammar items to the beginners and to correct their mistakes giving explanations.

After completing this exercise, the students wrote a short dialogue within their tandem,[9] using the model dialogue to help them. For writing this dialogue, the students were given certain roles to play, for example:

> BEG 1 doesn't want a cupboard, but insists that the table should go against the back wall.

> ADV 1 wants to put the cupboard against the free wall and the table in the middle of the room. They agree on the rest of the furniture.

Figure 6.2

The ADV were given the task of helping their partners find suitable phrases to express their intentions. At the same time, any relevant grammar items were to be practised and, if necessary, explained by the ADV. Though these phrases and expressions were learned within the restraints of the contextual situation – here: furniture, adverbs of space, making suggestions, etc. – the pairs were given a free hand in writing their dialogues, which were later checked by the teacher, and thus used a range of different words and phrases.

One of the dialogues written in tandem could thus look like the following:

ADV 1: I suggest we put the table in the middle of the room.
BEG 1: I don't like that. I'd put it against a wall.
ADV 1: But wouldn't it look better in the centre of the room?
BEG 1: I don't think so.

The students were then asked to simulate the dialogues in their tandem without the help of the written version,[10] before joining another pair to form an FSG (Phase 3).

Every FSG consisted of two tandems, i.e. four students. In an earlier lesson they had already assumed fictitious identities, such as the following:

> Wolfgang Johannsen,
> 35 years old, car mechanic,
> has got a motor-bike, likes reading
> detective stories, doesn't do
> any cleaning, doesn't like alcohol,
> often has headphones on, speaks loudly
> and has a speech impediment,
> dyes his hair blond . . . .

This 'biography' was hung up on the wall together with a photo so that it could be read and used for reference by the other learners.

Every FSG, consisting of two tandems, was given part of the classroom to furnish. The learners brought various items with them from home, such as table-cloths, flowers, pictures, small carpets, etc. The communicative function of this role play consisted of reaching a decision on how to furnish the flat, with every student sticking to his or her pre-assigned role. All the FSGs practised in the classroom simultaneously, the teacher only offering assistance where necessary. The correction of spoken errors was not carried out by the teacher, but by the advanced students alone. For the students, the challenge lay in being confronted by the foreign language utterances of the other tandem and having to react to them appropriately.

In Phase 4, this scene, which had been simulated in the tandems and practised in the FSGs, was acted out by one of the FSG groups in front of the whole class. The performance was filmed so that the participants could later use the video to discuss their own linguistic behaviour. The rest of the class was invited to contribute comments, too. As it turned out, at this point the participants had already departed quite considerably from the dialogues written in their tandems and increasingly began to speak spontaneously and freely. As they gained more confidence in speaking and enjoying the role play more and more, the learners also began to act more emotionally: they got angry or felt insulted, expressed reservations or agreement in different ways. The following dialogue on the topic of house rules will give an example of such enacted FSG role plays:

BEG 1: I think children shouldn't be allowed to play in the back yard between one o'clock and three o'clock.
ADV 1: Why not?
BEG 1: Because my flat-mate is studying for his exams and always takes a nap after lunch.
ADV 2: But that's stupid. Where else should the children play at that time?
BEG 2: In any case, I think we should compile an alternative set of house rules in which we write down everything that isn't forbidden.
BEG 1: Then we'll put in it that children can play in the back yard from 9 to 12 and 3 to 6.
ADV 1: You don't seem to like children, I must say!

The students did indeed write this set of 'house rules with a difference' and it was hung up in the classroom next to a 'typically German' set of house rules.

After this phase, the teacher held separate plenary sessions for the beginners or the advanced students, where necessary. In an earlier part of the course, the advanced students had already been trained in their role as co-teachers. The role play in the FSGs and in front of the whole class prompted the teacher to give the advanced students some additional instructions. The beginners were given exercises on grammar, useful phrases and language structures, etc. to work on, while the teacher talked with the advanced students.

The instructions for the advanced students concerned the students' language problems that were to be discussed later in tandem work. Importance was also attached to the cooperation within the group about which the teacher kept himself informed thoroughly, and any problems arising were discussed.

Some of the topics discussed with the ADV were:

• the role of the advanced students as co-teachers (for example, problems when practising certain items with the beginners),
• error correction,

- methodological aids for giving explanations,
- the beginners' grammar problems,
- their progress/impediments/level of competence,
- ways of encouraging the beginners' linguistic development/how to avoid becoming too dominant.

The structure of the course

The course as a whole needed a warm-up phase. The students were not used to learning a language in differing types of classroom interaction, and initially had to try and forget their accustomed ways of learning. During a period of familiarization, both the constant need – mainly of the beginners – for correction and supervision by the teacher as well as the unusual type of group work with a fellow student as co-teacher had to be taken into consideration.

As an introductory phase, two weeks (twelve lessons) were therefore devoted to work exclusively in the plenary sessions or in tandem. During this period, the advanced students attended plenary sessions without the beginners in order to familiarize themselves with their difficult task:

- how do I correct mistakes?
- how can I get the beginner to talk?
- how do I avoid becoming too dominant, especially in role play?
- how should I talk so that the beginner will answer me in German?
- how do I explain grammar?
- how should I prepare myself for class?

In other phases with the whole class, the learning process was discussed from the beginners' point of view:

- personal feelings about working with the advanced student,
- comprehension problems during explanations,
- fears and anxieties,
- exercises to do at home, etc.

The teacher's role comprised the additional tasks of

- breaking down the fear of speaking and role playing,
- making sure that the participants got to know each other,
- finding out the learners' level of competence,
- compensating for basic language problems or helping the students to do so (giving individual assistance),
- introducing and practising the different types of classroom interaction.

In the third week (lessons 13–18), the students formed FSGs and 'moved into the block of flats'. In the fourth week, they began role-playing the scenes in their FSGs.

Weeks 1–2:	plenary BEG + ADV silent work/plenary BEG/plenary ADV tandem
Weeks 3–4:	plenary BEG + ADV plenary BEG/plenary ADV tandem FSG
from Week 5 on:	plenary (if required) tandem FSG/contacts between FSGs plenary/FSG

After the fourth week, the students were used to the way the course was organized, so that the teacher could concentrate on working with weaker students individually. The students were now told to make contact with other FSGs: to introduce themselves, to ask for help, to arrange to meet, etc.

Methodological background

Though there are many aspects of the methodology worth discussing, I would like to concentrate on two points: the communication situations and the forms of classroom interaction.

Communication situations

All instances of listening and speaking in this course are motivated by their communicative function, i.e. language is learned with respect to the situation in which it is used to carry out a specific aim. Over the course of the semester, the situations that have to be mastered become more complex and the communicative requirements more demanding. In order to guarantee individual learning progress, the communicative exercises were structured according to the principle of repetition, but the requirements were always different. The dialogue written and enacted in tandem 1, for example, serves for initial practice purposes. In the FSG a new situation arises: the new communication partners (tandem 2) may use other, possibly unknown, expressions and their role-play instructions are not known to tandem 1. The learners have to react to both and try to achieve their communicative aim while adhering to their role-play instructions.

The language requirements are thus similar to those of an authentic communication situation, which can be successfully mastered even if not all the utterances are understood completely; but this has to be practised. In plenary sessions the learners can then watch and comment on a scene.[11]

To summarize: it could be said that the learning environment should be designed as a living environment and that aspects of living together should be made the topic of the learning process.[12]

Classroom interaction

Working in a stable social structure (having a fixed role in permanent pairs or groups of four), and without the supervision by a teacher, has different effects on the motivation of the two groups of participants, ADV and BEG. Through talking with a fellow student, the beginners' fear of speaking the foreign language is reduced, and they feel secure doing group work with one or three other students. As the tandems and FSGs practise speaking simultaneously, the individual student's 'speaking time' is increased considerably, without making the learning process unfocused or random. Getting weaker students in particular to participate orally in the classroom is one of the major problems of traditional forms of FLT. For the advanced students, hearing the beginners speak is not wasted time as it is appropriate for their level of competence for them to be thinking about types of mistakes, about how to classify mistakes – including their own – and how to avoid them.

The autonomy of the students when learning grammar, syntax and vocabulary or indeed learning to deal with communicative situations provides the motivation to find and use different kinds of learning aids, such as grammar books, dictionaries, textbooks and also the linguistic output of their fellow students. Of course, an important contributing factor is whether the students are enjoying the course.

The learners experience a structured order of different forms of classroom interaction, which are all designed to increase their level of competence. In tandem, the learners can familiarize themselves with the topic, practise useful expressions, correct errors and gain a certain amount of confidence. The role-play in the FSGs again provides the opportunity for language practice within a group and without an audience, before scenes are presented to the whole class. The aim was to enable the students to cope with unpredictable situations through having practised certain communicative structures. For this reason, the flat-mates from one FSG get to know the members of another FSG later on in the course. Through these conversations with different speakers the learners can practise mastering varying situations, as the others act differently, use different expressions and – due to their instructions or fictitious biographies – react differently.

Topics

The aim of the course was for the learners to practise situations from everyday life which they had personally experienced. The theme 'Living together' presented itself, having the advantage that it is not unlikely that a situation of this kind could occur in a foreign culture. Through the principle of a high frequency of repetition, the use of appropriate language can be consolidated.

The following topics were discussed in the course:

- looking for a flat (advertisement)/speaking to landlord or landlady on the phone,
- moving,
- inventing a fictitious biography,
- furnishing the flat,
- cooking together,
- arranging to meet someone,
- asking someone a favour,
- getting to know the neighbours/introducing oneself,
- establishing a set of house rules,
- making a complaint,
- preparing and giving a house party.

Treatment of the themes lasted for approximately four to eight lessons respectively. For example, in connection with the theme 'Establishing a set of "house rules with a difference"', the following tasks had to be accomplished:

- use of modal verbs and their paraphrases:
  man darf, es ist erlaubt, es ist gestattet,
  hat zu+Infinitiv, muß, es ist in keinem Fall erlaubt/gestattet . . .
  (you may, it is allowed/permitted, to have to do something,
  must, it is under no circumstances permitted, it is forbidden to . . .)
- infinitive constructions:
  die Reinigung der Treppe hat am Ersten eines jeden Monats zu erfolgen;
  es ist nicht erlaubt, im Hausflur zu rauchen;
  ab acht Uhr abends ist die Haustür geschlossen zu halten . . .
  (the staircase has to be cleaned on the first day of every month; smoking in the hall is forbidden;
  the main door has to be kept shut after 8 pm . . .)
- disagreeing vehemently:
  das ist doch Unsinn/Blödsinn;
  solch ein Quatsch;
  das finde ich bescheuert . . .
  (that's stupid; what a load of rubbish; I think that's crazy . . .)

- coming to an agreement:
  ich schlage folgenden Kompromiß vor;
  wie wärs, wenn wir uns darauf einigen . . .
  (I would suggest the following compromise;
  how about agreeing to/on . . .).

Concluding remarks

Finally I would like to comment on one of the questions most frequently asked concerning this project, namely how much did the participants actually learn.

Experience has shown that simply learning vocabulary, grammar and syntax, as is expected in many textbooks, can only achieve short-term learning effects, especially when the learner is only studying towards a specific exam. In the course described above, in which the teaching method was customized to the theme of 'Living together', it became apparent that through

- taking away the fear of speaking through a role-play (living) environment without assessment,
- creating an emotionally secure learning atmosphere,
- integrating the learning process into a stable social framework,
- using role play in which repetition and individual creation of content were underlying principles,

impediments to learning could be removed and a long-term learning effect achieved. The following study year confirmed this.

The remigrants' development in Germany, for the most part, appeared to have been arrested before they had reached a point at which they could speak without error. Their mistakes had become consolidated through their consistent use in school and with German-speaking peers. Thus the first task was to make the students aware of their mistakes. These students learned much through having to explain grammatical phenomena first to themselves and then to fellow students. Their own assessment of their German, particularly their written German, made it clear to them that their linguistic learning process was not yet completed. In addition, the motivation among students to cooperate in the project was very high, as most of them planned to become teachers themselves and therefore saw the methodological and didactic training they would receive as co-teachers as being useful preparation for their chosen profession.

The progress of the group of beginners was mainly oriented towards the long term. The students were speaking – simultaneously – throughout the major portion of the lessons, i.e. continuously practising what they had learned. Having to cope with the same situations repeatedly forced the students to react creatively to their conversation partners and not rely on standard phrases. Much emphasis was placed on developing a feeling for speaking and acting appropriately according to the communicative situations with various partners. Students who were afraid to speak during the first two weeks relaxed later, i.e. they communicated without fear. It was noticeable that having a clearly defined speech intention gave a sense of purpose to communication in the classroom. The fact that the BEG always had the ADV to turn to afforded them a degree of support which could not have been achieved even through intensive individual assistance in traditional teaching. The need to communicate a message, which developed out of identification with the role and the situation, was of enormous significance for the students' motivation. The privacy in the groups also motivated the students to speak. At the end of the course, the participants were able to witness their own progress by watching themselves on film.

It must be admitted that problems did arise during the course. It should be pointed out that classroom arrangements must be flexible, i.e. it must be possible to move tables and chairs around, and ideally two rooms should be available. Furthermore, it was difficult to change the students' learning habits, as the following two points illustrate. The beginners were supposed not to ask the teacher for advice but to try and solve the problem on their own, or seek assistance from the ADV. On the other hand, the ADV had to be convinced that their role as co-teachers had a positive effect on their own learning process, namely that when they explained something, they were also teaching themselves. It was important for the students to realize this in order for them to be able to develop a teacher–learner relationship. The students argued in class, told each other jokes, ate and drank together. They all agreed that they had enjoyed the course very much.

Notes

1   Cf. Hüllen, 1991: 431–435.
2   Methodological discussions have broadened communicative FLT through the inclusion of the intercultural concept. The following two publications offer an introduction for the foreign language teacher: Neuner/Hunfeld (1993), and the collection of articles edited by Henrici/Koreik (1994).
3   The word 'skills' is here taken to refer to the basic skills of reading, listening, writing and speaking, which in turn are the result of a complex interaction of different verbal and non-verbal partial skills.
4   In the course in question, the advanced learners were remigrants, i.e. Portuguese students who grew up in Germany and then returned to Portugal. Their level of competence can be classed as advanced, and they form about a quarter of all students starting to study German in Coimbra/Portugal. Though their spoken German seems to be flawless, their written German is often contaminated by colloquialisms. Their imprecise use of inflections in spoken German is usually reflected in their writing in the form of mistakes. Besides, when it comes to more demanding situations, further errors appear in their spoken German which again usually has a multiplying effect in writing. The German language courses are also obligatory for the remigrants during their German studies.

Traditionally, remigrants are grouped into special remigrant courses which mainly deal with literature. The project-oriented language course 'Living Together' is designed to do away with the separation of remigrant students and beginners. This measure is an attempt to turn the remigrants' linguistic potential into a teaching resource and make it possible for every beginner to have the chance of consistent contact with a near-native speaker.

5   The so-called 'WG' is a frequent living arrangement in Germany among young people, particularly students, who rent a flat together in which every occupant has his or her own room, and kitchen and bathroom are shared.

6   A useful aid to planning oral communication and collecting useful phrases is the book *Sprechplanung. Empirie, Theorie und Didaktik der Sprecherstrategien* by Klaus R. Wagner (1978), as it is written for practical use and contains an extensive section of teaching materials.

7   So-called two-way prepositions are prepositions which in German require either the dative or the accusative case depending on the context; as they occur very frequently, it is necessary to practise them intensively.

8   The exercise book *Wechselspiel* by M. Dreke and W. Kind (1986) is particularly useful for tandem work.

9   Manfred Arendt's article 'Zwei Wege zur Schulung des small talk' (1996: 25–31), which is based on actual classroom experience, is helpful for practising oral communication in the foreign language classroom.

10 This type of role play should be distinguished from other types of simulations or scenic presentations (cf. interactional pedagogy) and is to be understood as a learning method in which a situation is practised as closely to the authentic situation as is necessary for the learning process.

11 Compared to an authentic situation, the described classroom situations should be termed reductionist situations, as the complexity of the surrounding circumstances and possible utterances in natural situations is reduced through the teacher's instructions. Of importance here is a communicative context that is free from sanctions, as it can prove very beneficial for the learning process to allow learners to make mistakes.

12 This demand, already formulated by Hartmut von Hentig, seems not to have been taken into account in FLT so far.

Useful materials

Materials on the theme of 'Living (together)' can be found in almost every textbook and in collections of texts. The following titles have proved their worth in the classroom.

Bieler, K. H. (ed.) (1984) *Standpunkte. Texte und Übungen für die Oberstufe*, München: Max Hueber Verlag.

[This book contains a teaching sequence on the theme 'Living in the city' with activity materials as well as literary and non-literary texts.]

Blaasch, H.-W. (1985) 'Wohnen in der Großstadt – Überlegungen und Texte zu einem thematischen Baukasten für Fortgeschrittene', in Ch. Edelhoff (ed.) *Authentische Texte im Deutschunterricht*, Ismaning: Max Hueber Verlag.

[This contribution contains a model teaching sequence with didacticized materials that can be used in class. Various ways of working with authentic texts are demonstrated.]

Dreke, M. and Lind, W. (1986) *Wechselspiel. Sprachanlässe für die Partnerarbeit im kommunikativen Deutschunterricht. Arbeitsblätter für Anfänger und Fortgeschrittene*, München: Langenscheidt Verlag.

[This workbook provides numerous communicative situations within topics such as 'asking for information about apartments', 'furnishing an apartment', 'moving', etc. It is especially useful for work in small groups.]

Goethe-Institut (1984) *Unterrichtsmaterial zur Landeskunde. "Projekt Wohnen" I/ II*, München: Goethe-Institut.
[This book of materials especially developed for the classroom contains texts and pictures that can be used for different purposes. The texts are grouped thematically and presented along with suggestions for their use.]

Lohfert, W. (1982) *Kommunikative Spiele für Deutsch als Fremdsprache. Spielpläne und Materialien für die Grundstufe*, Ismaning: Max Hueber Verlag.

Authentic materials:

- brochures of Munich, courtesy of the Department of Tourism, Munich,
- city maps,
- road maps,
- house rules,
- photographs of blocks of flats and their surroundings.

References

Arendt, M. (1996) 'Zwei Wege zur Schulung des small talk', in *Fremdsprachenunterricht* 1, 25–31.

Dreke, M. and Lind, W. (1986) *Wechselspiel. Sprachanlässe für die Partnerarbeit im kommunikativen Deutschunterricht. Arbeitsblätter für Anfänger und Fortgeschrittene*, München: Langenscheidt Verlag.

Henrici, G. and Koreik, U. (1994) *Deutsch als Fremdsprache. Wo warst Du, wo bist Du, wohin gehst Du?*, Hohengehren: Schneider-Verlag.

Hüllen, W. (1991) 'Sprachliches Curriculum', in Bausch/Christ/Hüllen, W./Krumm (eds) *Handbuch Fremdsprachenunterricht*, Tübingen: Gunter Narr Verlag.

Neuner, G. and Hunfeld, H. (1993) *Methoden des fremdsprachlichen Deutschunterrichts*, Berlin: Langenscheidt Verlag.

Wagner, K. R. (1978) *Sprechplanung. Empirie, Theorie und Didaktik der Sprecherstrategien*, Frankfurt am Main: Hirschgraben-Verlag.

7

PORTRAYING THE COMPLEXITY OF L2 CLASSROOM INTERACTION

Paul Seedhouse

Introduction

L2 teachers from around the world may be familiar with the experience of speaking with teachers of 'content' subjects and finding that they have little idea of the difficulty and complexity of the work which L2 teachers do in the classroom. I often hear people say, 'if you can speak the language, then you can teach it'. An engineering colleague told me that his job was much more difficult than mine because engineering is in a constant state of change whereas languages never change!

The main point I would like to make in this chapter is that the methodology we have predominantly used to observe and describe L2 classroom interaction understates the complexity and fluidity of our interactional work to a considerable extent. It is suggested, however, that a change in methodology may be successful in revealing the extreme demands which the dual nature of language as subject and vehicle places upon us, as well as in portraying the interactional skill and professionalism of language teachers.

Theoretical background

According to Levinson (1983: 286), there are two major approaches to the study of naturally occurring interaction: *Discourse Analysis* (DA) and *Conversation Analysis* (CA). DA uses principles and methodology typical of linguistics to analyse classroom discourse in structural-functional linguistic terms (Chaudron, 1988: 14). According to DA, utterances can be translated into speech acts or interactional moves; for example, 'Could I borrow your pencil?' could be mapped as 'request'. Once sequences of speech acts or moves have been plotted, a set of rules can be written which show how the units fit together to form coherent discourse. Then, hierarchical systems which depict the overall organization of classroom discourse can be developed. The two outstanding studies of (first language) classroom interaction which take this DA approach are Sinclair and Coulthard (1975) and Mehan (1979). Perhaps their most significant finding as far as the teaching profession is concerned is their identification of the three-part sequence typical of classroom interaction. This sequence is known as teacher Initiation, learner Response and teacher Follow-Up (IRF) in the British school, or teacher Initiation, learner Response and teacher Evaluation (IRE) in the American school. I will refer to it as the IRF/IRE cycle in this study.

The DA system of analysing classroom interaction has proved highly appealing to the language teaching profession, to the extent that the vast majority of studies of classroom interaction have been based more or less explicitly on the DA approach. There are notable exceptions to this, including Allwright (1980) within the CA tradition, Peck (1988) with a pedagogical approach, and Van Lier (1988) within the ethnographic tradition.

The basis of the DA approach is that a teacher is making one pedagogic move on one level at a time. The move the teacher is making can be specified and coded as a pedagogic move, for example, 'initiates' or 'replies'. This 'one pedagogic move on one level at a time' coding approach is the basis of the following coding systems developed especially for the L2 classroom: the COLT instrument (Froehlich *et al.*, 1985), TALOS (Ullman and Geva, 1984), Mitchell *et al.* (1989), and FLINT (Moskowitz, 1976). A full list of observation instruments is given in Chaudron (1988: 18).

Some of the above coding systems involve coding on different dimensions of analysis, such as content, type of activity, skill focus, language used: see Chaudron (1988: 22) for a summary. However, the assumption is still that in each of these separate coding dimensions the teacher is making one pedagogical move at a time and the coder has to make a choice as to which slot the pedagogical move should be coded into. However, I will show in my analysis of extract 1 line 5 that the same single teacher utterance is simultaneously making moves of agreement, confirmation and correction and displaying an approved version of the learner utterance for the benefit of other learners.

Studies within the communicative approach (Dinsmore, 1985; Nunan, 1987) have also adopted DA methodology to examine classroom interaction. Both studies examine L2 classroom interaction and conclude that, although the teachers were using modern methods, there was little genuine communication taking place. Both Dinsmore (1985: 226) and Nunan (1987: 137) present the presence of the IRF cycle as *their initial reason* for asserting that there was little 'genuine' communication in the language classrooms which they observed. Dinsmore (1985: 227) claims that the prevalence of the IRF cycle and the unequal power distribution 'hardly seems compatible with a "communicative" language teaching methodology'. Nunan (1987: 137) writes:

> On the surface, the lessons appeared to conform to the sorts of communicative principles advocated in the literature. However,

when the patterns of interaction were examined more closely, they resembled traditional patterns of classroom interaction rather than genuine interaction. Thus, the most commonly occurring pattern of interaction was identical with the basic exchange structure ... Teacher initiation, Learner response, Teacher follow-up.

The DA approach has been subject to considerable criticism on a theoretical level (Levinson, 1983). However, I would like to focus on the problems inherent in the DA approach in a way which is relevant to language teachers.

1   A basic problem with the DA approach is that it portrays teachers as making one pedagogic move on one level at a time. I suggest in my analyses of L2 classroom extracts that teachers may be simultaneously orienting to multiple separate pedagogical concerns and that classroom interaction may be operating on multiple levels.

2   The focus and context of the interaction may switch with great fluidity, as I hope to show in my textual analyses. Halliday (1985: xxxiv) suggests that 'The context of spoken language is in a constant state of flux, and the language has to be mobile and alert ... The complexity of spoken language is more like that of a dance; it is not static and dense but mobile and intricate.' I hope to show that DA cannot portray the flow of interaction because it is essentially a static approach which portrays interaction as fixed and unidimensional coordinates on a conceptual map.

3   Since the DA approach was developed for L1 classrooms and transferred for use in L2 classrooms, it has difficulty in portraying the extra dimension which distinguishes L2 classroom interaction from L1 classroom interaction, namely that language is not only the vehicle but also the goal of the interaction. As Willis (1992: 162) states: 'language is used for two purposes; it serves both as the subject matter of the lesson, and as the medium of instruction. It is precisely this dual role that makes language lessons difficult to describe.' Some coding schemes have tried to adapt the DA approach to the L2 classroom. In order to try to make the DA approach cope with these two different levels of language use, Willis (1992) proposes coding on either an inner or an outer level. However, this still implies that an utterance is either being used on one level or another, whereas I hope to show that utterances often operate on both levels simultaneously.

In the following CA analyses of classroom extracts I attempt to show that, in contrast to DA, CA is able to capture the dynamic, fluid, complex interplay and dialectic between the different levels on which the L2 classroom operates and hence portray the complexity of the teacher's interactional work.

Analyses of transcripts of L2 lessons

In this section I will analyse, using a CA methodology, three extracts from L2 lessons around the world. My research is based on a database of published and unpublished transcripts (as well as videos) of L2 lessons, totalling 330 lessons or fragments of lessons from eight different European countries. These include English, French and German lessons. I apologize for the fact that the extracts I have chosen for discussion in this article come exclusively from English lessons.

Extract 1

1 *T:* Vin, have you ever been to the movies? What's your favourite movie?
2 *L:* Big.
3 *T:* Big, OK, that's a good movie, that was about a little boy inside a big man, wasn't it?
4 *L:* Yeah, boy get surprise all the time.
5 *T:* Yes, he was surprised, wasn't he? Usually little boys don't do the things that men do, do they?
6 *L:* No, little boy no drink.
7 *T:* That's right, little boys don't drink.

(Johnson, 1995: 23)

Taking first of all a conventional DA approach, this extract can be analysed quite straightforwardly. What we have is a sequence of consecutive IRF/IRE cycles which can be coded as follows: Line 1: Initiation. Line 2: Reply. Line 3: Follow-up and Initiation. Line 4: Reply. Line 5: Follow-up and Initiation. Line 6: Reply. Line 7: Follow-up. The analysis is simple and complete and we can confirm that this is traditional, lockstep classroom interaction of the type often criticized by the communicative approach (Dinsmore, 1985; Nunan 1987) because it is teacher-dominated and not like 'genuine' interaction.

I will now analyse the extract using a CA methodology and suggest that in fact this is a very complex and dynamic piece of interaction indeed. If we analyse turn-taking and topic at the same time, we can see that the learner is able to develop a topic and is allowed interactional space. In line 1 T introduces the carrier topic (films) and constrains L's turn in Line 2, which is a minimum response appropriate to the turn. In line 3 T shifts the topic slightly from the carrier topic (films) to the sub-topic of the specific film *Big*: this sub-topic has been nominated by L. In doing so T validates and approves L's sub-topic by calling it a good movie. T constrains L's next turn by making a general statement summarizing the plot of the movie (which was about a little boy inside a big man) together with a tag question. This allocates L a turn, constrains the topic of L's turn (the plot of the film *Big*) and simultaneously provides the other students in the class (who presumably may

111

not know the film) with sufficient information to be able to follow the evolving dialogue. The tag question effectively requires L to confirm the accuracy of T's summary of the film's plot, but also allows L the interactional space (if L wishes) to develop the sub-topic. L does confirm T's summary of the sub-topic and then chooses to contribute new information which develops the sub-topic (the film's plot), namely in line 4 (boy get surprise all the time). This utterance is linguistically incorrect, although the propositional content is clear. Since L is introducing 'new' information, L is effectively developing the sub-topic, to which T could respond in his/her next turn. At this point T could choose to (1) correct the learner's utterance; (2) continue to develop the sub-topic; (3) decline to adopt L's sub-topic and change the course of the interaction: T has superior interactional rights and is not obliged to adopt the direction in which L is pushing the interaction.

T effectively chooses to combine choices (1) and (2) in the first sentence of line 5: 'Yes, he was surprised, wasn't he?' There is positive evaluation of the propositional content of the learner utterance followed by an expansion of the learner utterance into a correct sequence of linguistic forms. The type of repair used is embedded correction, that is, a repair done in the context of a conversational move, which in this case is a move of agreement and confirmation:

> That is, the utterances are not occupied by the doing of correcting, but by whatever talk is in progress ... What we have, then, is embedded correction as a by-the-way occurence in some ongoing course of talk.
>
> (Jefferson, 1987: 95)

This form of correction and expansion is highly reminiscent of adult–child conversation.[1]

In the second sentence of line 5 T accepts L's invitation to develop the sub-topic, and T's statement 'usually little boys don't do the things that men do' also simultaneously provides the other students in the class with an explanation as to why the boy was surprised all the time, thus enabling them to continue to follow the evolving dialogue. The tag question (line 5) again allocates L a turn and effectively allots him the interactional space to continue to develop the sub-topic should he wish to do so. L uses 'no' in line 6 to agree with the negative tag-question and chooses to develop the sub-topic by providing an example from the film to illustrate T's previous generalized statement with 'little boy no drink'. Again his utterance is linguistically incorrect, although the propositional content is clear. Since L is again introducing 'new' information, L effectively invites T to respond to this elaboration of the sub-topic in T's next turn. T's response in line 7 is similar to line 5 in that T performs a move of agreement, simultaneously corrects L's utterance (using embedded correction) and displays a correct version for the other students.

What is clear from the analysis of the above extract is that, although it could at first sight be mistaken for a rigid, plodding, lockstep IRF cycle sequence in which everything is pre-planned and predictable, the interaction is in fact dynamic and locally managed on a turn-by-turn basis to a considerable extent. There is some degree of pre-planning in that the teacher has an overall idea of what is to be achieved in the interaction and in that it is the teacher who introduces the carrier topic of films and has overall control of the speech exchange system. However, the question in line 1 is an open or referential one – the teacher does not know how L will respond – and L is able to nominate and develop a sub-topic.

It will now be demonstrated how the teacher is balancing multiple and sometimes conflicting demands. The teacher is orienting to five separate (though related) concerns simultaneously:

1   The teacher's purpose (Johnson, 1995: 23) 'was to allow the students to share their ideas and possibly generate some new vocabulary words within the context of the discussion'. This implies that the teacher needs to control the topic while allowing the learners some interactional space. The teacher thus has to orient to an overall pedagogical plan.

2   The teacher also has to respond to the ideas and personal meanings which the learner chooses to share, and does so successfully in that he/she develops the sub-topic introduced by the learner. Thus in lines 5 and 7 the teacher responds to the learner utterance with a conversational move of agreement which validates the propositional content of the utterance as well as the introduction of the sub-topic.

3   The teacher also responds to linguistic incorrectness in the individual learner's utterances and conducts embedded repair on them. The linguistic repair is performed in a mitigated and non-face-threatening way because it is prefaced by a move of agreement and approval and because the correction is treated as a by-the-way matter.

4   The teacher must also orient to the other learners in the class. One problem frequently faced by teachers is that individual learners often produce responses which are inaudible or incomprehensible to the other students in the class. Thus in lines 5 and 7 the teacher is simultaneously displaying approved versions of learner utterances so that the other learners are able to follow the propositional content of the interaction and are also able to receive correctly formed linguistic input.

5   One of the most difficult feats in L2 teaching is to maintain a simultaneous dual focus on both form and meaning. Examination of classroom transcripts often shows that focusing on the correctness of linguistic forms leads to 'meaningless' discourse, whereas focusing on meaning leads to accepting incorrect forms, which may in turn lead to fossilized errors. I explore this issue in another study (Seedhouse, 1997), but at present I would like to argue that the teacher in the above extract

is skilfully managing to maintain a simultaneous dual focus on both form and meaning. There is a focus on form in that the teacher upgrades and expands the learner's utterances on a linguistic level, which means that the learners have a linguistically correct utterance to function as model and input. The focus is simultaneously also on meaning in that the learner is able to contribute 'new' information concerning his/her personal experiences.

In the following extract the teacher is orienting to an overall pedagogical plan which focuses on form. A learner, however, wants to express some personal meanings:

Extract 2

174 *T:* Yeah. OK. What does this mean? 'Get to'? Uh.
175 *SS:* [unintelligible]
     T: OK. It says the group has been trying to get the government, the city government, to help uhm draw special lanes, lanes like this [draws on board] on the street. OK. These are for cars. These are for bikes [points to blackboard].
180 *L:* You know, in Moscow they reproduce all all cab.
     T: Uhm?
     L: They reproduced all cabs.
     T: They produce?
     L: Reproduce.
185 *T:* D'you mean uh they they use old cabs, old taxis?
     L: No, no, no. They reproduced all ALL cabs.
     T: All the cabs?
     L: Yeah, all the cabs for electric (electric you know) electric points.
190 *T:* Cab. Oh you mean they made the cabs in down in downtown areas uh uh use electric uh motors?
     L: Yeah, no downtown, all cabs in Moscow.
     T: Where?
     L: In Moscow.
195 *T:* Oh. And it's successful?
     L: Yeah.
     T: OK. Uhm. Just a second, Igor. Let's what does this mean? If you get someone to do something. Uhm.

(Allwright, 1980: 180)

Up to line 179 T has been focusing on form, on the meaning of words in a text, so L is self-selecting, and in effect stealing a turn in line 180. L tries to make a statement designed to express personal meaning while remaining within the carrier topic of the lesson (traffic). L has therefore not only stolen a turn but has shifted the focus of the lesson from form to meaning. T has various choices here. T could simply regain control of the focus and of the turn-taking system by, for example, telling L that he is out of line; or T could validate L's attempt to express personal meanings by showing interest in the utterance or by engaging with the topic. However, there is an initial problem in that the meaning of L's utterance is unclear. The problem in communication is that L has made an error in lexis ('reproduce' instead of 'convert') which obscures the meaning. T in effect validates L's taking the floor and shifting the focus by helping to repair L's statement in order that the meaning should be clear. The repair process is complex and is certainly a cooperative effort: L repairs T's candidate rephrasings in lines 184, 186, 188 and 192 in an attempt to convey his meaning, while T initiates repair in lines 181, 183, 185, 187, 190 and 193. The repair was successfully managed on a cooperative basis in that L finally managed to make his personal meaning clear with the help of T: the meaning was 'negotiated'. Once the meaning has finally become clear in line 195 T shows interest in the utterance by engaging briefly with the topic and then shifts the focus of the lesson back to form (in line with the pedagogical lesson plan) in line 197.

In the case of extract 2 it is not claimed that the interaction is particularly complex, by comparison with extract 1. What extract 2 illustrates is the fluidity and mutability of L2 classroom interaction and the tension, interplay and dialectic between a focus on form and a focus on meaning. We should note that the meaning of L's utterance was obscured by a problem with linguistic form. Although the teacher has an overall pedagogical plan, he/she needs to react to interaction which is instantly transformable, as in extract 2. Further, the teacher needs to be able to repair a wide variety of errors of a linguistic nature. In extract 1 syntactical errors were repaired indirectly. In extract 2 a lexical error which hindered communication was repaired, and of course teachers also repair errors on the level of phonology, grammar, discourse, etc. Not only do teachers need to decide what to repair in learner utterances and how to repair them; they also need to be sensitive to the flow of interaction and decide whether or not to repair them: is the repair going to break the flow of the interaction, or does the error impede communciation? All of this complex interactional work has to be accomplished on a turn-by-turn basis, reacting to the discourse as it unfolds. Chaudron (1988: 146–148) lists thirty-one different types of corrective reaction that a teacher can make. Ellis (1994: 585) points out that 'Perhaps the main finding of studies of error treatment is that it is an enormously complex process'. Yet all a DA approach is able to tell us in the analysis of an extract is that 'teacher corrects'. The COLT instrument (Froehlich *et al.*, 1985) is perhaps the most sophisticated coding scheme developed for L2 classroom interaction, and yet it contains only one coding category termed 'correct' for teaching acts.

Extract 1 showed the teacher establishing the focus of the interaction and managing the turn-taking system, while extract 2 showed a learner temporarily shifting the focus of the interaction and stealing the floor. Extract 3 shows an amicable struggle between teacher and learners for control of the focus of the interaction and of the turn-taking system.

Extract 3

(L2 is male and L6 is female)

1 *T:*   okay do you have any questions about using these words?
        okay?
2 *L:*   okay
3 *L6:*   yeah
4 *T:*   what
5 *L6:*   how many – girlfriends do you have here? [to L2]
6 *L2:*   o::h
7 *T:*   how many girlfriends [stresses first syllable] does he have here?
8 *L6:*   yes
9 *L:*   [unint]
10 *L2:*   are you very interesting? [meaning: interested]
11 *LL:*   [unint]
12 *T:*   that's his business. he's not telling you
13 *LL:*   [modest laughter]
14 *L6:*   I cry
15 *T:*   You cry
16 *LL:*   [loud laughter]
17 *T:*   are you jealous?
18 *L6:*   ya

(Van Lier, 1988: 160)

According to Van Lier (ibid.), extract 3 shows learners attempting to change a specific interaction type into another one because they prefer 'just talking' to other, more regimented activities. From the point of view of this chapter, we can say that the learners would like to shift from a focus on form to a focus on the expression of personal meanings. In line 1 T constrains the next turn by specifying the next turn activity (asking a question) but does not select a speaker. T also implies that the interaction should remain focused on form in that he/she indicates that the questions should be about using specified words. L6 then self-selects and partly conforms to T's constraints by asking a question. However, the question is not within the allocated area (using specified words) and, more importantly, it shifts the focus to meaning. We can see from L2's 'oh' in line 6 that L2 was surprised by this sudden shift. Moreover, when T allocated interactional space to the learners in 1, it was clearly in order for the learners to ask T him/herself a question. L6 has in effect not only shifted the focus but also altered the turn-taking system by addressing a question to L2, thus cutting T out of the interaction. Part of the teacher's institutional authority is vested in his/her ability to control the focus of the interaction and the turn-taking system in the classroom. A learner who attempts to shift (or challenge) the focus or the turn-taking system introduced by the teacher is performing a face-threatening act (Brown and Levinson, 1987) or challenging the teacher's authority. I have numerous examples in my database of teachers taking corrective action to regain control of the focus and/or the turn-taking system.

At this stage, T could react in a number of ways. T could reject L6's attempt to change the focus and the speech exchange system in the authoritarian fashion described by Long (1983:15), for example, by insisting that only questions addressed to him/her and concerning the specified words would be allowed. At the other extreme, T could validate the shift of focus and speech exchange system by saying nothing and allowing the interaction to flow. What T elects to do in line 7 is a third, medial, alternative. T corrects L6's pronunciation, addressing the correction to L6. This initially appeared to me to be a very odd thing for T to do, since it is clear that L2 and T understood what L6 meant perfectly well. However, after studying the extract many times, it became clear to me that T's utterance in line 7 is doing a great deal of interactional work. It allows L6's limited right to alter the interaction to some extent but also reasserts T's right to have overall control to some extent. Specifically, T's original intention was to maintain a focus on form: the learner shifted the focus to meaning and T's correction is focused on linguistic form rather than on meaning. In other words, T has not yet validated a shift in focus.

There appears to be no communicative necessity for T to perform a correction because L2 in line 6 appears to have understood L6's question, even if it was mispronounced slightly. T has also clearly understood L6's question. In fact there is no interactional necessity for T to say anything at all if T wishes to validate the shift commenced by L6. We should also note that L6's question in line 5 uses 'you' addressed to L2, cutting T out of the interaction. T's correction in line 7 transforms 'you' to 'he', thus making it into a question which L6 could address to T as intermediary, which would put T back in the centre of the speech exchange system. Thus T is suggesting that L6 should ask instead, 'how many girlfriends does he have here?' Thus line 7 can best be interpreted as T asserting his/her right to control the focus of the interaction and refusing to be shut out of the speech exchange system.

The interaction continues in line 10 with L2 answering L6's question and addressing the answer 'are you very interesting?' to L6. In other words, L2 is attempting to continue in the context and speech exchange system which L6 established, and is relating back to L6's utterance in line 5. At this stage T could react in a number of ways. T could change the context and the speech exchange system back to the way it was in authoritarian fashion. At the other extreme, T could validate the shift of focus and speech exchange system by saying nothing and allowing the interaction to flow. Or T could follow the same strategy as in line 7 and correct the linguistic error which L2 has made in line 10. What T elects to do in lines 12 and 17 is a fourth alternative. T validates the shift of focus and the topic of 'classroom relationships' but does not validate the shift in speech exchange system. T does not correct the linguistic error in line 10 but in effect develops the topic by commenting on the classroom relationship. T takes back control of the speech exchange system and acts as an intermediary between L2 and L6, interpreting (in line 12) L2's reactions to L6. In line 17 T asks L2 a question related to the topic of classroom relationships which L6 introduced and by this point T has validated the shift in focus but has regained complete control of the speech exchange system within the new focus.

The extract demonstrates complex and fluid patterns of interaction with competition among the participants for control of the focus and the speech exchange system. The teacher can be seen to be orienting to multiple simultaneous concerns. The teacher is trying to manage the focus of the interaction and the organization of turn-taking, and is responding to the new topic and focus introduced by the learners as well as to their linguistic errors. We can see again the dialectic between form and meaning, with the teacher choosing to repair a linguistic error in line 7 but not in line 10, and the teacher is trying to maintain a balance between allowing the learners some interactional space and losing control of the lesson.

Conclusion

I hope to have shown in the above analyses that, by virtue of language being the object as well as the vehicle of instruction, L2 teachers are doing fantastically complex interactional work compared with 'content' teachers and professionals in other institutional settings. Yet the DA methodology which is predominantly used to represent their work tends to portray them as plodding from one monotonous IRF cycle to the next and as working on a single level.

The analyses of extracts 1–3 used a CA methodology, and were intended to demonstrate that CA is able to portray the complexity of the interactional work which L2 teachers do. Space does not permit me to elaborate on what CA methodology entails: interested readers may consult the references below for introductory accounts. My experience of using both CA and DA methodologies is as follows. I found DA methodology easy to learn and to use: extracts 1–3 could probably be coded and analysed in less than an hour. However, as I have argued, the analysis remains very much on the surface and oversimplifies the interaction. I found CA methodology extremely difficult to learn and use. Analysing extracts is very long and laborious work: it took me weeks to analyse the above data. However, I persist with CA because it enables me to get under the surface of the interaction and explore the complex, fluid, dynamic and multi-layered nature of L2 classroom interaction.

I would like to make clear that I am not suggesting that the DA approach is wrong and worthless. On the contrary, it has been successful in many ways and has proved popular with the language teaching profession. DA and CA approaches can to some extent be combined to explore a text in greater depth. However, I feel that the DA approach we have predominantly used up until now to portray what we do in the classroom has not done justice to the complexity of the interactional work we are engaged in. I would suggest that it has therefore not done sufficient justice to our profession. It may therefore ultimately be worthwhile to make the long and difficult shift to portraying our work by means of a CA methodology.

Note

1   For adult–child transcripts cf. Painter (1989: 38), Peccei (1994: 83), Wells Lindfor (1980: 114). The technique being used by the teacher here is often termed 'scaffolding'.

References

Allwright, R. L. (1980) 'Turns, Topics and Tasks: Patterns of Participation in Language Learning and Teaching', in D. Larsen-Freeman (ed.) *Discourse Analysis in Second Language Research*, Rowley: Newbury House.

Brown, P. and Levinson, S. (1987) *Politeness*, Cambridge: Cambridge University Press.

Chaudron, C. (1988) *Second Language Classrooms: Research on Teaching and Learning*, Cambridge: Cambridge University Press.

Dinsmore, D. (1985) 'Waiting for Godot in the EFL classroom', in *ELT Journal* 39/4: 225–234.

Ellis, R. (1994) *The Study of Second Language Acquisition*, Oxford: Oxford University Press.

Froehlich, M., Spada, N. and Allen, P. (1985) 'Differences in the Communicative Orientation of L2 Classrooms', *TESOL Quarterly* 19: 27–57.

Halliday, M. A. K. (1985) *An Introduction to Functional Grammar*, London: Arnold.

Jefferson, G. (1987) 'On Exposed and Embedded Correction in Conversation', in G. Button and J. Lee (eds) *Talk and Social Organisation*, Clevedon: Multilingual Matters.

Johnson, K. (1995) *Understanding Communication in Second Language Classrooms*, Cambridge: Cambridge University Press.

Levinson, S. (1983) *Pragmatics*, Cambridge: Cambridge University Press.

Long. M. (1983) 'Inside the *Black Box*', in H. Seliger and M. Long (eds) *Classroom Oriented Research in Second Language Acquisition*, Rowley: Newbury House.

Mehan, H. (1979) *Learning Lessons: Social Organization in the Classroom*, Cambridge, MA.: Harvard University Press.

Mitchell, R., Parkinson, B. and Johnstone, R. (1981) *The Foreign Language Classroom: An Observational Study*, University of Stirling monograph.

Moskowitz, G. (1976) 'The Classroom Interaction of Outstanding Language Teachers', in *Foreign Language Annals* 9/2.

Nunan, D. (1987) 'Communicative Language Teaching: Making It Work', in *ELT Journal* 41/2: 136–145.

Painter, C. (1989) *Learning the Mother Tongue*, Oxford: Oxford University Press.

Peccei, C. (1994) *Child Language*, London: Routledge.

Peck, A. (1988) *Language Teachers at Work*, Hemel Hempstead: Prentice Hall.

Seedhouse, P. (1997) 'Combining Form and Meaning', in *ELT Journal* 51/4.

Sinclair, J. and Coulthard, R. M. (1975) *Toward an Analysis of Discourse*, Oxford: Oxford University Press.

Ullman, R. and Geva, R. (1984) 'Approaches to Observation in Second Language Classes', in C. Brumfit (ed.) *Language Issues and Education Policies*, Oxford: Pergamon.

Van Lier, L. (1988) *The Classroom and the Language Learner*, New York: Longman.

Wells Lindfors, J. (1987) *Children's Language and Learning*, Englewood Cliffs, NJ: Prentice-Hall International.

Willis, J. (1992) 'Inner and Outer: Spoken Discourse in the Language Classroom', in M. Coulthard (ed.) *Advances in Spoken Discourse Analysis*, London: Routledge.

Introductory reading on conversation analysis

Drew, P. (1994) 'Conversation Analysis', in R. E. Asher (ed.) *The Encyclopedia of Languages and Linguistics*, Oxford: Pergamon.

Drew, P. and Heritage, J. (eds) (1992) *Talk at Work: Interaction in Institutional Settings*, Cambridge: Cambridge University Press.

Heritage, J. (1995) 'Conversation Analysis: Methodological Aspects', in U. Quasthoff (ed.) *Aspects of Oral Communication*, Berlin: Walter de Gruyter.

Psathas, G. (1995) *Conversation Analysis*, Thousand Oaks: Sage.

Part III

ASPECTS OF GRAMMAR IN
THE CLASSROOM

Grammar, however one defines it, has been central to the teaching of languages since that practice began, and central also to the debate about language teaching and its relationship to linguistics, and associated sciences, of the last quarter of a century.

This part of the book is interesting because, among other things, it represents the views of three people from a range of nationalities and background, all of whom address themselves to the place of grammar in language teaching. They share, however, the conviction that the purpose of language teaching is to permit people to communicate with each other.

The first contribution has been written by Antony Peck (Chapter 8). It is firmly situated in the classroom. It advocates no theories, it is pragmatic and eclectic, and attempts to apply common sense to the question of grammar teaching. It is placed first in the series of four because it takes as its starting point the question of why we should teach grammar at all. It continues by trying to throw some light on what grammar teaching actually is, and finally reaches the conclusion, founded on many years of experience, that teachers should be eclectic in their approach. While the chapter begins with generalities, it finishes with a precise and specific example of how a grammatical rule of English can be taught communicatively.

Georgia Catsimali sets herself a difficult, unenviable, but important task (Chapter 9). She tries to bridge the yawning gap between theoretical linguistics and language teaching. Her chapter brings the reader, full circle, back to generalities, but this time to the theoretical point of departure. Her point of view is one that many have paid lip-service to, but few have tried to implement. What conceivable relevance can a linguistic theory, such as that of Noam Chomsky, have to the classroom language teacher? Not much, it would seem at first sight. Yet Chomsky reminded us that children can learn any natural language with ease, and proposed a theory to account for this amazing ability. After a rapid review of the role of applied linguistics, contrastive analysis, universal grammar and such like, Catsimali makes the persuasive point that teachers cannot but be better prepared for their task by knowing something of the theoretical underpinning of the skill they profess. She is scrupulous in protecting language learners from the sweeping fire of linguistics, but argues that a deep knowledge of the complexity of a language will help teachers, and especially textbook writers and curriculum planners to plan a syllabus in such a way that the best path is followed through the data which a natural language presents. She concludes with practical exercises for students learning Greek.

The third contribution is by Linus Jung (Chapter 10), who teaches his mother tongue German in Spain, and writes about one of the central problems of teaching German. After the general approach of Chapter 8, the reader is metaphorically asked to take a microscope and study how a teacher tries to cope with some of the minutiae of a language, essential to effective communication. That is what English speakers increasingly refer to as 'nitty-gritty'. Jung writes about modal particles and how to teach them. As a native speaker of the language he teaches, he realizes the degree to which their appropriate use by students contributes to an authentic use of the language. Few abilities, other than having a perfect pronunciation, better give the impression of having mastered German than being able to use a range of modal particles in the right place at the right time. Jung does what few textbooks do, namely, he informs the reader what they really mean. He puts them into the contexts which every German recognizes as authentic, and concludes by offering some practical exercises to develop their use.

8

THE PLACE OF GRAMMAR IN MODERN LANGUAGE TEACHING

Antony J. Peck

Introduction

It should be obvious that we cannot learn by heart all the sentences we will ever need to use in a foreign language. Even if we could learn by heart a very large number of sentences, we would still need to be able to have a way of deciding in which situations we could use them appropriately.

We can see how absurd it is to rely exclusively on learning by heart phrases and sentences if we take at random some isolated sentences from a well-known phrase book.

The wash-basin is clogged.
The food is cold.
That man keeps following me.
Where are our drinks?
I need an axe.
Where is the British Consulate?

The absurdity of learning lists of sentences like these is clear because we know that each sentence fits a predetermined situation which we may or may not encounter. Since we cannot predict the situations in which we will find ourselves in a foreign country or when talking to foreigners, much of what we may learn by heart will be useless.

Grammar gives us the means of making up our own sentences, and expressing our own meanings. Grammatical rules allow us to respond creatively to whichever situation we find ourselves in. Grammar frees us from the expectations of the phrase-book author and the school textbook author; it allows us to send our very own messages.

123

Unconscious grammatical knowledge

When we say that somebody has an excellent knowledge of English, we do not necessarily mean that that person can explain the rule for using the words *some* or *any*, in English. A native speaker, for instance, uses the words *some* or *any* unconsciously and correctly without thinking about it. A learner must master the rule governing the use of these words. It is the same when it comes to deciding upon the correct sequence of adjectives. He/she will instinctively say 'an old blue jacket' rather than 'a blue old jacket'; but he/she will say 'a nice old jacket' rather than 'an old nice jacket'. The native speaker is unlikely to be able to explain exactly why one sentence is right and the other is wrong. Thus when we say that somebody has an excellent knowledge of English we mean that they have the ability to use the language with very few or no mistakes at all. Another way of putting this would be to say that this person has an ability to use the structural and grammatical resources of the language; or, yet again, that they have a very good knowledge of grammar. Native speakers are not only able to produce correct sentences; they are also able to produce a string of sentences, all of them correct, all of which may use a different grammatical rule. David Stern, in his book *The Fundamental Concepts of Language Teaching* (Stern, 1983), called this unconscious knowledge of grammar *Grammar A*. (For a more recent view on this, and other matters raised in this study, see Stern *et al.*, 1992.)

Children learn this grammar by the age of 5 on the basis of what parents, and especially mothers, say to them. Most parents are not language teachers, and language teachers who are also parents do not necessarily make a better job of it. This grammatical knowledge which children acquire in the early years is so complicated that it is rare for someone who learns the same grammar as a foreign language ever to become as proficient in it as is the child at this very early age.

Conscious grammatical knowledge

Conscious grammatical knowledge is knowing exactly what the rules are which allow correct sentences to be produced. Some of these underlying principles are regular; that is to say, a given principle will allow a large number of correct sentences to be produced; but very often the principles have deviants and exceptions which plague the life of the language learner. This knowledge we have about a language is expressed in terminology such as noun, verb, subject, complement, tense, aspect, stem, ending, agreement, etc.

One of the very few rules which native speakers of English know about their own language is that *i* comes before *e* except after *c*. This is a very good rule because it allows the person who knows it to spell correctly, when writing, those words which have an e and an i. We can say of adjectives in

French, for instance, that they usually come after the noun they describe, for instance, French people say *'tu aimes cette jupe noire'* but, on the other hand, they say *'c'est un bel homme'*. With reference to German we can say that the relative pronoun must agree with its antecedent in number and gender, but its case depends on its relation to the rest of its own clause. This is a rule which will allow correct sentences always to be produced, but unfortunately it is so complicated for the learner that it needs a lifetime of learning German to be able to get it right with the sure instinct of a German 5-year-old native speaker.

David Stern called this collection of rules, or conscious statements about the language, *Grammar B*. As language teachers, we know that we can only teach a small part of the language at any one time, and therefore we choose from Grammar A that part of the language which we wish our pupils to concentrate on in a given lesson or sequence of lessons. This is what David Stern calls *Grammar C*. The explicit statements about the regularities of the language which account for this selected portion that we wish to teach David Stern calls *Grammar D*. It is therefore our own selection of Grammars C and D with which we are concerned on a daily basis in our teaching.

Implicit or covert grammar teaching

The purpose of implicit grammar teaching is to induce students to produce a series of similar sentences, each based on an identical rule. Sometimes of course, we deliberately select two contrasting rules in order to highlight a particular aspect of the language. For instance:

> I was coming home when I had a puncture.
> She was driving to work when she saw an accident.
> She was listening to the radio when the telephone rang.
> He was mowing the lawn when it started to rain.

The reason for getting students to produce similar sentences like these is so that the regularities underlying them can be shown to be salient features of the language. Thus, the common features of the sentences above are the use of the past continuous tense in contrast to the use of the simple past tense. Sentences like this seldom need to be learned by heart because their function is to display how other, similar sentences may be produced, so that the learner can express what he/she wishes to say. We should notice in passing that in a real conversation one would never use these four sentences one after the other, because they refer to a number of different situations. However, we need to practise them as a group so that we can get our students to concentrate on the grammatical rules which account for them. The production of similar sentences like this is a step for the students towards a general knowledge of this aspect of the foreign language. We believe, as teachers, that if we give our students enough practice, and adequate explanations for these sentences, that they will be able to produce them correctly when it is appropriate to do so.

Littlewood calls this sort of implicit grammar teaching pre-communicative.

> The learning activities themselves are pre-communicative rather than communicative. That is, they aim to equip the learner with some of the skills required for communication, without actually requiring him to perform communicative acts. The criterion for success is therefore not so much whether he has managed to convey an intended meaning, but rather whether he has produced an acceptable piece of language.
>
> (Littlewood, 1981: 8)

It is important to note that I am concerned here with trying to define implicit grammar teaching. I am not trying to describe which sort of exercises are used, nor the various methods which teachers use in class. There are countless types of exercise which contribute to implicit grammar teaching, that is, the learning of rules, and every textbook has a good selection of them. There are also many different pedagogical procedures or teaching activities that teachers use in class, which range from question and answer, to drills, pair work or chains where one student asks another, and so on. All these exercises and teaching activities share a common feature: to induce students to produce a series of sentences similar to each other. And it is the similarities between the sentences which indicate the underlying grammatical rule.

It is sometimes the case that these key sentences are embedded in a text which includes many other types of sentence. This sometimes happens in textbooks which present the language in dialogue form or in narrative paragraphs, where only some of the sentences exemplify the grammatical rule which the teacher wishes to concentrate on. In cases like this, teachers develop an added skill, namely that of focusing the attention of their students on the sentences which are important because they are there for rule learning, and at the same time diverting their attention – so far as rule learning is concerned – from the other sentences in the text.

Explicit or overt grammar teaching

This is what most teachers mean when they speak about grammar or grammar teaching. You often hear teachers say:

There's no grammar in that book.
You can't teach that class any grammar.
We ought to be teaching more grammar.
They don't teach grammar any more in the primary school.

What do such statements mean? They refer almost always to statements about the rules of the language, or explanations. They refer to *Grammar B*, that is, conscious grammatical knowledge about the language. It is interesting to note that statements like the ones above refer almost always to knowledge which native speakers do not have about their own language. It is tempting, I know, to take the view that it is unnecessary to teach students of a foreign language that knowledge which the native speakers do not have themselves. I do not take this view myself, however. Nevertheless, the teaching of explicit grammar remains a controversial matter, and some teachers feel that they are acting rather immorally if they ask their students to learn a specific grammatical rule.

However, before we look at the pros and cons of explicit grammar teaching let us look a little more closely at what it is. Explicit grammar teaching can only be explicit by using terminology. We may call a verb a doing word and an adjective a describing word, but this is, in fact, terminology. Moreover, it is difficult to invent meaningful terms which account for the full range of even simple, everyday examples. How does the term 'a doing word' account for 'To be or not to be'? or 'I have a headache'? Explicit grammar teaching will, sooner or later, need terms like noun, verb, stem, ending.

Explicit grammar teaching gives explanations about the forms of the language. Look at the following example:

Give the plural of these nouns: table, shoe, foot, tooth, box, book, glass, plant, butter.

Any explanation given by the teacher about how these words make their plural will focus on the forms of the language. Of course, a grammatical explanation may also refer to meanings. For example, consider the two following sentences:

Sparta produced many great soldiers.
Nepal has produced many great soldiers.

A teacher who gives an explanation about the difference between these two sentences will not only be concerned with the formal differences between the simple past and the present perfect tense, but he/she will have to tell the students about their difference of meaning.

Learning by example

At this point I want to make a case for learning by heart some memorable sentences. The careful reader will realize that I am not contradicting what I said earlier about learning isolated sentences by heart. A teacher or a clever textbook author who knows that students will shortly have to study the present perfect tense, let us say, may introduce beforehand a number of sentences containing vivid examples of this tense. In this way a set of usable expressions may be introduced, and frequently used, without explanation or analysis, in order to provide a basis of linguistic experience for subsequent explanation either in explicit or implicit grammar teaching at a later stage.

Recommendation about implicit and explicit grammar teaching

In my personal view, implicit grammar teaching is essential. It is most likely to be successful, I believe, if a teacher has access to a wide range of different types of exercises, so that the language can be practised in different ways. Exercises which require students to speak to each other in two, four or six line exchanges are particularly useful, because they can be transferred completely to the students in the form of pair work once the teacher is convinced that the forms are likely to be used correctly. If possible, several different exercise types should be used on each grammatical point in order to show students that the rule can be used in different sorts of language exchange.

I think that explicit grammar teaching is essential, too. We need explanations because we have a very short time in which to learn the foreign language on the basis of only a very few utterances. We do not have as much time as a baby to learn a language, and most of us do not have time to go and live in a foreign country and be submerged in the language in order to learn it. Moreover, most adults and adolescents can perceive the regularities of a language when their attention is drawn to them, and if teachers are clever with their explanations, and do not require their students to learn too many different forms at once. However, we must face up to the fact that the use of technical terms and complicated explanations may be counterproductive with certain students. I believe therefore that the key to good practice is to match the degree of grammatical (morphological and syntactical) complexity to the ability level of the students concerned; and I further believe that it is very valuable to give visual support in the form of diagrams, wherever it can be done, in order to help students to understand grammatical explanations.

Two methods of grammar teaching

It is important to understand from the outset that the teaching of grammatical rules is not the first stage in the cyclical process of language teaching. The first stage is always the introduction and presentation of a piece of language. As Henry Sweet says:

> It is only the fully-developed mind of the adult that can plunge straight into the study of the grammar of a foreign language. A less-

developed mind, one which is less used to dealing with general and abstract statements, requires to start with something more individual and concrete. There is, besides, as we shall see hereafter, a pre-grammatical stage in every progressive course of linguistic study – whether for children or adults – in which no grammar is taught, but only the materials on which grammar is based; that is, sentences and short texts.

(Sweet, 1898/1964: 115)

The inductive method

In the inductive method of teaching grammar the teacher begins with implicit grammar teaching. That is to say, there is a substantial period of oral practice during which the teacher focuses on encouraging the students to produce a number of grammatically similar sentences by using a range of questions, cues, stimuli, etc.

Once this has been done to the teacher's satisfaction, a rule or general statement about the language may be given. Where this explanation comes after the practice it is said to be the inductive method.

If a teacher uses the inductive method it usually means that a lot of practice is guaranteed. It is also said that the inductive method leads students, step by step, towards a general understanding of the language point being studied. A further advantage claimed is that the inductive method follows the classical rule of all teaching, namely that it goes from the known to the unknown. By this is meant that the student begins with a few sentences or a short text with which he or she is familiar, and by practising the structural similarities of the language gradually moves towards an understanding of the general rule. Some teachers believe that practice can by itself help students to discover the rule which governs the structure of the sentences they have to produce, and a rule which is discovered by the students themselves is, it is said, more likely to be fixed in their memories.

There is frequently an unstated assumption about the inductive method of teaching that a sufficient number of induced, correct utterances will make it possible for learners to discover the rule, without the teacher having to state it explicitly. A modification of this point of view is held by certain teachers who believe that at some point, when there has been enough practice, an explanatory statement may be given, and it may use technical terms.

All these points of view have in common that the process starts with the intensive practice of structurally similar sentences. My own personal view is that it seems extremely risky to depend on students discovering a grammatical rule unless they are helped; it is risky to assume that they will understand a rule unless it is explained; and it seems risky to me to assume that students will remember unless they first understand.

The deductive method

In the deductive method the teacher gives essential information such as statements of the rule, concerning either the forms or the meanings to be practised, and the actual practice of the structurally similar sentences comes afterwards.

Those who believe in the deductive method of teaching grammar attach importance to students knowing what they are doing and why. It is claimed that the advantages of beginning a period of practice with a clear statement of a grammatical rule gives the students insight into what they are being asked to do; they are not left to learn by trial and error. It is also claimed that a clear statement of the rule at the beginning helps students to avoid mistakes.

My own view is that every teacher needs to decide for each group of students whether it it better to use the inductive or the deductive method. It may well be that certain grammatical rules are best taught one way, and others by a different method. What seems vital to me is that teachers should be aware of both methods, and be capable of using them whenever they think one or other is appropriate.

Presentation, practice, production

I should like to conclude this chapter by drawing readers' attention to a fundamental paradox of language teaching and learning. As we saw earlier, the teaching of grammar, whether it is conscious or unconscious; implicit or explicit; or whether it is done by the inductive or the deductive method, is concerned with trying to teach learners how to produce correct, appropriate sentences, sentences which obey the rules of the language in which they are trying to communicate, so that native speakers of that language will understand them. In order to learn a rule, most students need a certain number of practice sentences, some more than others, and some will need a formal statement of the rule, whether this is given before or after the practice. What is undeniable is that grammar learning and teaching is accomplished by focusing on examples of the rule. Unless the mind of the learner is focused on these similar examples, it is unlikely that learning will occur.

When we come to look at the use of language in communication, we see that each successive sentence uttered by the speakers, and writers, is almost certainly based on a different grammatical rule. In a genuine act of communication, therefore, the speaker-learner needs one grammatical rule for the first sentence, another for the second sentence and a third for the next sentence, and so on. Here then is a fundamental paradox. In order to learn grammatical rules, students need to be confronted with examples of structural similarity, i.e. sentences based on the rule to be learned, but on the other hand, in order to use the language authentically, learners have to have a wide range of grammatical rules at their fingertips so as to choose, at a remarkable speed, the one which will allow them to produce a correct sentence which is appropriate to whatever they wish to say next. Time has to be allocated specifically for this in the language teaching process. It is called production.

Summary

We see, therefore, that the cyclical process of language teaching has three stages, each beginning with the letter P: presentation, practice, production. In the first stage, the teacher presents examples of the language, i.e. sentences and short texts on which the grammar is based. In the second stage, the learners try to learn the rules governing the formation of the sentences to be focused on. In the third stage, students are given the chance to learn how to produce the language creatively, so that they can express their own meanings and send their own messages appropriately, using the grammar they have learned. This is sometimes called language learning by the three ps. I recommend it to everyone.

Teaching grammar communicatively

Communicative grammar teaching can be defined as the attempt to teach generative rules to learners while they are in the process of communicating with each other. The best point of departure for communications like this are behavioural specifications such as the following:

1   How to ask where someone lives.
2   How to ask what type of accommodation a person lives in.
3   How to ask how long someone has been living in the present accommodation.

Specifications such as these provide the framework for a short conversation of three exchanges.

1   How to ask where someone lives.

	do	you	
Where	does	John Mary	live?

I	live		Granada
			the centre of York
He		in	Paris
	lives		Athens
She			

2   How to ask what type of accommodation a person lives in.

Do	you		a house?
	he	live in	
Does			a flat?
	she		

Yes, I do.
No, I don't.

			a semi
I	live	in	a single room
			a bed-sitter

He		in	a hostel
	lives		a furnished flat
She			

3   How to ask how long someone has been living in the present accommodation.

How long	have	you	been living there?
		he	
	has		
		she	

I	have			living		two years
He		been			there for	ten months
	has			staying		three weeks
She						

133

It is the exponents of the functions which indicate the point of focus for grammar teaching. In the above example it is likely to be the use of the words 'do' and 'does' in English questions, and the form and usage of the present perfect tense. These rules are truly generative in the sense that they are sentence-producing. The rules are syntagmatic; that is, they are concerned with parts of the foreign language as they operate in given sentences.

References

Littlewood, W. (1981) *Communicative Language Teaching*, Cambridge: Cambridge University Press.

Stern, H. H. (1983) *The Fundamental Concepts of Language Teaching*, Oxford: Oxford University Press.

Stern, H. H., Allen, P. and Harley, B. (eds) (1992) *Issues and Options in Language Teaching*, Oxford: Oxford University Press.

Sweet, H. (1964) *The Practical Study of Languages*, Oxford: Oxford University Press. (First published by J.M. Dent and Sons Ltd, 1898.)

Further reading

Doyle, W. (1977) 'Paradigms for Research in Teacher Effectiveness', in *Review of Research in Education* 5, American Educational Research Association.

Dunkin, M. J. and Biddle, B. J. (1974) *The Study of Teaching*, New York: Holt, Reinhardt & Winston.

Flanders, N. A. (1970) *Analysing Teaching Behaviour*, Reading, MA: Addison-Wesley.

Grell, J. (1974) *Techniken des Lehrerverhaltens*, Weinheim: Beltz.

Hobbs, J. (1977) *Teaching Observed*, London: BBC.

Hoberg, G., Brabeck, H., Hoster, H. and Pesch, W. (eds) (1977) *Lehrerverhalten, Beobachtungs-Analyse-Training*, Heidelberg: Quelle und Meyer.

Palmer, H. E. (1968) *The Scientific Study and Teaching of Languages*, New York: Oxford University Press.

Peck, A. J. (1988) *Language Teachers at Work*, Englewood Cliffs, NJ: Prentice-Hall International.

Peck, A. J. and Westgate, D. (eds) (1994) *Language Teaching in the Mirror*, London: Centre for Information on Language Teaching.

9

FROM LINGUISTIC THEORY TO SYLLABUS DESIGN AND CLASSROOM PRACTICE

Georgia Catsimali

Introduction

The conflict between theoretical linguists and language teachers is well known. This derives from their different interests and objects of enquiry. Theoreticians are trying to describe the language system and to provide a theory which will account for the systematic character of language, while teachers are trying to find ways to teach the language more effectively.

In this chapter we address the question of whether some insights of recent theoretical linguistics could be used directly or indirectly in foreign language teaching. We will consider only those theoretical results that have strong empirical support and are accepted by the majority of the scientific community.

More specifically, we will focus on some theoretical claims of Chomsky's recent theory (1981) as they are illustrated in English and Modern Greek, and we will explore the way in which they can inform teaching methodology. This issue will be approached by comparing English and Modern Greek, and it will be argued that clusters of syntactic patterns which result from linguistic analysis could be used profitably in foreign language teaching. For each cluster of syntactic patterns we will propose teaching strategies.

Theoretical linguistics vs. applied linguistics

If we conceive of *theory* and *practice* as two sides of the same coin whose value lies in their coexistence, the question of which is more important than the other is reduced to a pseudo-problem. Theoretical linguistics is deeply involved in the study of language(s) in order to discover underlying theoretical principles, while applied linguistics looks for ways to teach language(s) more effectively. However, theoretical perspectives do not remain invariant and in fact often undergo radical changes, something which contributes to the unwillingness of teachers to put much faith in them. On the other hand, teachers should not reject linguistic theory categorically because it can often be immensely helpful in the language classroom.

Do teachers need theory?

The difficulties of teaching a language are well known. Teachers are inevitably confronted with the foreign language to be taught on the one hand, and the individual needs of their students on the other. In order for their students to attain a level of proficiency quickly and in the easiest possible way, teachers must possess talent, experience and a good knowledge of the foreign language in question. Proficiency in a foreign language is understood in terms of communicative, pragmatic and linguistic/grammatical competence. Communicative and pragmatic competence refers to the ability of the speaker to communicate effectively in everyday situations, to differentiate the pragmatic implications of an utterance; grammatical competence refers to the thorough knowledge of the grammatical system of the foreign language. There has been much discussion as to whether one kind of competence prevails over the others. In our view, communicative, pragmatic and grammatical competence all complement each other.

We might ask ourselves how theory can help the foreign language teacher. The purpose of linguistic theory is to observe, describe and explain data (Chomsky, 1986: 53), and thereby it might give the teacher a different perspective on the language. If the teacher has thoroughly understood the language system, he/she will try to choose an appropriate teaching method based on the students' profile (age, available time, special needs, mother tongue and community languages). If the teacher is familiar with linguistic theory this will help him/her feel confident in the management of the syllabus and the class. It will also help to detect the problem areas for students and to guide them by creative and imaginative techniques to more successfully acquire the foreign language.

Does theoretical linguistics intersect with applied linguistics?

Theoretical linguistics has indeed much in common with applied linguistics, especially in reference to grammar. In the past, grammar has been viewed as prescriptive, although there is now a greater tendency towards the description and explanation of linguistic data. Pedagogical grammars are distinct from linguistically oriented grammars (Odlin, 1994). For some teachers, grammar is not a central aspect of language teaching, whereas for others it is the most important part. Our view is that grammar is necessary in language teaching. Furthermore, teachers should be convinced of its importance and find ways to use it more effectively in the classroom and for the benefit of their students.

This means that several factors should be considered such as the manner of acquiring the foreign language (i.e. class instruction or learning within the community), the structure of the particular language, the students' motivation and specific needs, their age and the time available.

In recent years, researchers and practitioners have stressed the need to incorporate structural regularities of languages in the syllabus, either explicitly or implicitly. This idea is conveyed overtly in Rutherford's theory of consciousness raising, and is defined as 'a deliberate attempt to draw the learner's attention specifically to the formal properties of the target language' (Rutherford and Sharewood Smith, 1988: 107). For Rutherford, there are degrees of explicitness in teaching and degrees of elaboration of a grammatical feature.

Contrastive analysis: a previous approach to foreign language teaching

Contrastive analysis is based on the behaviourist view of language according to which language acquisition is habit formation. It relies on the similarities and differences between the mother tongue and the target language. It predicts the language errors made by the learner and the intermediate stages he/she goes through, explaining them as interference or transfer of knowledge from one language to the other. For example, Greeks learning English will use definite articles in front of proper names (*the Mary) and will misuse the causative construction.

(1)　a) *I am going to cut my hair/*to wash my car, instead of
　　　b) I am going to have my hair cut/to have my car washed.

Such errors are attributed to the fact that the causative construction is expressed differently in the two languages: in English it is a syntactic pattern, while in Modern Greek it is expressed lexically.

Contrastive analysis was heavily criticized, because it sometimes predicted errors which were not observed in the classroom while failing to predict others which were more common. Furthermore, interference was in doubt, because certain errors have no mother tongue equivalence. Mackey (1973: 250) wonders:

> what is the use of predicting mistakes already heard? Since anyone who has taught a language can predict from experience the sort of mistakes his students are likely to make a posteriori, is he any wiser for the a priori and less reliable prediction which the linguistic analysis makes on the basis of a differential analysis?

Chomsky's theory vs. pedagogical practice

Chomsky's linguistic model has not made strong claims in the area of teaching methodology. It is mainly interested in accounting for the acquisition of the mother tongue/first language (L1) by considering the short time span in which the acquisition of L1 takes place (the first four years) and the limited linguistic input to which the child is exposed. In other words, on the basis of degenerate and impoverished data which come from the family environment, the child acquires the correct grammar of the language. This is called poverty of stimulus or Plato's problem (Chomsky, 1986: xxv–xxix).

Chomsky believes that when humans acquire a language, they simply follow their internal bioprogram. In the earlier stages of his theory (1965), this was called the language acquisition device (LAD), while in the later stages (1981, 1986) it is called universal or core grammar or internalized language. Universal grammar (UG), it is argued, includes principles which constrain the structural properties of sentences. These principles mainly concern the syntax of the language and are reflected in the intuitions of native speakers on the grammaticality vs. ungrammaticality of sentences.

The periphery contains the special characteristics of individual languages. It is where language-specific differences are found. These differences refer to syntax and they are accounted for by distinct parameters for each language. Following UG principles, a structure could be unmarked or marked for specific language(s).

Universal grammar research in second/foreign language aquisition

In recent years, extended experimental research has been conducted to test the UG hypothesis for the acquisition of a second/foreign language (L2). Unlike

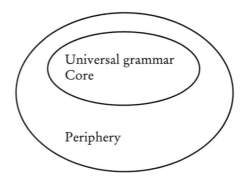

Figure 9.1

138

much earlier research where the primary goal was the description of the learner's language, UG-based research is trying to answer the following questions:

1 Is universal grammar available to the adult foreign language learner?
2 If the learner's first language differs from the target language with respect to certain parameters, then we have a mismatch between parameters. To what extent does this mismatch explain the errors which occur during the acquisition of the target language?

The results of such research are still inconclusive; some favour the UG hypothesis whereas others reject it.[1] Cook (1993: 210) summarizes the possible answers to the question whether UG is actually involved in L2 learning in Figure 9.2.

In a no-access position, L2 learners acquire the L2 grammar without any reference to UG; in a direct-access position, L2 learners learn in exactly the same way as L1 learners; in an indirect-access position, L2 learners have access to UG through what they know of L1.

One problem with the tests conducted is that they are mainly grammaticality judgement tests in the foreign language, and the learners' judgements vary greatly depending on their native language. In addition, we do not know if their responses are due to UG or to the fact that the learner has fully mastered the structures of the target language at the time of the test. Furthermore, there are cases where at different times the same subjects make different judgements on the same structures.

A proposal for the use of theory in foreign language teaching

In this section, the issue of second/foreign language learning is viewed from a slightly different perspective, always within the UG model. We share Newmeyer's (1982: 102) view that 'learning of fundamental syntactic

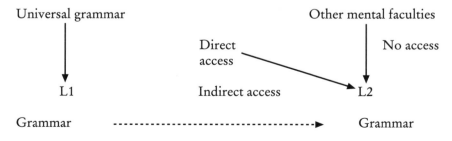

Figure 9.2

139

relations and processes cannot be accomplished by drill based on analysis of surface structure alone'.

We would argue that if a teacher knows that a specific parameter of the target language predicts a number of structural properties of the language, he/she can organize the grammar lesson associating the main parameter with the correlated structures. Obviously, we are not suggesting that the theory as such, its terminology, should be taught to the students, because such a practice will not really help students' performance but rather will distract them and burden them unnecessarily. What we actually claim is that the textbook writer and/or teacher should be aware of the clusters of similarities and differences between the languages and present the students with clusters of constructions. Interesting exercises could be devised that unify construc-tions. With this teaching technique of grouping together formerly disparate constructions, we implicitly draw the learner's attention to structural regularities of the target language. We believe that the student will induce the common element in the structures which are taught as a group, and he/she will correctly draw the relevant generalization. Students will be helped to organize the parameters in the target language and successfully to form the grammatical system of the language.[2]

This idea is being currently experimented with two groups of native speakers of American English who are taking intensive courses in Modern Greek at the University of Crete. One group is being taught grammar communicatively, while another group is being taught grammar in an explicit way where a few units are designed following the principles and parameters proposal.

Illustration of the technique

In what follows, we will consider only English vs. Modern Greek, having in mind teaching Modern Greek as a foreign language. We will present three examples in the following steps: first, we present the English data with the correlation of properties; second, we refer to the Modern Greek data which correspond to the English ones; third, we will provide a simplified explanation of the differences between English and Greek, always within Chomsky's (1981) framework. Finally, we will suggest some teaching techniques for Greek as a modern language.

Example A

It is a universal principle that we cannot have a sentence without the notion of subject. Thus in English the subject is present, either as a noun (2a) or as a pronoun (2b):

(2) a) Mary is dancing.
     b) She is dancing.

140

This observation is correlated with the following properties for English:

(i)   If the lexical subject is missing, a dummy element will hold the initial position of subject in the sentence to prevent ungrammaticality:

(3)   a) It is raining.
      b) There is God.
      c) * is dancing.

(ii)   The subject of the infinitive is obligatorily present if it is different from that of the main clause:

(4)   a) I want you to close the window.
      b) I want to close the window.

In (4a) *you* is the semantic subject of the complement clause, while in (4b) *I* is both the subject of the main and the complement clauses. On the contrary, in Greek, the lexical subject is optionally present. This means that in a conversation, if we ask the question 'What are you doing, John?', we will rarely hear the equivalent of '*I* am dancing' as an answer. Instead, we will hear only the inflected verb.

Linguistic theory explains the difference between English on the one hand, and Greek on the other, in terms of the variation in parameters. The difference between Greek and English in the above type of parameter regulates the appearance of the subject when the verb has 'rich inflection'. By 'rich inflection' we mean the possibility of indicating number and person (i.e. I, you, he/she). The subject pronoun only appears in a sentence if it receives emphasis in Greek. From this observation it follows that:

(i)   There is no dummy element in the initial position of subject:

(5)   --βρέχει (lit. rains)

(ii)   Movement of the subject out of a complement clause is possible.

(6)   ποιος   λες   έρχετάτ;
      (who [*nom.*]   say-you [*sing.*]   comes [*sing.*]?)

(iii) The subject of the complement clause does not appear, unless it receives emphasis:

(7) ....
    a) (want-I to-close-you [*sg./pl.*] the-window)
       I want you to close the window.
    b) (want-I to-close-he the-window [*acc.*] the-John [*nom.*])
       I want John to close the window.

In terms of application, the teacher of Modern Greek as a foreign language might take advantage of this clustering of properties in the target language and present them as a group to the students. A possible exercise could be based on the *triangle of communication*. By this we refer to an oral interaction in classroom where students take turns by asking their fellow-students simple questions such as 'What does John want to do on Mondays, Tuesdays, etc.?' In Modern Greek the answers are simple, involving just the verb without subject pronouns. In the next question 'When are you dancing?', the answer could involve 'weather verbs'. A third student continues the dialogue with a more complex question such as 'Who do you think is dancing?'

A question involving more structures could be:

(8)   a) What do they do when it rains/snows?
      b) Who does John say ——— (dance, read, sleep), when the weather is good/bad?
      c) (I, you, he/she, we, you, they) ——— (dance, read, sleep), when it is raining/snowing outside.

This strategy is that the teacher should start with sentences without lexical or pronominal subjects and present several patterns together. The student makes the generalization for Greek that the lexical or pronominal subject is not obligatory because it is implicit in the verb. The student arrives at this generalization more easily if he/she faces a group of structures rather than sporadic and isolated structures. Furthermore, it is simpler to add something to a structure already learned (e.g. the lexical or pronominal subject) rather than to delete it.

Example B

Let us take the case of verbs like 'give' in English. These verbs can form two alternative constructions:

(9)   a) The teacher gave the book *to Mary*.
    b) The teacher gave *Mary* the book.

In (9a), the indirect object is marked by the preposition *to* while in (9b) it is marked by its position next to the verb and the absence of a preposition. These syntactic alternations (10a and b) imply several properties of English.

(i) There is a bond between the verb and its direct object (*gave the book*), which can only be broken by shifting the position of the direct and indirect objects and deleting the preposition *to* (*gave Mary the book*).

(ii) These two alternative constructions can form two passive constructions, respectively.

(10) a) The book was given to Mary.   (Passive of (9a))
      b) Mary was given the book.   (Passive of (9b))

(iii) In questions for emphasis, the prepositional phrase can be moved to the beginning of the sentence.

(11)   *To whom* did the teacher give the book?

(iv) In questions, it is also possible to separate the indirect object from its preposition.

(12)   *Who* did the teacher give the book *to*?

In Modern Greek, the corresponding structures to (9a and b) are the following:

(14) a) δάσκαλος   έδωσε   τοβιβλίο   στη Μαρίαζ.
         (the-teacher [*nom.*]   gave-he   the-book [*acc.*]   to-the-Mary [*acc.*])

     b) δάσκαλος   έδωσε   της Μαρίας   το βιβλίο
        (the-teacher [*nom.*]   gave-he   the-Mary [*gen.*]   the-book [*acc.*])

In Modern Greek this type of construction is handled by using cases. The indirect object may be expressed in the genitive (της Μαρίας, lit. Mary's) which alternates with the prepositional phrase (στη Μαρία, lit. to-the-Mary).

In linguistic theory, languages like Greek, which have a rich morphological system, allow the sentence constituents to vary their position, according to the speaker's intention to present a specific constituent as a more prominent topic or for emphasis. On the contrary, in languages with a less complicated morphological system, like English, word order is more fixed. Therefore, the syntactic positions are associated with grammatical functions (such as subject, object(s)).

Since English differs from Modern Greek in the morphological marking of nouns, we would expect the opposite correlation. Indeed, in Modern Greek we would expect radical differences as can be seen in the following:

(i) The bond between verb and direct object is not close; other constituents may intervene:

(15) Ο δάσκαλος   έδωσε   χωρίς δισταγμό   το βιβλίο
      (the-teacher [*nom.*] gave-he   without-hesitation the-book {*acc.*}])

(ii) Passivization of the indirect object is impossible:

(16) *Η Μαρία   δόθηκε   το βιβλίο
      * the-Mary [*nom.*] was-given the-book {*acc.*}]

(iii) Preposition stranding is not possible: (?)

(17) ποιον   έδωσε   ο δάσκαλος   το βιβλίο   σε;
      (who [*acc.*] gave-he   the-teacher [*nom.*] the-book [*acc.*] to)

From the above observations, one might ask how the teacher of Modern Greek can organize his/her material. It is obvious that first of all he/she needs a list of the verbs which take two objects and indicate the alternative constructions; in Modern Greek such verbs are: δίνω 'give', χαρίζω 'donate', πιάρνω 'take away', etc. The structural alternation of these verbs motivates the teaching of noun morphology and freedom of word order. In other words, the grammar section will focus on morphological case and its reflexes in syntax. The students will then realize that case is associated with meaning by grouping together the different structures.

Possible teaching techniques could be either by means of *wh-questions* (e.g. 19) and *or-questions* (e.g. 20).

(18) Who did you give the book to?
      ποιανού έδωσες το βιβλίο;

(19) John or Mary did you give the book to?
      της Μαρίας ή του Γιάννη έδωσες το βιβλίο;

Undoubtedly, these questions trigger the appropriate answer for Greek. This will help students to generalize and understand what the form of indirect object is in Modern Greek.

Example C

Let us next consider the position of time, place and manner adverbs. In English, adverbs or adverbial phrases cannot be placed between the verb and its direct object:

(21) a) Mary saw John yesterday.
      b) Mary has a meeting in Athens.
      c) Mary speaks English very well.

In Modern Greek, manner and time adverbs are normally placed after the direct object, but they can also intervene between the verb and its direct object (21a,b,c).

(22) a) Η Μαρία   είδε χτες   το Γιάννη
          the-Mary [*nom.*] saw yesterday the-John [*acc.*]
      b) Η Μαρία   έχει στην Αθήνα μία συν άντηση
          the-Mary [*nom.*] has at-the-Athens   one-meeting [*acc.*]
      c) Η Μαρία   μιλάει   πολύκαλά   Αγγλικά
          the-Mary [*nom.*] speaks   very well   English [*acc.*]

The structures (22 a,b,c) illustrate that in Modern Greek the bond between verb and object(s) which exists in English is not equally strong. As a result, the order of constituents is free. Of course, there is a particular intonation associated with each arrangement which allows us to convey emphasis, contrast or focus on different constituents by placing them at the beginning or at the end of the sentence.

From the teacher's point of view, it follows that intonation will be taught in relation to different word orders and the meanings associated with them.

A possible exercise could be along the lines of *problem solving*. For example, we could give the students exercises such as:

Form all possible sentences with the words: αύριο, με χαράε, το Γιάννη, δω, θα (lit. tomorrow, with pleasure, the-John, see, will).

- Αύριο
- θαδω
- Μεχαρά

How many sentences can you form? Could you read them providing an appropriate context?

Conclusion

Linguistic theory attempts to explain the facts of language(s) in a formal way. Applied linguists, that is, syllabus designers and language teachers, should be aware of the developments of linguistic theory. Syllabus designers could reorganize the teaching material on the basis that universal grammar principles do not need to be taught extensively, since they generalize across languages. An innovative idea is that constructions related in every target language should be grouped together in line with findings in theoretical linguistics. The structural differences of the target language, which are accounted for in terms of parameters, could be taught in clusters. While linguistic theory analyses structures in isolation, syllabus designers could infer clusters of properties which are usually interconnected by parameters. Thus syntax becomes the element of the curriculum upon which morphology and intonation will be based along it. This means that, for example, noun morphology will be taught within sentences, and it will be associated with an appropriate meaning and intonation according to the context.

Our proposal predicts that these students will acquire the grammatical system of the target language faster than others who are taught in a conventional way, thus offering indirect evidence of the existence of universal grammar. The issues raised here definitely merit further study and research.

Notes

1 Proponents of universal grammar hypothesis: Flynn (1987); White (1989); du Plessis *et al.* (1987). Against the universal hypothesis: Felix *et al.* (1991).

2 This proposal is in line with the teaching of grammar in an explicit way, following the inductive method which is also illustrated by Peck in Chapter 8.

References

Chomsky, N. (1965) *Aspects of the Theory of Syntax*, Cambridge, MA.: MIT Press.

Chomsky, N. (1981) *Lectures on Government and Binding. The Pisa Lectures*, Dordrecht: FORIS.

Chomsky, N. (1986) *Knowledge of Language*, New York: Praeger.

Cook, V. (1993) *Linguistics and Second Language Acquisition*, London: The Macmillan Press.

Dirdsong, D. (1994) 'Asymmetrical Knowledge of Ungrammaticality in SLA Theory', in *Studies in Second Language Acquisition*, 16/4: 463–473.

Dulay, H. C. and Burt, M. (1973) 'Should we Teach Children Syntax?' in *Language Learning* 23/2: 245–258.

du Plessis, J. D., Solin, L. T. and White, L. (1987) 'UG or not UG, that is the Question: A reply to Clashen and Muysken', in *Second Language Research* 3: 56–75.

Eckman, F., Bell, L. and Nelson, D. (eds) (1994) *Universals of Second Language Acquisition*, Rowley, MA.: Newbury House.

Ellis, R. (1993) 'The Structural Syllabus and Second Language Acquisition', in *TESOL Quarterly* 27/1: 91–113.

Ellis, R. (1994) *The Study of Second Language Acquisition*, Oxford: Oxford University Press.

Felix, S.W. and Weigl, W. (1991) 'Universal Grammar in the Classroom: The Effects of Formal Instruction on Second Language Acquisition', in *Second Language Research* 7/2: 162–181.

Fotos, S. (1993) 'Consciousness Raising and Noticing through Focus on Form: Grammar Task Performance versus Formal Instruction', in *Applied Linguistics* 14 /4: 385–407.

Flynn, S. (1987) *A Parameter Setting Model of L2 Acquisition. Experimental Studies in Anaphora*, Dordrecht: D. Reidel.

Gass, S. and Schachter, J. (eds) (1989) *Linguistic Perspectives on Second Language Acquisition*, Cambridge: Cambridge University Press.

Hellinger, M. (1977) *Kontrastive Grammatik Deutsch/Englisch*, Tübingen: Max Niemeyer Verlag.

Mackey, W. F. (1973) 'Applied Linguistics', in J. P. Allen and S. P. Corder (eds) *The Edinburgh Course in Applied Linguistics*, Vol.1, pp. 247–255.

Newmeyer, F. J. (1982) 'On the Applicability of Transformational Grammar' in *Applied Linguistics*, 8/2: 89–121.

Odlin, T. (ed.) (1994) *Perspectives on Pedagogical Grammar*, Cambridge: Cambridge University Press.

Rutherford, W. and Sharewood Smith, M. (1988) *Grammar and Second Language Teaching*, Boston, MA: Heinle & Heinle.

Sharewood Smith, M. (1993) 'Input Enhancement in Instructed SLA: Theoretical Basis', in *Studies in Second Language Acquisition*, 15: 165–179.

Tomlin, R. and Villo, V. (1994) 'Attention in Cognitive Science and Second Language Acquisition', in *Studies in Second Language Acquisition*, 16/2: 203.

Towell, R. and Hawkins, R. (1994) *Approaches to Second Language Acquisition*, UK: Multilingual Matters Ltd.

Tsimpli, I-M. and Smith, N. (1991) 'Second Language Learning: Evidence from a Polyglot Savant', in *UCL Working Papers* 3: 171–183.

White, L. (1989) *Universal Grammar and Second Language Acquisition*, Amsterdam: John Benjamins Publishing Company.

10

SPICE UP YOUR GERMAN!

Teaching modal particles

Linus Jung

Introduction

Modal particles (*Modalpartikel* in German, also known as *Würzwörter* ('spicing particles'), *Abtönungspartikel*, *Satzpartikel* or *Modaladverbien* (Schemann, 1982; Acosta, 1984; Thurmair, 1989; Helbig, 1990; Weinrich, 1993: 843–856; Duden, 1995: 371–2)), are a source of confusion for students because of the many different types of meaning they can express. These words, which are so frequent in colloquial German, are extremely difficult to explain to foreign language learners. Incredible as it may seem, German grammars barely mention these words, and German language textbooks use them without offering any type of explanation (Neuner *et al.*, 1987: 50; Aufderstrasse *et al.*, 1993: 18). However, students who wish to attain an appropriate level of communicative competence in German must be aware of the wide range of functions these words possess as well as their importance in spoken discourse.

This chapter offers a structured explanation of modal particles for use in the second language classroom, and discusses their usefulness in ascertaining the broader meaning of the context of the situation. First, we describe the grammatical and pragmatic functions of some of the most common modal particles in spoken discourse where a good understanding of the context is essential to comprehension. The second part of our study is an explanation of some of the most relevant meanings of each of these words (e.g. *aber*, *auch*, *bloß*, *denn*, *doch*, *eben*, *eigentlich*, *etwa*, *halt*, *ja*, *mal*, *nur*, *schon*, *ruhig*, *vielleicht*, *wohl*), as well as the different attitudes they can convey. This explanation is followed by a series of exercises through which students can practise the identification, function and general usage of these terms.

Classification of the modal particles

All modal particles are function words, and thus belong to the same category as adverbs, prepositions and conjunctions. Students must be made aware of the fact that many of these words have homonyms in other word-classes and thus may be difficult to identify. One means of differentiating a modal particle from its corresponding homonym is to see whether or not the word in question is stressed. If the word is not stressed, it is a modal particle (the only exceptions to this rule are *ja* in orders and *eigentlich*).

(1) Er hat *auch* immer was zu meckern. (*Auch* is not stressed because it is a modal particle.)
(2) Er war *auch* dabei. (*Auch* is stressed because it is an adverb.)

One logical consequence of this characterization is that a modal particle always modifies the predicate. In this way, such words add to the meaning of the entire sentence and do not only modify one word in the clause. The position of the modal particle in a sentence is after the personal pronouns, if there are any, and before *nicht* if the sentence is negative. Word order is important here as a means of identifying word-class. If any of these words *can* appear in another position, they *cannot* be modal particles but rather homonyms having another function and meaning. For example, in sentence (3) *mal* is a modal particle. In contrast, in (4) its change of position means that it is an adverb.

(3) Komm *mal* her. (Modal particle)
(4) *Mal* war er da, *mal* war er nicht da. (Adverb)

Another difference is that it is impossible for speakers to answer a question with a modal particle because in that case it would be stressed, as can be seen in the following example:

(5) Hast du das nicht gewußt? – *Doch*.

By way of a summary, it is worthwhile pointing out that the meaning of modal particles is strictly a function of the context. Moreover, they have a very definite position in the sentence. They always come after the finite verb and, again if there are any, after the personal pronouns and before the negation. Finally, it is also impossible to ask a question which would have a modal particle as its answer (Helbig, 1990: 21–28).

The function of the modal particles

Modal particles have two main functions. First, they enhance textual coherence and cohesion (Helbig, 1990: 32–36), as they refer to something already mentioned and, in spoken language, often have more or less the same function as conjunctions:

149

(6)   Ich habe meine Uhr zu Hause vergessen. Dann muß ich *eben* noch einmal zurück. (*Eben* connects the two sentences in much the same way as the conjunction *deshalb*.)

However, even more important is the second function. More specifically when a speaker uses a modal particle, he adds pragmatic meaning to the text. He is indicating his own assessment or point of view concerning the contents of the sentence and, in a manner of speaking, widens the context. In other words, through modal particles he is able to express surprise (*aber, ja, vielleicht*), disagreement (*auch, doch, etwa, vielleicht*) or warning (*auch, bloß, nur, etwa, vielleicht*). Notwithstanding, from the logical-grammatical point of view, modal particles do not alter the information content or truth value of the sentence. This means that the use of these words is optional and the speaker could eliminate them and still preserve grammatical coherence. In this sense, there is no difference in meaning between examples (7) and (8):

(7)   Du hättest mich anrufen können.
(8)   Du hättest mich *auch* anrufen können.

Nevertheless, from a more pragmatic perspective, the modal particle is meaningful because it adds a 'subjective touch', conveying a clear intentionality on the part of the speaker. The speaker thus communicates his/her intentions and attitude towards what is being said. It cannot be overstressed that by using modal particles the speaker can convey a wide range of possible meanings which show his feelings, perceptions, evaluations, expectations and attitude with great lexical economy. Helbig and Buscha (1986: 479) underline the potential illocutionary force that modal particles can add to the utterance. This illocutionary force is obvious when we compare the following examples (9) and (10):

(9)   Der Tee ist heiß.
(10) Der Tee ist *aber* heiß.

In (9) the speaker only wishes to say that the temperature of the tea is hot and he does not give any more information. In contrast, in example (10) he indicates that the tea is so hot that one can burn oneself, and through the modal particle, *aber*, he shows his surprise. In this way the illocutionary force of *aber* transforms the speech act. The same is also true for (8) where the presence of *auch* expresses anger and reproach.

Actually, the function of the modal particles is more communicative than semantic. Examples (11) to (13) show us some of the different types of meaning these words convey, indicative of the speaker's attitude:

(11)   Der Kaffee schmeckt *aber* gut! (The speaker did not expect such good coffee and expresses surprise).

(12)   Schmeckt der Kaffee *etwa* gut? (The speaker believes that the coffee is not good enough and hopes that the addressee shares his opinion).

(13)   Komm *mal* her! (Although this is a command, *mal* attenuates its pragmatic force, making it more polite and even familiar).

These examples are clear evidence of how difficult it is to deduce the meaning of modal particles. In fact, it can be said that the use of these words shows the speaker's command of the language and his communicative competence. The students' only salvation is a knowledge of the context of the utterance along with a good grasp of the different functions which modal particles can have.

Types of uses of modal particles

Modal particles are usually classified according to their use in different kinds of sentences, something which can help us to identify and apply them correctly. However, not all of them can be used in all kinds of sentences; for example, we can only find *eben* as a modal particle in statements, because it indicates resignation concerning an event or fact, something which is normally expressed in a statement.

You can use *aber, doch, eben, ja, schon, vielleicht* and *wohl* in statements; *auch, bloß, etwa, denn, nur, schon* and *wohl* in questions; and *aber, bloß, doch, eigentlich, ja, mal, nur, schon* and *ruhig* in commands (Acosta, 1984: 18).

The explanation of the different modal particles

In this explanation, our objective is not to give an exhaustive description of all the possible uses of modal particles, but rather one that will be useful for foreign language learners who may find these words highly confusing and difficult to use correctly (Kourukmas, 1987: 105).

aber   *Aber* expresses praise, surprise or irony:

(14)   Er ist *aber* alt geworden! (Surprise)
(15)   Der Kuchen schmeckt *aber* gut! (Praise)
(16)   Was bist du heute *aber* wieder nett zu mir! (Irony)
(17)   Wer tut *aber* auch so etwas? (Surprise)

Although the above examples are all technically exclamations, (14) and (15) are actually statements, while (17) is a question (Acosta, 1984: 17–18; Helbig, 1990: 80).

151

bloß/nur   In an order, *bloß* and *nur* indicate warning and, in other types of speech acts, they express emphasis. Such emphasis is indicative of a special interest or wish with a nuance of worry or reproach (Acosta, 1984: 21).

(21)   Wo bleibt er *bloß/nur?* (Emphasis, worry)
(22)   Mach *bloß/nur* schnell! (Warning)
(23)   Wenn er *bloß/nur* nicht zu spät kommt! (Worry)

denn   *Denn* only appears in questions and expresses astonishment or surprise. It indicates the expectation of an affirmative answer.

(24)   Kannst du mir etwas zu essen machen? – Hast du *denn* Hunger? (Astonishment)

doch   *Doch* is one of the most frequently used modal particles. It appears in all types of sentences and refers to something once known but now forgotten. It expresses reproach or disagreement, but can also be a form of polite urging (Acosta, 1984: 23–24).

(25)   Nimm *doch* noch ein Stückchen Kuchen! (Urging)
(26)   Warum willst du mir das Buch nicht geben? – Ich habe es *doch* gar nicht mehr. (Reproach)

eben/halt   *Eben* and *halt* both express a logical consequence. They comment on a previous statement, explaining it and even transmitting the speaker's resignation concerning a state of affairs he/she cannot change (Thurmair, 1989: 120).

(27)   Mir reicht nie mein Geld.
Du gibst es *eben/halt* für unnützes Zeug aus.(Explanation)
(28)   Ich bekomme immer mehr Falten. – Du wirst *eben/halt* älter. (Explanation)

eigentlich   The function of *eigentlich* is to indicate a change in the subject by a polite question. The speaker introduces another subject, but also shows a possible lack of certainty about the contents of the utterance (Weinrich, 1993: 852; Thurmair, 1989: 175). In affirmative sentences *eigentlich* expresses disagreement (Helbig, 1990: 128).

(29)   Peter ist gekommen. Kennst du ihn *eigentlich*? (Uncertainty)
(30)   (In the airport) Mehr als 20 Kilogramm! Der Koffer ist *eigentlich* zu schwer. (Disagreement)

etwa   *Etwa* appears in questions and indicates surprise and criticism when the addressee does not share the speaker's opinion. Therefore, the use of *etwa* means the expectation of a negative answer. Sometimes it can even give the utterance a slightly reproachful tone (Weinrich, 1993: 853).

(31)   Willst du *etwa* mit dreckigen Schuhen ins Theater? (Reproach, surprise)
(32)   Findest du das Bild *etwa* schön? (Disagreement)

ja   *Ja* is used very frequently. It never appears in questions since it refers to something very well known. The function of *ja* in an exclamation is to show astonishment, although it can also express irony. In commands (where it is stressed), it expresses emphasis and warning (Weinrich, 1993: 844–845).

(33)   Das ist *ja* teuer! (Astonishment)
(34)   Das hast du *ja* wieder fabelhaft hingekriegt! (Irony)
(35)   Komm *ja* pünktlich! (Emphasis)

mal   *Mal* usually weakens a command or a yes–no question which is a polite wish or request. The use of *mal* is also indicative of the speaker's familiarity.

(36)   Helfen Sie mir *mal*, bitte? (Politeness)
(37)   Kann ich *mal* den Zucker haben? (Politeness)

schon   *Schon* appears in statements, questions and commands. Normally, in an imperative sentence it urges someone to do something. However, its use in a statement means that the speaker wishes to reassure the addressee (Helbig, 1990: 201).

(38)   Er wird *schon* kommen!(Calming down)
(39)   Komm *schon*! (Urging)

ruhig   *Ruhig* is mainly used in orders and expresses permission (Thurmair, 1989: 187).

(40)   Trink *ruhig* noch ein Bier! (Permission)
(41)   Du kannst *ruhig* ohne mich ins Kino gehen! (Permission)

vielleicht   *Vielleicht* can express a wide range of different meanings, such as surprise, praise, criticism, probability or irony. However, these can only be deduced from the context (Acosta, 1984: 29–30).

(42) Du bist *vielleicht* ein komischer Kerl.(Surprise)
(43) Du hast *vielleicht* ein schönes Bild gemalt. (Praise)
(44) Das ist *vielleicht* ein dummer Vorschlag. (Criticism)
(45) Siehst du das *vielleicht* anders? (Probability)
(46) Du bist *vielleicht* ein großer Künstler. (Irony)

wohl   *Wohl* shows that the speaker is not sure about what he is saying.
In this sense it is also used in rhetorical questions (Acosta, 1984: 30).

(47) Wo werden sie jetzt *wohl* sein? (Uncertainty)
(48) Sie wird *wohl* zu Hause sein. (Probability)

Summary of the use of modal particles

Appeasement:	*nur, ruhig, schon*
Confirmation:	*auch*
Disagreement, criticism:	*auch, doch, etwa, vielleicht*
Emphasis:	*aber, auch, bloß, denn, doch, eben, eigentlich, etwa, halt, ja, mal, nur, schon, ruhig, vielleicht, wohl*[1]
Justification, agreement:	*ja*
Praise:	*aber, vielleicht*
Permission:	*ruhig*
Politeness:	*doch, eigentlich, mal*
Probability:	*etwa, vielleicht, wohl*
Resignation:	*eben, halt*
Rhetorical question:	*auch, denn, doch, wohl*
Surprise:	*aber, ja, vielleicht*
Uncertainty:	*eigentlich, wohl*
Urging:	*doch, nur, ruhig, schon*
Warning, threat:	*auch, bloß, etwa, ja, nur, vielleicht*
Worry:	*bloß, nur*

Conclusion

In this chapter we have described the different meanings, use and functions of German modal particles. These words are often a nightmare for the foreign language learner because they express states of mind, and thus are difficult to use correctly. Furthermore, German language textbooks make little or no attempt to offer an explanation for these words.

To help students gain competence in their use, we have provided three types of exercises (see Appendix, p. 155). In the first exercise, students must determine the function of modal particles. In the second, they must insert the option which is in accordance with the attitude to be conveyed.

In the third, they must distinguish between modal particles and homonyms.

Exercises with modal particles go hand in hand with the practice of a very important language skill, the deduction of meaning from context. It can even be said that the knowledge of the correct use of modal particles enhances communicative competence because the essentially pragmatic function of these words signifies that their meaning is to a great extent context-dependent. Consequently, when the students work with modal particles, they are also working with the whole communicative framework of the discourse.

Appendix

I. Erklären Sie die Funktion der Modalpartikel im Satz!
– Hast du ihn *etwa* nicht angerufen? – (Criticism, disagreement)
– Bleib du *ruhig* zu Hause! – (Permission, urging)
– Das ist *doch* nett von ihm. – (Disagreement)
– Das ist *vielleicht* ein schüchterner Kerl! – (Surprise)
– Dir geht es *wohl* nicht so gut heute. – (Probability)
– Mach das *bloß* nicht noch mal! – (Warning)
– Du hast *eben* nicht aufgepaßt. Jetzt ist es kaputt. – (Resignation)
– Ich habe Monika getroffen. Kennst du sie *eigentlich*? – (Insecurity)
– Wieder kein Sechser im Lotto! Wir haben *auch* ein Pech! – (Confirmation)
– Der Chef! Was hat er *denn* wieder für eine Laune? – (Rhetorical question)

II. Setzen Sie entsprechend ein!
(Surprise) – Du kommst . . . spät! – (> *aber, ja, vielleicht*)
(Resignation) – Er hat es . . . nie gelernt. – (> *eben/halt*)
(Justification, agreement) – Herr Kuhn, er ist . . . allen bekannt, hält heute einen Vortrag. (> *ja*)
(Warning) – Geh . . . nicht bei Rot über die Straße! – (> *bloß, ja, nur*)
(Urging) – Du nimmst . . . noch ein Stückchen Torte?! – (> *doch*)
(Permission) – Er soll . . . nach Hause gehen. – (> *ruhig*)
(Uncertainty) – Wir sind . . . gegen 14 Uhr zurück. – (> *wohl*)

III. Entscheiden Sie: Modalpartikel oder nicht?
– Niemand war zu Hause. Warum *nur*? – (Ja)
– Wo ist Peter? – *Vielleicht* kommt er noch. – (Nein)
– Warst du nicht in der Schule? – *Doch*. – (Nein)
– Wir hatten dieses Jahr *auch* keinen Urlaub. – (Nein)
– Was bist du *auch* so neugierig! – (Ja)
– Dieser Bach ist *etwa* 12 Kilometer lang. – (Nein)
– Hast du das *denn* vergessen? – (Ja)
– Sie konnten ihn nicht erkennen, *denn* es war dunkel. – (Nein)

155

– Wo ist Maria? – *Eben* hatte ich sie noch gesehen. – (Nein)
– Du bist *ja* so klug! – (Ja)

Note

1   While these particles can express emphasis in certain contexts, they cannot be used indiscriminately.

References

Acosta, L. (1984) 'Las partículas modales del Alemán Y Español', in *Studia Philologica Salamaticensia* 7–8: 7–41.

Aufderstrasse, H., Bock, H., Gerdes, M., Müller, H. and Müller, J. (1993) *Themen neu. Lehrwerk für Deutsch als Fremdsprache*, Ismaning: Max Hueber Verlag. 3 Bde.

Duden (1995) *Grammatik der deutschen Gegenwartssprache* 5, neu bearb. Aufl. Mannheim: Bibliographisches Institut and F. A. Brockhaus AG.

Helbig, G. (1990) *Lexikon deutscher Partikeln*, Leipzig: Verlag Enzyklopädie.

Helbig, G. and Buscha, J. (1986) *Deutsche Grammatik. Ein Handbuch für den Ausländerunterricht*, Leipzig: Verlag Enzyklopädie.

Kourukmas, P. (1987) 'Sind Modalpartikeln lehrbar geworden? Partikellehren für Deutsch als Fremdsprache aus den Jahren 1979 bis 1984', in *Info DaF* 2, 99–110.

Neuner, G., Scherling, T., Schmidt, R. and Wilms, H. (1987) *Deutsch Aktiv Neu. Ein Lehrwerk für Erwachsene*, München: Langenscheidt. 3 Bde.

Schemann, H. (1982) 'Die Modalpartikel und ihre funktionale Äquivalente. Untersuchung anhand des Deutschen, Französischen und Portugiesischen', in *Archiv* 219, 2–18.

Thurmair, M. (1989) *Modalpartikeln und ihre Kombinationen*, Tübingen: Niemeyer.

Weinrich, H. (1993) *Textgrammatik der deutschen Sprache*, Mannheim: Dudenverlag.

Part IV

VOCABULARY TRAINING

Teachers of modern languages know from experience that it is necessary to look up words and find the appropriate equivalents in the target language. Different types of dictionaries are their main tools. Nobody can expect a language teacher to be familiar with every word in the texts which he/she reads in class in the target language. The teacher must, moreover, be in the position to offer stylistic alternatives to his/her pupils when they write an essay in the foreign language or attempt to translate a text from L1 into L2 or vice versa. The teacher would never be able to do this without having access to a selection of useful dictionaries.

The learner of a foreign language should be just as aware of any lexical assistance he/she can get from dictionaries in order to improve his/her ability to express ideas in the target language. Finding the right expression in a certain context is not just a matter of going through some storage of internalized words, but also requires the appropriate coordination of word combinations in a given situation and social context. Thus looking up a word like 'claustraphobia' may be a frustrating experience for a beginner or even for a somewhat advanced student of English as a foreign language. A two-way pocket dictionary may not have registered this word at all, as has been tested by the editor of this book. If the learner looks up this word in a monolingual dictionary such as *The Oxford Universal Dictionary Illustrated* or *The Concise Oxford Dictionary*, he will find that this is a modern Latin word with its first occurrence in 1879 and that it is explained as a 'morbid dread of confined places'. But what is the meaning of words like *morbid*, *dread* or *confined*, the learner may wonder. If an unknown word is explained by other unfamiliar words, the frustrated language learner may be tempted to give up on dictionaries altogether and to make his own guess, which may not always turn out to be the wisest decision.

Marquez Linares (Chapter 11) shows how Spaniards learning English as their target language can easily be trapped by misinterpretation of a dictionary entry if they are not trained to use it properly. So, quite obviously, it takes some training to find the adequate information from a dictionary, provided that one has picked the right type of dictionary. Linares removes the fear of learners consulting a dictionary which some used to consider more or less an act of 'cheating'. On the contrary, the foreign language learner is very much encouraged to use a dictionary at every given opportunity, because it will enrich his variety of expressions to a great extent. He shows what is meant by 'dictionary awareness' and how this can be an important factor in language acquisition. Advice is given for selecting the right dictionary for specific learning operations. After presenting the various types of dictionaries, the author discusses the advantages and disadvantages of using thematic vs. alphabetical, and monolingual vs. bilingual dictionaries, and he finally pursues the question of how dictionary awareness should be taught.

The traditional way of teaching vocabulary is by using bilingual or (for more advanced learners) monolingual dictionaries in order to find the closest equivalent to a word or expression in the respective language. However, Jiménez Hurtado (Chapter 12) illustrates the process of learning vocabulary by lexical fields which form semantic hierarchies. Instead of learning words without a view to how they are organized in the mental lexicon, Hurtado argues that it would be much better for a student to learn the basic concept of a lexical field which can be expanded by increasing experience.

Another problem for the learner of a foreign language is how to master the use of metaphorical and idiomatic expressions which cannot be literally translated into L1, and whose syntactic patterns are inflexible. Gewehr (Chapter 13) focuses on the genesis and occurrence of idiomatic phrases in various languages, and shows that the metaphoric nucleus is often identical, and that in some cases even the semantic and syntactic features are similar or even identical. A number of proverbs from the Bible show that metaphorical language is several thousand years old, and only a few have been preserved in the form of idiomatic phrases in modern languages. If we accept that a phraseological unit is a lexicalized word group which has syntactic and semantic stability, then this means that such expressions do not allow any variation and must be memorized as complete phraseological units. This takes some special effort on the part of the learner, and it is therefore suggested that illustrations of the image of an idiomatic phrase may support memorization.

In the final section of his chapter, Gewehr suggests some sample exercises which could perhaps be done in a class of advanced L2 students. The presented materials are in several European languages because it is one of the purposes of this book to compare cultural differences and how they are reflected in semantic structures. Phraseology is certainly an area where this aspect becomes most relevant.

This idea is also taken up by Zevgoli (Chapter 14), who discusses idioms in foreign language teaching. Starting with the distinction of primary properties (such as conventionality and invariability) and secondary properties (such as analysability, grammaticality, figurative property, etc.), she establishes some kind of typology of idioms. However, her prime objective is to draw the teacher's attention to the teachability of idioms. Like Gewehr, Zevgoli argues that a student should learn at least a limited number of idioms in order to approach the communicative competence of a native speaker. For methodological reasons, it is being suggested that idioms should generally be taught by the degree of their compositionality and grammaticality, because the more regular the syntactic features of an idiom, the easier it may appear to the learner to memorize it. A sentence like 'Tom spilled the beans' could be conceived literally as a 'normal' sentence containing a subject, an object and a predicate. Its semantic content indicates that Tom may have stumbled or may be a clumsy guy who spilled beans all over the floor. Even a beginning EFL learner does not have any problem with such a simple sentence. However, the crux is that the learner must comprehend that this very simple sentence can at the same time express a figurative idea, i.e. that Tom revealed a secret. This process of metaphorization must be learned by the L2 student in fitting situations. The author suggests that only at a later stage should more conventionalized idioms be presented to the learner, ones which do not have a simple grammatical structure. Some exercises include this contribution which should give the teacher help with teaching idioms.

11

DICTIONARY AWARENESS

Carlos F. Márquez Linares

Introduction

A junior high school Spanish student of English produced the following text:
'He *see* a tall man. His hair *see* grey and he *see* old.' The teacher was initially
astonished at this shocking display of visual perception on the part of the
'man', only to discover after some thinking that the reason for it was very
simple. The student meant to say that the man *was* tall, grey-haired and old.
He knew that the Spanish verb for 'was', is *'era'*, third-person singular of *'ser'*
(to be), so he looked up the translation of *'era'* in a dictionary, where he found:
'see ser'. He obviously chose the most English-looking translation.

Mistakes based on inadequate use of dictionaries are not limited to the
beginning stages of language learning. An English-speaking lecturer at a
Spanish university was surprised to find that many of her students wrote
'overcoat' when they meant 'above all'. Puzzled by the recurrence of this
mistake, she did some lexicographic research, only to find that what her
students had done was to look up in their bilingual dictionaries *'sobre todo'*,
the Spanish equivalent of 'above all'. There they found an entry for *'sobretodo'*,
and they obviously thought the fact that it was a single word was an irrelevant
detail, and they incorporated its translation, 'overcoat', into their compositions, with results such as 'I liked the book very much, and, *overcoat*, the
description of . . .'. Every language teacher can probably recall some examples
of his/her own of this type of 'dictionary-generated' mistake, which, in fact,
emphasizes the importance of the role that dictionaries play in language
teaching and learning.

Dictionaries have traditionally been essential tools for language learning
and have consistently been considered as such by most lexicographers,
language teachers and language learners. In addition, publishing companies
have become increasingly aware that language learners around the world
represent a huge market whose needs deserve attention. Thus a considerable
number of dictionaries specially designed for language learners have appeared
in the last decades creating a tradition which fulfils one of the basic maxims
of lexicography, as formulated by Householder and Saporta (1975: 279):

'Dictionaries should be designed with a special set of users in mind and for their specific needs.'

Learners have at their disposal a whole battery of lexicographic works, such as the learner's dictionary, the traditional bilingual dictionary, or a complete set of special area dictionaries. It is because of this attention that it seems the more surprising that both teachers and lexicographers find that language learners do not take full advantage of the possibilities their dictionaries offer. Indeed, studies on dictionary use aim at the fact that 'many students are not aware of the riches that their monolingual dictionaries contain' (Bejoint, 1981: 219), nor 'of the variety of dictionaries available, and of the differences between them' (Bejoint, 1989: 208). It therefore seems necessary to pause and try to find a reason why this should be so.

We will limit ourselves to exemplifying our points with respect to the teaching of the English language. However, the importance of dictionary awareness and the need for it exceeds the limits of the English language, and so most of what is said here can be extrapolated for use in the teaching of languages other than English.

It is the intention of this chapter to provide an answer to the following questions: (1) *What is dictionary awareness?* (2) *Why dictionaries?* (3) *Which dictionaries?* This means showing to what extent dictionaries are useful and necessary in the process of language learning, discussing some of the different dictionary types available in the market, and finally demonstrating the immense wealth of information in dictionaries. The final section suggests some means of improving dictionary awareness of foreign language learners.

What is dictionary awareness?

Some lexicographers have ventured that teachers do not always encourage dictionary use on the part of their students. Hartmann (1989: 181) asks: 'Are teachers sceptical, or possibly afraid, that learners ... might acquire independence from the taught course too soon?' Herbst and Stein (1987: 120) state that German teachers 'seem rather sceptical about their students' ability to use the dictionary appropriately'. Thus a vicious circle is produced: students do not apparently know how to use their dictionaries, so teachers discourage their use (Jiménez Raya, Chapter 1, Lamb, Chapter 2, this volume).

On the other hand, dictionaries do not always meet the requirements of language learners as users. This is something which both language teachers and especially lexicographers are aware of, as can be seen in the reference section. Thus the problem of inadequate dictionary use by learners becomes more serious, for there is no one single cause. Rundell (1988: 127) writes

> the reference needs of people learning English are not adequately met
> by existing monolingual learner's dictionaries ... Either the diction-
> aries themselves are deficient, or their target users have not yet

162

learned how to use them effectively; ... and the truth is probably somewhere in between.

It is the task of lexicographers to improve their dictionaries so that they become increasingly better tools for language learners. The task of teaching language learners how to take full advantage of the wealth of linguistic – and even cultural – information in their dictionaries should be undertaken by their teachers. It is therefore necessary for teachers to raise their own *dictionary awareness* so that they will be able to enhance their students' awareness.

Returning to the initial question, a person with *dictionary awareness* is one who knows *where* to find the information he needs and *how* to extract it. This implies that such a person must be, on the one hand, at least fairly familiar with the range of lexicographic works at his disposal so that he can discern which one is most suitable for the task at hand. On the other hand, a person with dictionary awareness should also be able to find the exact bit of information required within the particular dictionary in use (provided that it is there).

Why dictionaries?

Some of the reasons why dictionaries must be a part of language learning have already been hinted at. The first reason is one of circulation. One of the first questions a teacher must be ready to answer when facing a beginners' class is advising them as to which dictionary they should buy. Indeed, not only do all language learners use dictionaries as a learning tool, but they probably own at least one, which implies a certain familiarity with its use. It would seem illogical to ignore this fact and to neglect such an obvious and widespread tool.

However, dictionaries are not only useful because everybody owns one, although that reason alone certainly justifies their importance. Hartmann (1989: 181) stresses the universal recognition that dictionaries are a common and useful teaching tool:

> Currently the dictionary is regarded as one of the several 'teaching aids' (with text-book, grammar exercises, visual aids, games, tests, etc.) as well as a potential 'liberator' in the trend towards individualised instruction.

The core importance of dictionaries lies in their status closer to the learning than to the teaching of a language. It is not necessary for the teacher to be present when a dictionary is being consulted. This actually seldom occurs. It is not even necessary for him/her to assess the learner's methods in the same way as grammar exercises should be assessed, unless dictionary use itself is being taught. Dictionaries are tools to be used primarily by the individual when working and learning individually, and so they encourage and facilitate learner autonomy.

This characteristic of autonomous learning inherent to dictionary use may explain why some teachers are reluctant to use them extensively. Herbst and Stein (1987: 120) mention that the widespread attitude of German teachers is that 'it is sometimes better for the student to solve linguistic problems without consulting a dictionary . . . finding the solution to a problem in this way is regarded "second best"'. After all, dictionary use means non-controlled learning with all the risks that such learning implies. However, given that an important educational goal in language learning is learner autonomy, it is essential that dictionaries be taken into account. Teachers must be aware that autonomous learning does not imply non-controlled learning, but the teaching of techniques to avoid the pitfalls of independent learning. When it comes to the dictionary as a learning aid, learner autonomy implies raising the dictionary awareness of learners and the actual teaching of techniques for dictionary use.

However, though dictionaries are an important tool for language learning, they are far from being the panacea that some students consider them to be. Looking something up in the dictionary is often the easy way out when in doubt, and consequently other more productive ways of finding solutions are disregarded. In addition, there is nothing more dangerous where dictionaries are concerned than the non-critical dictionary consultation, since this invariably leads to disaster. Dictionaries can never substitute for the teacher or the learner, and obviously must be accompanied by the learner's judgement. Students must be made aware that judgement must be exerted both when deciding whether it is necessary to consult a dictionary, and when assessing how useful or pertinent the information thus found is. Bejoint (1989: 209) writes: 'it is clear that the dictionary is meant to help the students find what they do not know or verify what they think they know, but not to do all the work in their place.'

The role of the dictionary in language learning is a basic point to be taken into account in the teaching of dictionary use. Students have to be aware of why and when dictionaries can be profitably consulted.

Which dictionaries?

Talking about 'dictionaries' in an abstract way implies at least some degree of vagueness. There are many types of dictionaries which in turn differ from each other enormously. Dictionary awareness implies, on the one hand, knowing that dictionaries are important and useful, and on the other, knowing how to use them. A language learner with dictionary awareness should also be familiar with the existence of a wide range of dictionaries on the market, as well as with the differences between them. At the same time, he/she should be able to discern which dictionary is more useful for each learning situation. Learning how to choose a good dictionary must be one of the aims of the teaching of language awareness. However, what is a good dictionary? According to Haas, as quoted by Bejoint (1981: 211):

> A good dictionary is not only one which has all the information one needs, it is also 'one in which you can find the information you are looking for – preferably in the first place you look'.

Thus, knowing what an ideal dictionary should provide, our aim now is to analyse which is the most appropriate dictionary for each particular learning need. Hartmann (1989: 187) analyses the factors to be taken into account when dealing with dictionaries for language learners:

1   level of proficiency
2   type of activity,
3   language base and directionality,[1]
4   category of information.

In the light of these factors, the next step is to analyse some of the dictionary types available on the market so as to make a decision as to which is the most suitable for each learner and situation.

Dictionary typology

There is ample bibliography on dictionary typology (Malkiel, 1975). In this study, dictionaries available for language learners will be classified according to three main criteria: (1) the number of languages involved; (2) macro-structure or general layout; (3) coverage. In no case is it our intention to present an exhaustive classification of the dictionaries on the market. This would lie beyond the scope and length of the present study. The aim of this section is to help language teachers and learners to understand what kind of dictionary they are handling, in order to get as much advantage as possible from it.

According to the number of languages involved, a dictionary will be *monolingual*, if it is written all in one language; or *multilingual*, if correspondences between two or possibly more languages are established. The most usual example is bilingual dictionaries, where correspondences between just two languages are given. A third less usual case is that of bilingualized dictionaries, which usually combine the monolingual dictionary definition style with a translation into the target language.

If we take macrostructure (the general organization of the entries in a dictionary) as the criterion for classification, dictionaries can be labelled as either *semasiological* or *onomasiological*. Semasiological dictionaries present the traditional alphabetical arrangement, where the user is expected to go from the lexical item to the meaning. Onomasiological dictionaries go back to the much older tradition of thematic organization. Information in these dictionaries is organized so that the user is expected to go from the meaning to the lexical item.

Typical examples of onomasiological dictionaries are *Roget's Thesaurus* or the *Longman Lexicon of Contemporary English*. Most onomasiological dictionaries include the semasiological element in the form of alphabetical appendices, for reasons of ease of access. Similarly, some monolingual dictionaries incorporate an onomasiological component by providing synonyms. This is the case of *Collins COBUILD*. A more innovative format can be represented by the *Longman Activator*, which attempts to combine both onomasiological and semasiological arrangements with considerable success. An example of a completely different type of macrostructure is that of pictorial dictionaries, for example, those of the 'Duden' series. In this type of dictionary words are not defined, but matched with a drawing of the object or part of an object they stand for. Although they are useful for concrete vocabulary, they turn out to be rather less useful when dealing with abstract vocabulary because of the difficulty of pictorial representation.

The third criterion discussed is *coverage*. Coverage can be interpreted in at least two different ways: in terms of the type of information offered and in terms of the number of dictionary entries. In the first case, the dictionary can be designed to either cover only one type of information (e.g. meaning, pronunciation, synonyms, collocation, culture, etc.), or several types of information. In the second case, the criteria for the inclusion of entries in a dictionary can be one of frequency of use, or one of morphosyntactic category (e.g. a dictionary of phrasal verbs, a dictionary of idioms). If a dictionary is designed to include all the lexical items in a language it will be unabridged (*Oxford English Dictionary*). If some selection of entries is made, it will be abridged (*Concise English Dictionary*). A very popular type of dictionary including only some of the lexical units in a language is the pocket dictionary, a convenient book to handle for its small size. However, its narrow coverage and superficial treatment of information render it an inconvenient tool for learning.

Thus, according to these criteria, a dictionary could be classified as monolingual onomasiological abridged (*Longman Lexicon of Contemporary English*), monolingual semasiological unabridged (*Oxford English Dictionary*), etc. Once a typology is established, one of the big controversies in dictionary use by language learners arises precisely from the difficulty in choosing between different dictionary types. The importance of the teacher's advice in choosing a dictionary is emphasized by Bejoint (1988: 145): 'The main conclusion is that one should be extremely careful when advising L2 learners on which dictionaries to use and how to use them.'

The answer to this question, the same as with all the questions dealt with in this chapter, will be given taking into account the user as a learner and his particular needs in the different learning situations.

Thematic vs. alphabetical dictionaries

One of our basic premises is that it is never bad to use a selection of dictionaries, as long as the learner knows how to use them. Indeed, it is convenient for the learner consistently to consult as many dictionaries as possible and to be encouraged not to rely on a single source. However, it must be taken into account that it is not always the case that several dictionaries are available to a single learner unless he owns them, something which seldom happens.

As far as the opposition thematic (onomasiological) vs. alphabetical (semasiological) dictionaries is concerned, it is not a good idea to encourage beginners to use onomasiological dictionaries, first because they usually demand a higher command of the target language, and second because they will surely be more motivated to use the kind of dictionaries with which they are most familiar in their native language, that is, alphabetical dictionaries. However, when it comes to more advanced learners, dictionaries with an onomasiological component can be of great help, especially if they have been designed with language learners in mind. In my opinion, onomasiological dictionaries are more useful for encoding activities, such as writing, where the user can find information on words with a similar meaning, which is usually absent in semasiological dictionaries. The latter, however, are usually more helpful for decoding purposes. In any case, the learner must be familiar with both types of dictionaries, and actively encouraged to use both. It is always necessary to make learners aware of their comparative advantages and disadvantages depending on the task at hand.

Monolingual vs. bilingual dictionaries

A long-standing controversy both among language teaching experts and lexicographers is the question of whether it is better to use a monolingual or a bilingual dictionary. It is not easy to answer this question, because the preference for one type of dictionary or the other will depend on the characteristics of the learner and his/her particular needs.

It is a fact that language learners favour the use of bilingual over monolingual dictionaries. Zöfgen (1991: 2888) writes: 'Research in various countries on the use of dictionaries has confirmed that a vast majority of foreign language learners tend to turn to the bilingual rather than to the monolingual dictionary.'

However, when analysing the comparative usefulness of both types, dictionary users are not so sure that bilingual dictionaries are on the whole better than monolingual ones. On the contrary, research carried out by Bejoint (1981: 219) among advanced students of English showed that: 'Monolingual dictionaries are on the whole considered satisfactory and useful, and more so than bilingual dictionaries.'

Bilingual dictionaries are more useful for students who are still not very proficient in the target language, if only for the reason that beginners would not be able to understand the definitions in a monolingual dictionary. However, as students advance in their knowledge of the target language, they should be encouraged to rely increasingly on monolingual dictionaries, especially on those designed for language learners, which will be analysed in the following section. Obviously, this is in consonance with the idea that language learners should work as much as possible in the target language environment, which is just what monolingual dictionaries provide. Still, some authors express their doubts on this issue. Bejoint (Bejoint and Moulin, 1987: 99) writes: 'The superiority of the monolingual over the bilingual dictionary is not as obvious as many people think.'

One of the reasons that these authors adduce is that bilingual dictionaries are easier to use and provide a quicker answer than monolingual dictionaries. Besides, what learners very often demand and find most useful is the equivalence into or from their own language. Again, if the learner's task involves translation, a bilingual dictionary will be more useful than a monolingual one. However, the ease and speed of access in bilingual dictionaries frequently involves a trap caused by the unisomorphism of languages; in other words, the fact that two different languages organize semantic space in different ways. This is why full equivalence between items from different languages is difficult to find. Learners of a foreign language must be made aware of that fact, so that they know they must look up the word twice in the bilingual dictionary, once in each language, and then read the *whole* set of equivalents. It is often a good idea to look up these words in a monolingual dictionary to ensure a deeper understanding of the lexical item in question.

From what we have seen, it is difficult to give a straightforward recommendation as to the choice between monolingual and bilingual dictionaries. Both present advantages and disadvantages. Some guidelines, can be suggested however, along the lines of what Bejoint (Bejoint and Moulin, 1987: 104) writes:

> bilingual dictionaries are ideal for quick consultation in many cases, and . . . monolingual dictionaries, though more difficult to use, have the extra merit of introducing the user right into the lexical system of the L2 . . . thereby contributing to the development of lexical competence.

In conclusion, it can be said that it is necessary to encourage the use of monolingual dictionaries, which should increase in relation to the student's level of proficiency in the target language. Bilingual dictionaries may prove most useful at the initial stages of language learning and in activities that involve translation. However, they can still be used all through the learning process, provided that the learners' problems stemming from the uni-somorphism of languages are lessened by their being specifically taught how to use this type of dictionary effectively.

The learner's dictionary

Until now, we have discussed monolingual dictionaries as a whole, but it would be difficult to ask language learners to use the *Oxford English Dictionary*, probably considered *the* monolingual dictionary in English, as an aid to language learning. In contrast, the *Learner's Dictionary* is a whole new genre of dictionaries designed and written with language learners as their target users.

When A. S. Hornby first published his *Idiomatic and Syntactic English Dictionary* in Japan in 1948, he probably did not foresee that one later edition, already under the name of *The Oxford Advanced Learner's Dictionary* (*OALD*), would be the first token of a fertile new genre of dictionaries. Many more 'learner's dictionaries' have appeared following in the footsteps of Hornby's *OALD*, some of which have in turn become classics of the genre and introduced additions and improvements to the original model. This is the case of the *Longman Dictionary of Contemporary English* (*LDOCE*), the *Cambridge Universal Dictionary of English* (*CUDE*) and the *Collins COBUILD Dictionary of the English Language* (*COBUILD*). For a detailed discussion of some of their relative merits and drawbacks, see Herbst (1990).

Our aim in this section is to show what we mean when we say that these dictionaries are made for learners and also to show what kind of information can be obtained from them. The extent to which learners' dictionaries are compiled for learners can be demonstrated by the very principles that underlie them. According to Herbst (1990: 1379): 'The rationale behind the general learner's dictionary is the insight that the foreign user's demands are *fundamentally* different from those of a native speaker.'

Indeed, the very arrangement and presentation of the information in learners' dictionaries takes the particular characteristics of their users into account. According to Zöfgen (1991: 2899):

> the organisation of the content and formal arrangement of the dictionary article must be governed by the principle that not only the linguistic information, but also the means of access provided to it must correspond to the limited reference skills of an intermediate learner.

The type of information included is ample. As an example, we will provide a short entry from *LDOCE* including some of the information it offers. Some items of information, such as language variety, regional variant or register are not present, since the word chosen for the example is one belonging to the standard variety of the language, which presents no regional variation, but they do exist in the dictionary:

re-prove /ri'pruːv/ *v* [T (**for**)] *fml* to talk to angrily or express disapproval of: *She reproved him for telling lies.*

LDOCE

spelling, syllabication: re.prove *,*
accentuation, pronunciation: /rO'pruːv/.
morphology: No information on inflection means it is a regular verb.
grammatical category: *n* (noun).
syntactic information: [T (for)] (a transitive verb governing an optional preposition *for*).
register: *fml.* (formal).
meaning: to talk angrily or express disapproval of.
example of use: *she reproved him for telling lies.*
collocation: The verb collocates with a human subject and the cause for disapproval, introduced by the preposition *for*.
other words from the same lexical set: Immediately above this entry, we can find the entry for the noun *reproof*.

reprove /rɪ pruːv /, **reproves, reproving, reproved**. If you **reprove** someone, you tell them that they have behaved wrongly or foolishly; a formal word. ✧ **reproving**. EG *All she got was a reproving letter from her Aunt Agnes.*

v + o : IF + PREP
THEN *for*
⇑ criticize
= rebuke
✧ADJ CLASSIF

COBUILD

Other dictionaries may even expand the amount of information included. Thus *COBUILD*, in its famous 'extra column', also provides synonyms (rebuke), antonyms and hyperonyms (superordinate terms: criticize). This information is included exclusively on the grounds that it is useful for learners. Bejoint (1981: 208) states: 'Foreign learner's dictionaries should only include the kind of information that helps improve their communicative performance, and not etymology, which is just information about the language.' Learners must be made aware of this wealth of information at their disposal, and they must also be taught how to access it.

Learners' dictionaries are abridged. Lexical items are included mainly on the basis of their frequency of use. Their coverage of the language is very limited if compared to dictionaries for native speakers, such as the *Oxford English Dictionary*, or even the *Concise English Dictionary*. This allows learners' dictionaries to include all the information enumerated above, precisely the kind of information that is absent from dictionaries for native speakers, who do not need it to the extent that learners do. However, very proficient learners will find that some of the words they look up do not appear in their dictionaries. This emphasizes the idea that very proficient learners should use dictionaries designed for native speakers. Thus, the scale of progress in language proficiency should be mirrored in progress in the type of dictionary used. This scale starts with the bilingual dictionary, as has been suggested above, and ends in the dictionary for native speakers, with learners' dictionaries in the middle of the scale. Of course, the use of a more 'advanced' dictionary does not imply the abandonment of the previous ones, but their assuming an auxiliary role. The proficient learner will thus benefit from the whole scale of dictionaries at his/her disposal.

Teaching 'dictionary awareness'

This study is based on the premise that if dictionary use is viewed as unsatisfactory, one reason is that learners do not know how to extract the information in their dictionaries, in many cases simply because they are not aware of their possibilities (see Jiménez Hurtado, Chapter 1, this volume). The causes lie beyond the scope of the language classroom. According to Kipfer (1987: 50), the 'problems that exist probably stem from a lack of dictionary instruction in schools and homes and a low level of enthusiasm for dictionary use.'

Raising dictionary awareness is therefore not exclusively a task of language teachers, though they are the ones who are primarily involved in it. Although it is often the case that teaching dictionary use is included in general education syllabuses, it is still necessary to emphasize that

> linguistic awareness and skill in [monolingual] dictionary consultation should first be developed in relation to the learning of the mother tongue at primary school level. This would not only facilitate the task of the FL teacher but, more importantly, enable him to build on a much firmer foundation.
>
> (Bejoint and Moulin, 1987: 114)

Teaching dictionary awareness implies a whole range of activities. Bejoint (1989) suggests that these should be practical rather than theoretical, language-oriented rather than dictionary-oriented and spread over the learning period rather than concentrated. These activities could be based on the existing dictionary brochures, booklets, books or manuals on the market. According to Herbst and Stein (1987), the objectives of teaching dictionary use are the following:

1   The acquisition of reference skills (outline of dictionaries, types of macrostructure, cross-referencing, etc.).
2   The discrimination of faculties and skills (what information students need).
3   Establishing language achievement control (dictionaries must help the students to check how much they know and whether it is correct).
4   Self-study and self-education.

Activities

Some activities can be devised which respond to these objectives. One of the first problems that early dictionary users meet is the difficulty of finding information on words, starting from the difficulty in recognizing the base form of a word in a dictionary, that is, which particular form of the word is at the head of the entry. Thus, students will have to be made aware that the information on words is to be found under the infinitive for the verbs and the masculine singular for nouns and adjectives, in languages where nouns and adjectives have both gender and number, such as Spanish. Special attention will have to be paid to irregular forms. A possible exercise may be to ask the students to find the meaning of the following words in the dictionary: *book, good, come, is, books, cars, went, classes, knives, better, lying*. This exercise is also useful for reviewing the students' knowledge of morphology.

The problem of a word belonging to different syntactic categories (noun, verb, etc.) is also related to the difficulty of finding certain words in the dictionary. Students must be made aware that many words can be used as nouns, adjectives, etc. An activity which enables them to realize this fact would be one of asking them to look up the following words in their dictionaries and say to what parts of speech they can be allocated. They could then be asked to produce one sentence for every part of speech: *pay* (noun, verb); *fine* (adjective, adverb, verb, noun); *cool* (adjective, verb, noun, adverb); *last* (adverb, adjective, pronoun, verb); *back* (noun, adverb, adjective, verb).

One last activity related to the kind of information often easily missed in dictionaries refers to countabilty. Students are seldom aware that some words present both countable and uncountable uses. In order to correct this, students could again be asked to look up the following words in a dictionary and produce one sentence for their countable use and another for their uncountable use: *iron, egg, glass, paper, beer*.

However, not all activities concerning dictionary use involve looking up unordered lists of words. The second type of exercise proposed here is intended to make students aware that a word may have different meanings, and that it is often the case that the first meaning listed in the entry is not the one they are looking for. Students will be asked to give the meaning that the word in italics has *in that context*:

1   The boys *eyed* the toys on the floor.
    Their *eyes* were wide open.
2   The temperature in the room was *cool* and pleasant.
    The man's expression was *cool* and unfriendly.
3   It is not often that we *cook* puddings.
    She is an excellent *cook*.
4   There was a hole in the shoe's *sole*.
    I love fish in general, but I don't like *sole*.
5   The ball hit him on the *head*.
    She is the *head* of the department.

The third type of activity proposed here is more complex, since it involves motivation for self-study. One of the most usual activities that language students engage in is undoubtedly writing compositions, and one of the teacher's most usual activities is correcting them. Our proposal is that the teacher may want to try to correct one of these compositions in a different way. Instead of crossing out a wrong expression and writing the correct one beside it, the teacher may just underline the mistaken expression, and perhaps point out the type of mistake (spelling, meaning, grammar). The students will then be asked to correct their own mistakes with the help of a dictionary or several dictionaries. The teacher's task will be to assist them when they meet difficulties and to make sure that the corrections are correct! The aim of this activity is to show students how much useful information they can find in dictionaries, and how helpful dictionaries are as aids to independent study.

Conclusion

Emphasis must be laid on teaching the student the use of as many different types of dictionaries as possible, since 'a bilingual dictionary presupposes a different competence from that needed to consult a monolingual learner's dictionary, just as a non-alphabetical dictionary' (Herbst and Stein, 1987: 115). This is why the above activities must be carried out simultaneously with as many different types of dictionary as possible.

In the end, good dictionary users will become better language learners. What is more, a language user must master reference skills before he/she can be said to be proficient in a language. Herbst (Herbst and Stein, 1987: 127) underlines that 'for foreign learners competence in dictionary use is part of their wider competence as speakers, readers or writers of the foreign language.'

Dictionary skills are only a part of the more general reference skills, which are not exclusive to language learning. We live in a society where information is power, yet citizens are seldom taught how to extract information from their reference books. The problem is even greater if we consider information technology. Teaching where and how to find information, and how to process it is a task that must be undertaken by the educational system.

Note

1   *Language learning* implies the existence of a source language (the learners' first language) and a target language (the language they are learning). *Language base* refers to the language they are working on in a specific activity. *Directionality* makes reference to whether they are working from source language into target language or vice versa.

References

Bejoint, H. (1981) 'The Foreign Student's Use of the Monolingual English Dictionaries: A Study of Language Needs and Reference Skills', in *Applied Linguistics II* 5: 207–222.

Bejoint, H. (1988) 'Psycholinguistic Evidence and the Use of Dictionaries by L2 learners', in M. Snell-Hornby (ed.) *Zürilex '86 Proceedings*. Tübingen: A. Francke.

Bejoint, H. (1989) 'The Teaching of Dictionary Use', in F. J. Hausmann *et al.* (eds) *Wörterbücher/Dictionaries/Dictionnaires*, Vol. I. Berlin/New York: de Gruyter.

Bejoint, H. and Moulin, A. (1987) 'The Place of the Dictionary in an EFL Programme', in A. Cowie (ed.) *The Dictionary and the Language Learner*. Tübingen: Niemeyer.

Cowie, A. (ed.) (1987) *The Dictionary and the Language Learner*. Tübingen: Niemeyer.

Hartmann, R. R. K. (1989) 'The Dictionary as an Aid to Foreign Language Teaching', in F. J. Hausmann *et al.* (eds) *Wörterbücher/Dictionaries/Dictionnaires*, Vol. I. Berlin/New York: de Gruyter.

Herbst, T. (1990) 'Dictionaries for Foreign Language Teaching: English', in F. J. Hausmann *et al.* (eds) *Wörterbücher/Dictionaries/Dictionnaires*, Vol. II. Berlin/New York: de Gruyter.

Herbst, T. and Stein, G. (1987) 'Dictionary-using Skills: A Plea for a New Orientation in Language Learning', in A. Cowie (ed.) *The Dictionary and the Language Learner*. Tübingen: Niemeyer.

Householder, F. and Saporta, S. (eds) (1975) *Problems in Lexicography*. Bloomington: Indiana UP.

Kipfer, B. (1987) 'Dictionaries and the Intermediate Student: Communicative Needs and the Development of User Reference Skills', in A. Cowie (ed.) *The Dictionary and the Language Learner*. Tübingen: Niemeyer.

Malkiel, Y. (1975) 'A Typological Classification of Dictionaries on the Basis of Distinctive Features', in F. Householder and S. Saporta (eds) *Problems in Lexicography*. Bloomington: Indiana UP.

Rundell, M. (1988) 'Changing the Rules: Why the Monolingual Learner's Dictionary should Move away from the Native-Speaker Tradition', in M. Snell-Hornby (ed.) *Zürilex '86 Proceedings*. Tübingen: Francke.

Snell-Hornby, M. (ed.) (1988) *Zürilex '86 Proceedings*. Tübingen: Francke.

Zöfgen, E. (1991) 'Bilingual Learner's Dictionaries', in F. J. Hausmann *et al.* (eds) *Wörterbücher/ Dictionaries/Dictionnaires*, Vol. III. Berlin/New York: de Gruyter.

Further reading

Cowie, A. (1984) 'EFL Dictionaries: Past Achievements and Present Needs', in R. R. K. Hartmann (ed.) *Lexeter '83 Proceedings*. Tübingen: Niemeyer.

Hartmann, R. R. K. (ed.) (1984) *Lexeter '83 Proceedings*, Tübingen: Niemeyer.

Hatherall, G. (1984) 'Studying Dictionary Use: Some Findings and Proposals', in R. R. K. Hartmann (ed.) *Lexeter '83 Proceedings*. Tübingen: Niemeyer.

Hausmann, F. J. *et al.* (eds) (1989–1991) *Wörterbücher/Dictionaries/Dictionnaires. Ein Internationales Handbuch zur Lexikographie. International Encyclopaedia of Lexicography. Encyclopédie Internationale de Lexicographie*, Berlin/New York: W. de Gruyter.

Magay, T. (1988) 'On some Problems of the Bilingual Learner's Dictionary', in M. Snell-Hornby (ed.) *Zürilex '86 Proceedings*. Tübingen: A. Francke.

12

LEXICAL HIERARCHIES AS A STRATEGY OF TEACHING VOCABULARY

Catalina Jiménez Hurtado

Introduction

For many years, vocabulary was not given the recognition and attention it deserved in the foreign language classroom. This was undoubtedly related to the fact that in linguistic theory, the lexicon was mainly considered to be a list of irregularities unable to be explained by syntax. In the last decade, however, the lexicon has come to have an increasingly prominent role in linguistics and, not surprisingly, greater emphasis has also been placed on vocabulary in foreign language teaching.

One of the paradoxes in vocabulary teaching in the FL classroom is that despite the amount of time devoted to explaining and defining words, vocabulary is rarely presented to students in a systematic way. If students are lucky, they are given a context in which the word can be inserted, but this is often not the case, and such examples are invariably a source of confusion.

Our objective in this chapter is to offer a coherent form of lexical organization and presentation which will help students to understand vocabulary better. In order to introduce a maximum of relevant information, words are presented in terms of how they are related to other words with a similar meaning.

The importance of vocabulary in language learning cannot be overstressed, if only because of the fact that foreign language learners believe that knowledge of words is essential. In other words, the lack of lexical competence gives them a feeling of insecurity and eventually leads to the breakdown in communication, something which can be avoided if words are explained to students in a structured way. An example of this type of structure is given in Table 12.1. This is in line with what Morgan and Rinvolucri (1989: 5) mean when they write: 'We conceive of vocabulary learning as a relational process; it could be described as *making friends with the words of the target language*.' All the examples and exercises in this chapter have been used in the teaching of

Table 12.1 Hierarchical organization

(a) German

> fühlen mit den Sinnen oder mit der Psyche fühlen.
> empfinden etwas ganz bestimmtes fühlen.
> mögen etwas positiv empfinden.
> lieben intensiv mögen.
> liebhaben (infantil) lieben (restriktiver Gebrauch).
> liebgewinnen anfangen etwas lieb zu haben.
> schwärmen für vorübergehend, meist in der Pubertät lieben.
> anhimmeln unverhohlen für jemanden schwärmen.

(b) Spanish

> sentir experimentar cualquier tipo de sentimiento.
> gustar sentir un sentimiento positivo.
> querer sentir amor en general por alguien.
> estimar sentir afecto por alguien.
> apreciar estimar a alguien por sus cualidades.

German to students whose native language was Spanish.

This way of organizing words and their meanings for use in the FL classroom can help teachers to present vocabulary in such a way that students understand its meaning better. To this end, the vocabulary items to be taught must be carefully selected. Rather than using frequency as a criterion for selection, we have chosen the words within each area of meaning which best highlight the different lexical relations. This is the result of findings in psycholinguistic research on first and second language acquisition, and more concretely on the way people store information in their memory (Aitchison, 1987; Levin and Pinker, 1991).

Such research can be of great use to FL teachers and can enable them to be more creative in classroom procedures. On the one hand, vocabulary exercises based on lexical structure are a vast improvement over long lists of miscellaneous vocabulary items, and, on the other, vocabulary presented in such a way enhances its memorability.

The organization of vocabulary

It is generally agreed that words are not stored in our minds in a random way. Psycholinguistic experiments of association and retrieval show that our mental lexicon is organized in terms of meaning relationships. In other words, our mental dictionaries are organized more along the lines of a thesaurus than a traditional alphabetical dictionary.

We[1] have organized vocabulary in lexical fields based on definitional similarity. A lexical field is thus defined as the set of words whose definitions all have the same nuclear term. The inventory of the lexical units belonging to each field was determined by consulting both German dictionaries (*Duden* and *Wahrig*) and Spanish dictionaries (*María Moliner* and *M. Alvar*) and analysing the definitions in both languages.

Once the basic semantic information in each definition was established, encyclopaedic information was also inserted, as can been seen in the example of the paradigm of the verbs of *eating* in German and Spanish given in Table 12.2.

Table 12.2 Paradigm of the verbs of *eating*

(a) German

> **zu sich nehmen** dem eigenen Körper zuführen.
> **essen** feste Nahrung zu sich nehmen.
> **speisen** *in kultiviertem Rahmen* essen.
> **verzehren** Nahrung zu sich nehmen (*auch Fachsprache*). *Oft im Gaststättengewerbe, wo das Essen und Trinken bezahlt wird.*
> **konsumieren** Konsumgüter verzehren.
> **genießen** *mit Genuß* verzehren.
> **schlemmen** *sehr gutes Essen* genießen (*gute Qualität, gemütliche Atmosphäre*).
> **schmausen** *in angenehmer Atmosphäre ausgiebig* schlemmen. (± *Gemütlichkeit*).
> **schlecken** süße, breiartige Speisen genießen.

(b) Spanish

> **comer** ingerir alimentos sólidos.
> **banquetear** comer mucho y bien, como en un banquete. Darse un banquete.
> **zahorar** comer, generalmente mucho, con amigos en un ambiente agradable.
> **hartarse** comer generalmente *mucho hasta saciarse*.
> **hincharse** hartarse hasta sentirse *excesivamente lleno*.
> **atiparse** hincharse. Catalanismo. Costa Rica.
> **atiborrarse** hincharse generalmente de alimentos poco adecuados, *sin sustancia*.
> **atracarse** hincharse rápidamente hasta no poder seguir comiendo por *impedimentos físicos*.
> **engullir** comer rápidamente *sin apenas masticarlo*.
> **devorar** engullir como los animales.

This paradigm also includes the different contexts in which these words can appear, as is evident in the underlined parts of each definition. These contexts are of two main types: intralinguistic (e.g. *Fachsprache, salopp, lokal*) and extralinguistic (e.g. *in angenehmer Atmosphäre*; *oft im Gaststättengewerbe, wo das Essen und Trinken bezahlt wird*; *gute Qualität, gemütliche Atmosphäre*).

We have applied this model to the basic vocabulary in English, German and Spanish, comparing the three languages and analysing the cross-cultural validity of the superordinate terms in each field.

Table 12.3 is an example of an extract of a lexical field. In the FL classroom, words with related meanings are presented in this way. In a brain-storming session, the teacher asks students to extract all the information they can draw

Table 12.3 Extract of a lexical field

(a) German

> **sprechen** Wörter einer Sprache hervorbringen.
>   **stammeln** stockend sprechen; z.B. vor Aufregung.
>   **stottern** immer stammeln aufgrund eines Sprachdefektes.
>   **radebrechen** eine Sprache nur sehr schlecht, mühsam und unvollkommen sprechen.
>   **lispeln** mit Zischlaut und fehlerhaft mit der Zunge an die oberen Vorderzähne stoßend sprechen.
>   **näseln** durch die Nase sprechen.
>   **krächzen** heiser sprechen. (Metapher: wie ein Rabe sprechen.)

(b) English

> **stutter** to speak with difficulty (with short stops one cannot control).
> **stammer** to speak with difficulty (hesitating and repeating sounds and words).
> **lisp** to speak with difficulty (using 's' sounds which are not clear).

(c) Spanish

> **balbucir** hablar algo vacilando y con pronunciación entrecortada.
> **chapurrear** hablar mal o con dificultad un idioma.
> **balbucear** hablar imperfectamente como los niños.
> **mascullar** hablar sin pronunciar distintivamente como titubeando o gruñendo.
> **tartamudear** hablar con dificultad repitiendo los sonidos.
> **trabarse** hablar con dificultad por confusión de ideas.

from this paradigm. Students, with appropiate guidance from the teacher, should then be able to deduce that all these verbs come from the lexical field of *speech* verbs, and that they all encode some type of difficulty or impediment that prevents the speaker from speaking clearly.[2]

Table 12.3 tells us that the nuclear word, *sprechen*, is the main part of the definition of all the other words in the group. The adverbial modification within the definitions shows us the differences between the words. In this particular hierarchy, *radebrechen* and *lispeln* are subordinates of *sprechen*; they, in turn, become the nuclear part of the definitions of other words at more specific levels of the hierarchy, like *stammeln* for *stottern*.

This is how students become aware of the differences between verbs in the same area of meaning, and are thus able to acquire a fuller understanding of each lexical item. When contrasting two languages, FL students should be made aware of the lack of equivalence, and in some cases, even approximate correspondence in different languages. That way they can see for themselves that in the majority of cases a one-to-one equivalence does not exist, and that meaning can only be conveyed through the adaptation of each language to a particular situation.

Applications for vocabulary teaching

This lexicological model applied to vocabulary teaching has four main objectives: (1) the elaboration of vocabulary exercises based on lexical hierarchies as the principal structural pattern in each lexical field; (2) increasing the students' awareness of the similarities and differences between different languages; (3) showing students that each language lexicalizes its own cultural values, thus imposing different types of norms on its speakers; (4) the enhancement of the students' ability to understand how words are systematically interrelated through different types of meaning relations.

Consequently students should be taught how to compare words, concepts and even possible worlds creatively. In this way, students also learn how to use dictionaries more effectively and critically. Although there is no doubt that learners' dictionaries help to a certain extent, foreign language students must be encouraged to go beyond them in order to learn how mind, values and culture are encoded in language.

What language teachers should be aware of

It is the task of foreign language teachers to foment curiosity about language in general, and more specifically about the two languages under examination in the specific teaching context. This means looking at language as a means of communication and interpretation of experience in a particular context, dependent on a specific frame and contingent upon an observer's perspective (Givón, 1989: xvii).

180

Through the study of vocabulary, the students come to realize the truth of Wittgenstein's maxim that 'to imagine a language is to imagine a form of life' (Wittgenstein, 1953/1988: 8). The following contrast set of verbs of *change* in Spanish and German is a relevant example. Because change is one of the most basic domains in the lexicon, one might suppose that its structure is almost identical in both languages. However, a look at the paradigms in Spanish and German shows us that this is not so. Spanish students learning German as a foreign language can look at Table 12.4 and see the differences in the lexicalization of *change* in both languages. This brings home the fact that different languages make different distinctions in the construction of reality.

The existence of a gap in the chart means the language has no words to cover that particular semantic area. The study of lexical items in contrastive hierarchies leads to greater awareness on the part of the students of the behaviour and norms within a language community. Students thus become aware of language differences, and again, whenever they try to establish a one-to-one equivalence between lexemes, they will find that it is almost impossible because of the different norms and perceptions shared by people belonging to different societies.

How to teach cultural and/or pragmatic information

Pragmatic information is socio-cultural information, positive/negative evaluation, as well as usage. It encodes the cultural context of each lexical item, the knowledge of which enables students to know when and how to use words correctly.

Certain types of pragmatic information are specific to a certain area of meaning, while others are present throughout the lexicon. For example, in verbs of *eating*, apart from certain types of differences present throughout language, such as stylistic variants (*salopp*), words encoding negative/positive evaluation (*negative Bewertung*), etc., there are certain differences which are present because of the type of meaning expressed. For instance, 'manner of movement', 'quality of food' and 'social setting' are particularly relevant in the elaboration of cross-linguistic studies (Vilar Sánchez and Jiménez Hurtado, 1993). In Table 12.5, 'manner of the movement' as well as 'quantity of food' are determining factors in establishing differences between different verbs. In fact, in reference to the activity of eating there are important cultural differences between Spanish and German, and these appear codified in the lexical paradigm.

When first presented with these verbs in contrastive field structure, students are inevitably struck by the fact that in German there are a number of positively evaluated verbs indicating 'to eat a lot and very well'. In contrast, there are many verbs in Spanish whose meaning indicates that eating a lot is socially unacceptable.

Table 12.4 Differences in the lexicalization of change in Spanish and German

CAMBIO: llegar a ser. **hacerse** llegar a ser [proceso].	*VERÄNDERUNG*: werden. **werden** in einen best. Zustand kommen.

cambiar llegar a ser de otra manera
[proceso].
   convertirse en cambiar
   totalmente [foco resultado].
   transformarse cambiar totalmente
   [foco proceso].
	sich (ver)ändern anders werden.
	   sich verwandeln sich total
	   verändern.

crecer hacerse más *grande*, intenso,
numeroso.
aumentar hacerse más prot. en *intensidad*
o volumen.
   ampliarse crecer prot. en *volumen*.
     extenderse crecer prot. de forma
     horizontal.
	wachsen größer werden.
	zunehmen größer oder mehr werden.
	   sich ausbreiten flächenmäßig
	   wachsen.
	     sich breitmachen sich
	     ausbreiten (meist neg).
	   sich ausdehnen in alle Richtungen
	   wachsen.
	   sich ausweiten wachsen (Krieg,
	   Unruhen).

alargarse crecer en longitud.
   prolongarse crecer prot. en el
   tiempo.
   desarrollarse crecer prot. en
   calidad tamaño.
	sich verlängern länger werden (meist
	temporal).
	sich entwickeln stufenweise größer
	oder perfekter werden.
	   sich entfalten sich voll entwickeln.
	   sich weiterentwickeln sich zu einer
	   höheren Stufe entwickeln.
	     sich fortentwickeln sich
	     weiterentwickeln (pos).

multiplicarse crecer en número.
HACERSE MENOS O MENOR
decrecer ser menos en tamaño,
cantidad, intensidad o importancia.
	sich vermehren mehr werden.
	WENIGER ODER KLEINER WERDEN
	sich verringern weniger werden (meist
	+ abstr).
	   sich reduzieren sich verringern
	   (geh).

aminorar decrecer en intensidad.
   disminuir decrecer prot. en
   número.
   menguar decrecer en tamaño.
   reducirse cantidad y número.
   adelgazar ser menos en peso.
   mermar decrecer en tamaño y
   cantidad.
   empequeñecerse ser menos en
   altura.
   desfallecer decrecer en fuerzas una
   persona.
	abnehmen weniger, leichter werden.
	
	sich verkleinern kleiner werden.
	
	verkümmern stufenweise kleiner
	und/oder minderwertiger werden (neg).

182

Within this approach to lexical pragmatics, the extralinguistic information that a lexical item contains is systematized in the following way:

- Information about the positive or negative evaluation of the action.
- Deviation from the established norm: for example, in Spanish the action of *eating a lot* is negatively evaluated as can be seen in lexemes such as *zamparse*, *atiborrarse* and *atracarse*.

Table 12.5 Differences between different verbs

(a) Spanish and German compared

comer ingerir alimentos sólidos.	**essen** feste Nahrung zu sich nehmen.
tragar comer mucho *vulgar*.	
	schlingen viel und unzerkaut essen. (*neg.*)
	fressen viel und *unkultiviert* essen. (*unästhetisch, neg.*)
	mümmeln mit schnellen Bewegungen, mit den Vorderzähnen fressen (*Hasen, Kaninchen*).
	äsen fressen (beim Wild; *Jägersprache*).
hartarse comer generalmente *mucho hasta saciarse*.	**futtern** (viel) essen (*salopp*).
hincharse hartarse hasta sentirse *excesivamente lleno*.	**reinhauen** mit Appetit futtern. (salopp, neg.)
atiparse hincharse.	**spachteln** reinhauen (lokal, neg.)
atiborrarse hincharse de alimentos *sin sustancia*.	**sich vollstopfen** zu viel futtern. (*unästhetisch,neg.*)
atracarse hincharse rápidamente.	**sich vollpfropfen** sich *über die Maßen* vollstopfen.
empacharse atracarse hasta enfermar.	
glotonear comer mucho con ansia.	
cebarse comer mucho hasta *engordar* excesivamente.	
	verzehren Nahrung zu sich nehmen (auch Fachsprache) (tr.).
	konsumieren Konsumgüter verzehren.
	genießen mit Genuß verzehren.
banquetear comer mucho y bien, como en un banquete.	**schlemmen** sehr gutes Essen genießen.
zahorar comer mucho con amigos, en un ambiente agradable.	**schmausen** in angenehmer Atmosphäre ausgiebig schlemmen.
	schlecken süße, breiartige Speisen genießen.

Table 12.5 continued

(b) English

eat to take in solid food for nourishment.
 eat up to eat more of something or more quickly in order to finish.
  dispatch to eat up very quickly.
 overeat to eat more than one needs or is healthy.
 feed on
  browse (of cows, goats) feed on plants.
 swallow eat very quickly without chewing.
  get down (informal) to swallow food with difficulty, usu. unwillingly.
  bolt (down) to swallow food quickly.
 tuck in (informal) to eat with pleasure.
 tuck away (informal) to eat too much.
 scoff to eat quickly and greedily.
 wolf down to eat quickly and esp. greedily as if you were an animal /like a wolf.
 devour to eat something quickly and with great eagerness.
  gormandize to eat greedily for pleasure, devour like a glutton.
 gobble (up) eat a lot greedily, noisily, and very quickly.

- Contextual information: this information specifies the type of situation in which the action takes place.
- Cultural information: this information is specific to the type of society which sanctions the action in question.
- Intention of the speaker: as we can see in Table 12.6, the meanings of each verb are almost the same. The only difference between them lies in the pragmatic component (i.e. the kind of speech act they codify). *Losziehen gegen jdn* codifies trying to hurt and humiliate somebody, whereas *herziehen über jdn* codifies the speech act of making somebody feel ashamed.
- Text-type in which the verb is most likely to be found.

It is interesting for students to realize that whenever a speaker chooses a lexeme as part of the message he wishes to send it is a choice which, apart from the message content, also transmits the speaker's *intentions, evaluation* of the context of the situation, as well as his *cultural world view*.

Whenever students are faced with different verbs belonging to a certain lexical field, they have to know why they choose one term instead of another, and they also have to reason their decision, taking into account the context and communicative situation. This use will no doubt reflect the norms created by the language community, norms which echo its assumptions of reality. By this, we mean how people lexicalize the impact that the external world has on their processing of information as well as how they interact with other people.

Table 12.6 German

---

losziehen gegen jdn hemmungslos ausschimpfen.
(To scold somebody trying to *hurt* and *humiliate* him.)
herziehen über jdn hemmungslos ausschimpfen.
(To scold somebody *making him feel ashamed*.)
heruntermachen bis zur Erniedrigung ausschimpfen.
(To scold somebody from a position of physical and psychological power. From a cognitive point of view the speaker has a higher position and wants to make the addressee feel his inferiority.)
   herunterkanzeln von oben herab heruntermachen.
   (To scold somebody from a position of physical and psychological power as if the speaker were in a pulpit.)

Vocabulary activities

In this section, we shall present different kinds of vocabulary exercises based on the organization of verbs in structured lexical hierarchies.

Exercise 1

Explain the following table in your own language and how it compares with the language you are learning. Classify the following words in terms of their connotation.

Übung 1
Erklären Sie den Aufbau der folgenden Wortgruppen und vergleichen Sie sie mit der deutschen!

Negative	Neutral			Positive	
cebarse tragar hartarse	*comer*	amamantar	degustar	repapilar	banquetear
devorar engullir soplarse	picar	saborear		paladear tapear	
atestarse atiborrarse	sustentar	paladear		zahorar	
atizarse atracarse				golosinear	
glotonear zamparse					

185

Negative	Neutral	Positive
schlingen	schlucken	genießen
fressen	essen	schlemmen
mümmeln	verzehren	schmausen
mampfen	löffeln	kosten
schmatzen	trinken	schlecken

Exercise 2

Explain the difference between these verbs. What situation would you use them in?

I

probieren	den Geschmack prüfen, bevor man etwas verzehrt.
kosten	etwas Eßbares oder Trinkbares probieren.
speisen	in kultiviertem Rahmen essen.
konsumieren	Kosumgüter verzehren.
schlemmen	sehr gutes Essen genießen.
schmausen	in angenehmer Atmosphäre ausgiebig schlemmen.
ernähren	mit Nahrung versorgen.
füttern	ein Tier/Kind/Kranken ernähren.

II

reden viel sprechen.
　quatschen Unsinn reden; vulg.
　daherreden ohne Überlegung reden.
　　labern dumm daherreden; modern.
　　faseln dumm daherreden.
　　plappern viel und schnell naiv daherreden.
　schwatzen reden, salopp.

Exercise 3

Compare the following table, indicating differences and similarities in both languages. Which verbs correspond to each other?
Example:　endiosar / vergöttern.
　　　　　amar / lieben.

SENTIR (ESPAÑOL)	FÜHLEN (DEUTSCH)
enamorarse empezar a sentir amor.	**mögen** etwas positiv empfinden
encapricharse enamorarse de forma poco razonable de algo o alguien.	**lieben** intensiv mögen (meist eine Person) (restriktiver Gebrauch).
encandilarse enamorarse y expresarlo a través de la mirada con ojos brillantes.	**liebhaben** (infantil) lieben.
apasionarse sentir pasión por algo o alguien.	**schwärmen für** vorübergehend, meist in der Pubertät lieben.
querer sentir la tendencia a la posesión de algo.	**stehen auf** (Jugendsprache) lieben.
desear sentir apetito sexual hacia alguien.	**vergöttern** (met.) intensiv anbeten.
obsesionarse desear intensamente algo sin poderlo apartar de su mente.	**verlieben (sich)** anfangen, eine meist andersgeschlechtliche Person zu lieben.
amar sentir amor, enamoramiento.	**verknallen (sich)** (salopp) sich verlieben.
adorar amar profundamente.	**schätzen** rational mögen.
endiosar amar a una persona como si fuese un dios.	

Conclusion

Vocabulary teaching has come a long way in recent years and is no longer the Cinderella of the FL classroom. However, for words to be learned effectively, they must be placed within a meaningful context. Such a context must be psychologically adequate and reflect the idea of the lexicon as a structured whole divided into lexical fields, the elements of which are interconnected by a rich network of relations.

To this end, lexical sets of contrastive meaning hierarchies are particularly useful as a basis for the elaboration of vocabulary exercises. Such hierarchies include many different types of information within the definitional structure of lexemes, the study of which necessarily enhances students' awareness of the close relation between cognition, language and culture.

Notes

1   The members of the research group of the Department of Translation and Interpreting
    at the University of Granada (Spain).
2   As an example, this is of course only a section of the whole lexical field.

References

Aitchison, J. (1987) *Words in the Mind: An Introduction to the Mental Lexicon*, Oxford: Basil
    Blackwell.
Givón, T. (1989) *Mind, Code and Context. Essays in Pragmatics*, Hillsdale, NJ: Lawrence
    Erlbaum.
Jiménez Hurtado, C. and Vilar-Sánchez, K. (1993) 'Los rasgos pragmáticos en los diccionarios
    bilingües español-alemán. Una propuesta contrastiva sistematizada en los verbos de
    alimentación', in J. Fernández (ed.) *I" Conferencia Internacional de Lingüística Aplicada*,
    Granada: Centro de Publicaciones de la Universidad de Granada.
Levin, B. and Pinker, St (eds) (1991) *Lexical and Conceptual Semantics*, Cambridge, MA. and
    Oxford: Basil Blackwell.
Morgan, J. and Rinvolucri, M. (1989) *Vocabulary* (4th edn), Oxford: Oxford University Press.
Wittgenstein, L. (1953/1988) *Investigaciones Filosóficas.*, Barcelona: Editorial Crítica.

Further reading

Coseriu, E. (1977) *Principios de Semántica Estructural*, Madrid: Gredos.
Dik, S. C. (1989) *The Theory of Functional Grammar*, Dordrecht: Foris Publication.
Faber, P. (1994) 'The Semantic Architecture of the Lexicon', in K. Hyldgaard-Jensen and V.
    H. Pedersen (eds) *Symposium on Lexicography VI. Proceedings of the Sixth International
    Symposium on Lexicography May 7–9, 1992 at the University of Copenhagen. Lexicographica. Series
    Maior.* Tübingen: Niemeyer.
Faber, P. and Pérez, Ch. (1993) 'Image Schemata and Light: A Study of Contrastive Lexical
    Domains in English and Spanish', in *Atlantis XV* 1–2, May–November 1993:
    117–134.
Felices-Lago, A. M. (1991) *El componente axiológico en el lenguaje. Su configuración en los adjetivos
    que expresan emociones y conducta en la lengua inglesa*, Granada: Centro de Publicaciones de la
    Universidad de Granada.
Jiménez Hurtado, C. (1994) 'The Integration of Pragmatic Information in Lexical Entries:
    A Programmatic Proposal', in K. Hyldgaard-Jensen and V. H. Pedersen (eds) *Symposium
    on Lexicography VI. Proceedings of the Sixth International Symposium on Lexicography May
    7–9, 1992 at the University of Copenhagen. Lexicographica. Series Maior.* Tübingen:
    Niemeyer.
Levinson, St C. (1983) *Pragmatics*, Cambridge: Cambridge University Press.
Mairal-Usón, R. (1993) 'Complementation Patterns of Cognitive, Physical Perception and
    Speech Act Verbs in the English Language. A Functional-Cognitive Approach', unpub-
    lished Ph.D. thesis, Universidad de Zaragoza.
Martín-Mingorance, L. (1984) 'Lexical Fields and Stepwise Lexical Decomposition in a
    Contrastive English-Spanish Verb Valency Dictionary', in R. R. K. Hartmann (ed.)
    Proceedings from the International Conference on Lexicography Vol. II, Tübingen: Niemeyer.

Martín-Mingorance, L. (1987) 'Classematics in a Functional-Lexematic Grammar of English', in *Actas del X Congreso Nacional de la A.E.D.E.A.N.*, Zaragoza: AEDEAN.

Martín-Mingorance, L. (1990) 'Functional Grammar and Lexematics in Lexicography', in J. Tomaszcyk and B. Lewandowska Tomaszscyk (eds) *Meaning and Lexicography.* Amsterdam: John Benjamins.

Martín-Mingorance, L. (1995) 'Lexical Logic and Structural Semantics', in U. Hoinkes (ed.) *Panorama der lexikalischen Semantik*, Tübingen: Gunter Narr Verlag.

13

'LET'S TAKE THE BULL BY THE HORNS!'

Phraseology in modern language teaching

Wolf Gewehr

Introduction

Phraseology is without a doubt a widely neglected area in foreign language teaching and most certainly deserves closer attention. Imagine that a teacher of English as a foreign language is greeting his students with the following remarks:

'Good morning, class!

Believe it or not: I have been up with the lark this morning. But I can see that obviously all of us are early birds and busy bees. Whether we are poor as a church mouse or whether we were born with a silver spoon in our mouth, when it comes to learning a foreign language, we are all in the same boat.

Although some of you may already smell a rat, this is not a rat race, believe me! And those of you who might think I could possibly be a wolf in sheep's clothing, I assure you that I will not monkey around, but rather talk turkey with you. That's cold turkey indeed.

What's really bugging me at the moment is that I have so many experts around me that I am afraid I may behave like a bull in a china shop. Who among you does not know that strange feeling like having butterflies in your stomach. But after all, we all have some common interest, or as the true Brits are used to saying: "Birds of a feather flock together."

Just ask Lindsay as she is from England – then you will get it straight from the horse's mouth! And trust me: we are not talking about the Trojan Horse in this context! Come on: let's not change horses in mid-stream, let's not go on a wild goose chase, let us not chicken out . . . oh no! – Let's rather take the bull by the horns!'

Although we should not put all our eggs in one basket, it can be easily visualized that the English language is full of idiomatic phrases from the animal farm alone, and there cannot be any doubt that this is very similarly the case with all European languages and most certainly with German, Spanish and also Modern Greek.

Of course, in natural speech nobody would use such massive clusters of idiomatic expressions as that language teacher did just for demonstration.[1] As a matter of fact, in the academic world it is often considered bad style to use idiomatic phrases in writing, although metaphorical language is largely used in scientific texts as well as in fiction. Although idioms and idiomatic phrases are not necessarily identical with metaphors, they certainly have some similarity, because they all use images for expressing the semantic content. Josef Fliegner suggests the following diagram which shows how lexical or phrasal idioms, even certain texts, are related to the term 'metaphor' (cf. Abraham, 1975; Emig, 1972; Guenthner, 1975).

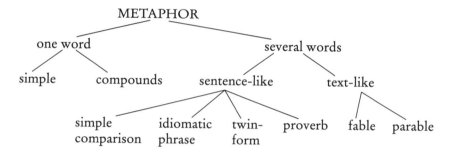

An example of a one-word metaphor is *head* as in a letter (letterhead) or *chicken* (coward). A compound metaphor would be *guinea-pig* or *scapegoat*. A simple comparison for a sentence-like metaphor or idiomatic phrase would be: *He is a nervous wreck* or *He is as cool as a cucumber*. A twin-form or a word-pair would be something like *sooner or later*. A proverb is more stable than an idiomatic phrase. For instance, a proverb is *Birds of a feather flock together*, while a phrasal idiom or an idiomatic phrase would be *That is a feather in his cap* which can be modified according to the person it refers to, for example: 'Finally, the French Prime Minister ended the nuclear tests. 'Le Monde' considers this another *feather in his cap*.'

In recent years, linguists or rather phraseologists have put a lot of effort into research of this widely neglected territory. A number of workshops and conferences on this subject have recently stimulated considerable interest on the part of Western lexicologists, while for Soviet linguists (and consequently for linguists in the former GDR) phraseology has always been considered a part of lexicology (cf. Häusermann, 1977; Klappenbach, 1968; Fleischer,

1982; Wotjak, 1992). In this chapter, however, we are not concerned with any semantic or structural approach to phraseology. Rather we try to determine whether idioms or idiomatic phrases should be part of foreign language teaching and, if so, how they can be taught and to what purpose. After all, even Johann Christoph Gottsched (1700–1766) pointed out the necessity of considering idiomatic phrases in language teaching and that purely grammatical knowledge is insufficient (cf. Palm, 1995: 108).

If we follow the distinction between *langue* and *parole* of Ferdinand de Saussure, phraseology is certainly a field that is more closely affiliated with the use of language (*parole*) than with the language system (*langue*). In his *Traité de stilistique Française*, Charles Bally (1909) differentiated between *séries phraséologiques* (stable word groups without idiomaticity) and *unités phraséologiques* (stable word groups with idiomaticity). Ludwig Wittgenstein defines the meaning of a word as its use in spoken or written language, and this definition can certainly be applied to idiomatic phrases. Harald Burger calls idiomatic phrases that cannot simply be explained by regular syntactic and semantic rules, 'idiosyncratic word chains' (Burger, 1973: 3) which may vary more or less from one language to the other. For instance, a French speaker will have no problem in understanding the meaning of the German idiom *mit den Wölfen heulen*, because it corresponds literally with the French idiom *hurler avec les loups*, while 'to howl with the wolves' is obviously not an English idiom, although a native speaker may still understand its meaning.

Metaphorical use of idioms

Idiomatic phrases have much in common with metaphors. In his treatise *Poetics*, Aristotle uses the expression 'metaphor' (derived from the verb meta-phérein = to transfer) when referring to samples taken from Homer's *Ulysses* as well as from some tragedies by Empedocles. He specifically mentions samples such as the following: *This ship is standing still, does not move any more, has anchored*, all of which refer to someone old whose life is no longer active. Interestingly enough, our modern economic terminology still makes use of such naval imagery as can be seen from the cover of a German magazine recently issued by the International Chamber of Commerce (Figure 13.1).

In Roman times, Cicero conceived the metaphor as a concept type of comparison where the so-called *tertium comparationis* points to the semantic crux. Quintilian even went so far as to say everything is basically metaphorical. If you think he exaggerated, let us examine the meaning of 'to exaggerate'. This English verb can be traced back to Latin *ex aggero* (*esse*) = lit. 'to be beyond the city mound', meaning to have surpassed certain limits, to have left a safely protected area. In fact, many words are conventionalized original metaphors.

192

Some characteristics of idiomatic phrases

Idiomatic phrases in the strict sense differ from any other utterances, particularly in three aspects:

1 Their verbal elements cannot be altered;
2 The position of the verbal elements is stable;
3 They use an image which is compared to a certain situation in real life.

Let us consider the following example: *An early bird catches the worm.* Certain verbal elements in this utterance can be changed, for instance:

Figure 13.1

- A morning bird catches the worm.
- An early sparrow catches the worm.
- An early bird snatches the worm.
- An early bird catches the fly, etc.

These sentences are still recognizable as a somewhat distorted idiomatic phrase, but they will not be accepted by any native speaker. If you change the position of the verbal elements, the proposition remains still the same, but the idiomatic character of the phrase is totally lost:

- The worm is caught by an early bird.
- Does an early bird catch the worm?
- A bird that gets up early catches the worm.

The image of an early bird catching a worm can be easily identified with a real situation in a human life. Someone who gets up early can get more things accomplished. Let us assume you are going to the airport two hours prior to the plane's departure; you will have a good chance of getting a window or aisle seat, while late-comers have to settle for the uncomfortable middle seats.

As is well known, the Bible is full of ornamental metaphors and idioms. The *Proverbs* of King Solomon for instance is a large collection of words of wisdom, some of which are still used nowadays, although many have not survived. This is unfortunate, because they are really inimitable, like the following:

> Don't talk so much. Every time you open your mouth you put your
> foot in it. Be sensible and turn off the flow.
>
> (*Proverbs* 10, 19)

Chatterboxes can be tiresome when they never stop talking. The English idiomatic phrase *to put one's foot in it* may originally be derived from the biblical proverb, but its meaning has changed and indicates embarrassment.

> It is better to eat soup with someone you love than steak with
> someone you hate.
>
> (*Proverbs* 15, 17)

Who likes to eat well with someone they cannot stand? The appetite disappears immediately. This proverb can be applied to many real-life situations, for instance, when you are looking for a new job. If the social atmosphere is cold, even the most luxurious office can be a torture chamber. A good relationship with colleagues is worth more than anything else.

A faithful employee is as refreshing as a cool day in the hot summertime.

(Proverbs 25, 11)

Anyone who has had an attentive secretary or assistant knows what a relief it is if you can totally rely on such a person.

Be patient and you will finally win, for a soft tongue can break hard bones.

(Proverbs 25, 15)

This proverb matches the German saying *Steter Tropfen höhlt den Stein* ('Steady drops excavate the rock'), which can be found as early as in German medieval literature of the twelfth century, e.g. Hartmann von Aue (Zutt, 1968).

However, a metaphor is not necessarily an idiom. The question is: what is an idiom? The *Oxford English Dictionary* (OED) defines 'idiom' as 'the form of speech peculiar or proper to a people or country'; or as 'the specific character, property or genius of a language; the manner of expression which is natural or peculiar to it'. Finally, the OED gives the following definition:

A form of expression, grammatical construction, phrase, etc. peculiar to a language; a peculiarity of phraseology approved by the usage of a language, and often having a significance other than its grammatical or logical one.

One of the most convincing explanations is by Rosemarie Gläser (1986) who defines a phraseological unit as 'a lexicalized word-group which has syntactic and semantic stability and optionally an intensifying function in the text. . . . The idiom may be regarded as the prototype of the phraseological unit.' Fillmore *et al.* (1988) seem to share this point of view when they argue:

We think of a locution or manner of speaking as idiomatic if it is assigned an interpretation by the speech community but if somebody who merely knew the grammar and the vocabulary of the language could *not*, by virtue of that knowledge, know
(i) how to say it, or
(ii) what it means, or
(iii) whether it is a conventional thing to say.
Put differently, an idiomatic expression or construction is something a language user could fail to know while knowing everything else in the language.

In the past few years, numerous publications on phraseology have appeared; they underline the interest of linguists in this topic. However, didactic aspects of phraseology have rarely been discussed extensively. From the perspective of a foreign language teacher the area of phraseology could be very attractive, because any FL learner who can use idiomatic phrases in fitting situations is closer to a native speaker's competence than ever.[2] For example, in a somewhat shaky situation a non-native speaker may say:

1   Alright, John, let's not rock the boat; or
2   Alright, John, let sleeping dogs lie.

Such a person proves that he is familiar with the most sensitive parts of speech in the English language. However, it is impossible to change any of the elements of such idiomatic phrases without destroying the effect. It would therefore be incorrect to say:

3   *Alright, John, let's not *shake* the boat; or
4   *Alright, John, let's not rock the *car*; or
5   *Alright, John, let sleeping *cats* lie; or
6   *Alright, John, let *dozing* dogs lie.

Such utterances would no doubt be understood by a native speaker, but they would not be acceptable because (even if the meaning of the exchanged elements is almost identical with the genuine idiomatic phrase) a native speaker would never use such a phrase unless he/she wanted to make a joke.
    This can be easily demonstrated by using a German example. If I want to say:

7   Maria, you drive me nuts!

I cannot translate this idiomatic phrase literally into German, i.e.:

8   *Maria, du treibst mich Nüsse!

No German native speaker would have the slightest idea what this utterance might mean. On the other hand, it is unlikely that an English native speaker would understand what is meant by:

9   *You can drive me up the palm-tree with your nonsense-talk.

This is a literal (though unacceptable) translation of the German idiomatic phrase:

10   Du kannst mich auf die Palme bringen mit deinem dummen Geschwätz!

Let us briefly return to a sample which was mentioned before:

11 Listen, Charley, you behave *like a bull in a china shop*.

The imagery of this sample is perfectly clear in contrast to the English idiom:

12 *Shall we go Dutch?*

This suggests to everyone that they will have to pay for their own meal. This idiom can only be understood through experience, because its meaning is not clear. A bull, however, smashes everything in its path. In German, we find an almost identical idiomatic phrase for someone's clumsy behaviour, but instead of a *bull* it is an *elephant* that causes the destruction. However, the results, namely piles of broken china, are more or less the same.

Our cat Lissy is a quite remarkable creature. She is used to walking elegantly through piles of precious vases on our window-sills, but she has never broken a vase in her life. Of course, cats are not bulls or elephants, but if you think that the main character of a phraseological unit can be exchanged at random, this assumption is wrong. In other words, if you say the following, it is not necessarily understood to describe someone as being an over-cautious person:

13 *Listen, Charley, you behave like a *cat* in a china shop.

In this sense, we have to accept that the syntactic and semantic stability of an idiomatic phrase cannot be altered by exchanging or replacing any element.

Similarly, example 14 is almost identical in German, and yet there are slight differences, because literally translated the German version:

14 Alright, John, let sleeping dogs *lie*.

would be:

15 Alright, John, let's not *wake up* sleeping dogs.

Idiomatic equivalents in European languages

It would be interesting to find out from other European native speakers the following:

- What are the equivalents in their own native language?
- Do other languages have literal or almost literal equivalents for some or for most English idiomatic phrases?
- If not, how do other languages express respective situations? Do they use any idiomatic phrases? If so, are they completely different or do they deviate only partially from their respective English idioms?
- Are there any specific national traits that are reflected in the respective idiomatic phrases? If so, how can this be explained?

For instance, in German you say 'ein Sturm im Wasserglas' (*a storm in the water glass*), while characteristically the English say *a storm in a teacup*. Is this just a coincidence or a cultural difference?

It sometimes helps if we look further than our own backyard or, as a German idiomatic phrase puts it literally, 'if we look beyond the rim of our plate' (*wenn wir über unseren Tellerrand gucken*), in order to see whether speakers of non-European languages also use phraseological units. For an example of a Turkish idiom, see Figure 13.2. The metaphorical meaning is 'to kill someone by talking to him continuously'. Or if there is not a single soul in the street, the Turks use the idiomatic phrase given in Figure 13.3.

In an article that has recently been published, Makoto Itoh (1995) shows how some idiomatic expressions in Japanese are literally identical with German phraseological units, while others differ from them by using different analogies (Itoh, 1995). The following idiom is taken from the Bible. Thus it does not surprise us if we find more or less the same wording in most European languages – even in Japanese:

English	*an eye for an eye, a tooth for a tooth*
Japanese	*me niwa me wo, ha niwa ha wo* (me = eye; ha = tooth)
German	*Auge um Auge, Zahn um Zahn*
French	*oeil pour oeil, dent pour dent*
Greek	*ofthalmón andi ofthalmú ke odónda andi odóndos*
	(lit. eye for eye and tooth for tooth)
Spanish	*ojo por ojo, diente por diente*

Much more surprising is that an image such as fetching chestnuts out of the fire for someone is not only used in all five European languages, but also in Japanese:

English	*to fetch the chestnuts out of the fire for someone*
Japanese	*notameni katyuu no kuri wo hirou* (notameni = for someone; katyuu-no = out of the fire; kuri = chestnuts; hirou = to fetch)
German	*für jemand die Kastanien aus dem Feuer holen*
French	*sortir les marrones du feu*
Greek	*vjázo ta kástana apó ti fotcá*
	(lit. I take the chestnuts from the fire)
Spanish	*sacarle a alguien las castañas de fuego*

Complete analogies can be found in the following idiomatic phrase in English, Spanish and Japanese, while the German idiom uses a slightly different image:

198

Figure 13.2 Turkish: *Kafa utulemek* (lit. to iron someone's head)

Figure 13.3 Turkish: *In cin top oynuyov* (lit. the ghosts are playing ball)

English   *to kill two birds with one stone*
Japanese *isseki nityou*   (isseki = with one stone; nityou = two birds)
             (lit. to kill two birds with one stone)
Spanish   *matar dos pájaros con un tiro*
             (lit. to kill two birds with one throw)
German   *zwei Fliegen mit einer Klappe schlagen*
             (lit. to kill two flies with one swat)

In the following example the English and German images are identical, while Japanese, like Spanish, uses *bees* instead of *wasps*. The Greek use an entirely different image by saying 'whoever is dealing with the bean, him are eating the chickens'.

English   *to stir up a wasps' nest/to put one's foot in a wasps' nest*
Japanese *hatsi no su wo tutuku*   (hatsi = bee; su = nest; tutuku = to
             stir up)
German   *in ein Wespennest stechen*
             (lit. to stir up a wasps' nest)
Spanish   *meterse en un nido de avispas*   (nido de avispas = wasps nest)

Idiomaticity and background knowledge

One of the most fascinating questions in phraseology is to determine the cultural provenance of an idiomatic phrase. In some cases, it requires some historical and cultural knowledge for a correct interpretation. Let's take a look at one example for illustration. When a girl rejects a boy's attempt of courting or dating her, a German idiom says: *She gave him a basket.* (Sie hat ihm einen Korb gegeben.) This idiomatic phrase can be traced back to the Middle Ages where a noble lady used to be kept in a firmly protected upper room of a castle. The only way she could see her lover was by pulling him up in a basket.[3] This is also attractively illustrated in the famous Manesse Manuscript from the fourteenth century (see Figure 13.4).

However, if the lady was approached by an admirer whom she resented, she would let down a basket with a very thin bottom. When she pulled it up, the unwanted lover would *fall through* (an expression still used in German schools if someone fails to fulfil the teachers' expectations at the end of a school year). It is reported that later on the basket for unwanted lovers was made without any bottom, which caused considerable embarrassment to the poor victim (and possibly some bruises). Perhaps the expression *bottomless infamy* is also related to such a lover's misfortune. I would not be surprised if the English idiom *not to let someone down* can also be traced to a similar source.

Interestingly enough, even old-fashioned lifts resemble a basket. Technically, they are nothing more than a modern version of such a basket. The idiomatic phrase *to give someone a lift* is probably derived from this image,

200

Figure 13.4

although it has changed its vertical motion to horizontal motion meaning *to give someone a ride*, while the idiomatic phrase *to take someone for a ride* has a totally different connotation, meaning 'to cheat someone'.

The number of publications on phraseology which have appeared in recent years is overwhelming. The *Penguin Dictionary of English Idioms* alone (1986; rev. 1994) contains several thousand idiomatic phrases with examples of usage or explanations. A remarkable collection of English idioms is the one by Jennifer Seidl, where she marks those idiomatic phrases which are only used in the United States or in Britain. A special warning is given to the learner, however:

> Above all, remember that it is extremely unwise to translate idioms into or from one's native language. One may be lucky that the two languages have the same form and vocabulary, but in most cases the result will be utterly bewildering to the English native speaker – and possibly highly amusing.
>
> (Seidl and McMordie, 1988: 13)

Antica Menac (1987) observed that Slavic, Germanic and Romance languages share a number of common structural features in idiomatic phrases. For our studies we will neglect the Slavic languages (Russian and Croatian); instead we will concentrate on word-pairs in English, German, French and Italian.

English	He is nothing but *skin and bones*.
German	Er ist nur (noch) *Haut und Knochen*.
French	N'a que *la peau et les os*.
Italian	[. . .] *pelle e ossa*.

English	*sooner or later*
German	*früher oder später*
French	*tôt ou tard*
Italian	*prima o dopo (poi)*

English	*neither fish nor fowl*
German	*weder Fisch noch Fleisch*
French	*ni chair ni poisson*
Italian	*né carne né pesce*

Other similarities may be observed in the following examples which are almost complete equivalents.

English	*with the naked eye*
German	*mit bloßem Auge*
French	*à l'oeil nu*
Italian	*a occhio nude*

English	*to the last breath*
German	*bis zum letzten Atemzug*
French	*jusqu'au dernier souffle*
Italian	*fino all'ultimo respiro*

English	*to receive with open arms*
German	*mit offenen Armen empfangen*
French	*recevoir à bras ouverts*

Italian   *ricevere a bracchia aperte*

English   *to play with fire*
German   *mit dem Feuer spielen*
French   *jouer avec la feu*
Italian   *giocare col fuoco*

English   *to buy a pig in a poke*
German   *eine Katze im Sack kaufen*
French   *acheter un chat en sac*
Italian   *comperare un gatto in sacco*

Although communication in a foreign language can function extremely well without using a single idiom or idiomatic phrase, a foreign language speaker can conquer the hearts of a language community if he/she has at least a passive and perhaps some active command of idiomatic phrases in the foreign language. Therefore, European modern language teaching should not entirely neglect idiomatic phrases which should be taught gradually throughout the respective curriculum.

Methodology

The first question which naturally arises is what methodology should be applied, because modern language teachers all over Europe have little experience in this field. It may be necessary to build some mental bridges for the learner to memorize some striking idiomatic phrases. Such a catalytic function may be achieved by illustrations that assist the learner to store certain idiomatic phrases in his memory. Others, however, have to be memorized and practised in a natural or simulated environment. Research on language teaching will have to do a lot of empirical work to verify or modify the hypothesis that mental bridges, like visual aids, can support memorization of idiomatic phrases in a foreign language. Recent language acquisition theory does not leave any doubt that recognition and memorization of idiomatic phrases and proverbs in a foreign language can only be successfully accomplished by encountering them in actual speech and to associate them with some realistic situation in which they are fittingly applied by the native speakers. It is up to the theories on language learning (e.g. McLaughlin, 1987; Littlewood, 1984) to explain the interrelations between visual and linguistic memory, but one thing is absolutely certain: idiomatic phrases have to be memorized literally, otherwise they are totally ineffective.

In order to test the hypothesis that visual aids may support the human mind to remember the wording of certain idiomatic phrases, the teacher could start with some activity that the learners may especially enjoy. The instructor may wish to use the following illustrations for making transparencies and let the students find the proper idiom. Of course, this can also be done in groups. In multinational classes, it will be interesting to see what the non-native learners contribute in their own language. At this point, however, we should only be interested in the *image* of an idiomatic phrase or proverb rather than with the exact wording in another language, although a literal translation is often very useful in understanding the approximate meaning of the respective idiom.

The teacher may wish to ask the students whether any of the illustrated images of idiomatic phrases 'rings a bell'. If so, it should be written down. It would be useful to compare the learners' findings with an appropriate idiomatic dictionary in order to make sure of the precise wording of the idiom.

Recognition exercises

1 (a) Write down an English idiomatic phrase that comes to mind when you see this picture.
   (b) Can you think of a similar idiomatic phrase in another language?

2 (a) Which English idiom is depicted here?
(b) Express this idiom in your mother tongue and give a literal English translation.

3 (a) Guess which English idiom is represented by this picture.
(b) Can you think of a similar idiomatic phrase in your mother tongue?

4 (a) Does this picture 'ring a bell'? What is the English idiom?
  (b) Is there a similar idiom in your mother tongue?

5 (a) This idiom is taken from the Bible. Do you recognize it?
  (b) Illustrate a fitting situation for this idiom.

6 (a) Heavy rain is expressed in different languages. Which English idiomatic phrase do you connect with this illustration?
   (b) How do you express this in your own language?

7 Which idiomatic phrase are you reminded of when you see this drawing, be it in English or in your mother tongue?

8   (a) This bachelor sweeps everything under the table/bed/rug/carpet/...
Find the correct form and name the English idiom.
(b) How do you say it in your own language? Is there an idiomatic
phrase?

9   Describe the embarrassing situation of the poor girl. Express it in the
form of an idiomatic phrase in any language.

10 (a) Guess what is in this sack. Would you buy it without inspecting its content? Why not?
(b) Write down an idiom in English or in another language that fits the situation.

11 (a) In a dispute it can easily happen that a speaker is going just a bit too far with his comments. What do you say in English if a speaker has reached such a point?
(b) This idiom occurs in several languages. How do *you* express it?

Comparison exercises

The following examples may stimulate modern language teachers in Europe to draft their own exercises for memorizing idiomatic phrases and perhaps explain their origin or find idiomatic equivalents in their students' native tongue.

A Compare the following idiomatic phrases which are all translated fairly literally into English for better identification:

English   *He behaves like a bull in a china shop.*
German   *He behaves like an elephant in a china shop.*
Greek   *He acts like a bull in a glassware shop.*

- What is identical? What is different in the given languages?
- How do you say it in your own language?

B It is reported that President Gorbatchev on his last visit to East Germany in 1989 said to Erich Honecker: 'Whoever is acting too late, will be punished by life.'

- Relate this political word of wisdom to the following proverb.
- How do the images differ from each other in the given languages?
- Explain each of these idioms. Which one do you like best? Why?

English   *An early bird catches the worm.*
German   *Morning hour has gold in its mouth.*
Greek   *Whoever wakes up {early} in the morning, he finds the florin (= coin).*
Spanish   *God helps those who get up early.*

C Any person who has experienced the construction of his house knows what happens when the contractor or superior leaves his craftsmen behind. Likewise, any teacher knows what usually happens when he/she leaves the class unattended. Such a situation is well reflected by the image of mice which celebrate the absence of their worst enemy.

English   *When the cat is away, the mice will play.*
German   *When the cat is not at home, the mice dance on tables and benches.*
Greek   *When the cat is absent, the mice dance.*

- Explain the differences of the above idioms in the three languages.
- Make up an applicable situation.
- Why is this image so popular in all three languages?

D Various European cultures experience the blessing of constant rain quite differently, as is reflected in idiomatic phrases of different languages:

English	*It's raining cats and dogs.*
German	*It's raining strings.*
Greek	*It's raining chair-legs.*
Spanish	*It's raining pitchers.*

- Which language reflects the image of heavy rain most figuratively?
- Do you happen to know this idiom in any other language?

E If someone gives you his old car as a gift, you don't care too much about its condition as long as it does not fall apart and runs without too many repair bills. The image of a horse with rotten teeth given as a present illustrates quite nicely a situation where you don't complain about the gift which you did not choose yourself.

English	*You don't look a gift-horse in the mouth.*
German	*A given old jade you don't look into its mouth.*
Greek	*A given donkey you don't look at its teeth.*
Spanish	*You don't look at the teeth of a gift-horse.*

- Make up a situation where you have been given an unwanted gift that you must accept.
- Explain the cultural differences which are reflected in the respective idioms in the four languages.

F Nobody will rent an appartment or buy a second-hand car which he/she has only heard of, but never seen. It would be stupid to rely on what people tell you as long as you have not inspected whether all the verbal promises of the broker or seller are true. This everyday experience is aptly mirrored in the following German and Greek idiomatic phrases.

German	Kaufe nie eine Katze im Sack!
	Never buy a cat in the sack.
Greek	Aghorazo ghuruni sto saki.
	Never buy a pig in the sack.

- What are the English and/or Spanish equivalents?
- What are the main differences? Can you explain them?
- Have you ever experienced a situation when this idiomatic phrase was fitting?

G One of the so-called *winged words* can be found in the Bible. God's message is too precious to be ignored by people who could not care less. This idiomatic phrase is often used nowadays.

English	*Don't cast pearls before swine.*
German	*Don't cast pearls before sows.*
Greek	*Don't give the saint to the dogs.*

- What have the animals used in the three languages in common?
- Explain why this idiomatic phrase occurs in all three languages in a similar way.

H When someone is getting illusions about his/her real situation and believes that a miracle will happen, for example, that he/she will become a millionaire overnight, various languages express this idea by using different picturesque idiomatic phrases.

English	Yes, sure! *And pigs might fly!*
German	Yes, sure! *And I will be Emperor of China!*
Greek	Yes, sure! *And I will become a bishop!*
Spanish	Yes, sure! *And I am the Queen of Sheba.*

- What idea do these expressions have in common?

Remember the exact wording

By carrying out the following sample exercises students can test themselves on whether they have memorized the precise language of an idiomatic phrase or whether they have just got a vague idea of it.

- Which of the following structures forms a correct idiomatic phrase?
- What does the idiom mean? Put it into a context which brings out its meaning.

(1) He managed to kill:

    (a) three sparrows with one stone.
    (b) two humming-birds with one arrow.
    (c) two flies with one swat.
    (d) two birds with one stone.

- Is there any equivalent in your own language?

(2) Come on! I know exactly what happened. Just don't sweep:

    (a) things under the carpet.
    (b) the dust under the table.
    (c) the burnt milk under the oven.
    (d) the dirt under the mat.

- Is there a comparable expression in your own language? If not, how would you express this in your language?

(3) You have absolutely ruined my new dress by spilling that soup over it! – Oh, come on! It's only a tiny stain which can be quickly removed. For heaven's sake, don't make:

(a) a mountain out of a molehill!
(b) an ocean out of a pond!
(c) a skyscraper out of a cabin!
(d) a giraffe out of a rabbit!

- How do you express this idiom in your own language? Give a literal English translation of it.

(4) He didn't want to let:

(a) the cat out of the sack.
(b) the bird out of the cage.
(c) the cat out of the bag.
(d) the dog out of the kennel.

- How do you explain the origin of this idiom?
- Is there an equivalent in your own language?

(5) Come to the main point and tell me the truth. Just stop:

(a) beating the carpet.
(b) hiding behind the trees.
(c) beating about the bush.
(d) hiding in the cornfield.

- Explain the origin of this idiom. What is meant by it?
- Do you know an equivalent in any other language?

(6) He will be giving his first public concert tomorrow. That is why he has got:

(a) ants in his trousers.
(b) pebbles in his shoes.
(c) butterflies in his stomach.
(d) worms in his ears.

- This is a unique way of expressing nervousness. How is this expressed in

213

other than your own mother tongue? Can you translate it literally into English?

Parts of the body exercises

Write down any idiomatic phrases relating to parts of the body in your own language. Can you think of any in your target language?

Samples

Head	Greek:	*I hit my head against the wall.*
		(to regret something)
Face	German:	*I must not lose my face.*
		(not to lose one's reputation)
Eyes	French:	*He threw powder in my eyes.*
		(to cheat someone)
Nose	English:	*Why does she stick her nose into my affairs?*
		(to interfere)
Ears	Italian:	Alright, tell me: *I am all ears.*
		(to pay full attention)
Mouth	German:	*You put the words in my mouth.*
		(to anticipate somebody's utterance)
Teeth	Greek:	*She gnashed her teeth at her poor husband.*
		(to threaten)
Hair	English:	*He did not turn a hair.*
		(to stay calm)
Finger	Italian:	*He did not move a finger.*
		(to be lazy)

Other parts of the body or inner organs are just as suitable for idiomatic phrases such as the neck, arm, hand, fist, thumb, leg, knee, foot, toe, back, heart, liver, kidney, stomach, lungs, etc. Similar exercises can be done with tame or wild animals, birds, tools, clothes, colours, etc. Students can find proverbs or idiomatic phrases from such areas and can explain their meaning or possibly even their origin. A number of excellent dictionaries, some of them contrasting idiomatic phrases in two or even more European languages, are available (e.g. Kettridge, 1980; Delicostopoulos, 1993; Taylor and Gottschalk, 1973; Lister, 1993, Goodale, 1995; Morris, 1995; Frenzel, 1978; Werny and Snyckers, 1976; Witnitzer, 1975).

We are in no way suggesting that learners studying a second language should be tortured with idiomatic phrases in foreign languages, but rather that they should detect similarities with and differences to their own mother tongue. This will increase their sensitivity to recognizing the meaning of an idiomatic phrase when used by a native speaker, and it may even stimulate them to memorize some, and to use them in a fitting situation. If this target can be reached any teacher should be more than happy, and should give up hope that pigs might fly.

Notes

1 Cf. Glaap (1979). He states: 'On the one hand idioms must be integral parts of the English lesson, but at the same time their function should not be so overemphasized that they become distorting features' (p. 485).

2 Some authors recognized this problem, but did not receive much feedback from the foreign language teachers. Cf. Brandt, 1965; Daniels, 1975; Heesch, 1977; Mrosowski and Coulon, 1978; Trübner, 1970.

3 This technique is already reported in the Bible: when St Paul was in Damascus and was threatened with arrest, his friends let him down from the city wall in a basket; this way, he managed to escape (2 Corinthians 11, 33).

4 This is the largest collection of minnesongs to have been preserved. It contains love songs of 140 medieval poets and is decorated with 137 beautiful paintings showing the minnesingers or medieval life-style. The unique manuscript is called after the Swiss collectors Rüdiger and Johannes Manesse. It can be seen in the university library at Heidelberg.

References

Abraham, W. (1975) 'Zur Linguistik der Metaphor', in *Poetica* 4: 133–172.

Brandt, B. (1965) 'Die idiomatische Wendung als Bestandteil der Kenntnisminima', in *Fremdsprachenunterricht* 9: 578–586.

Burger, H. (1973) *Idiomatik des Deutschen* (Germanistische Arbeitshefte 16). Tübingen: Niemeyer.

Daniels, K. (1975) 'Phraseologie als Aufgabe der Sprachdidaktik', in U. Engel and H. Schumacher (eds) *Linguistik / Beschreibung der Gegenwartssprache (GAL)* 6, Heidelberg: Julius Groos Verlag.

Delicostopoulos, A. (1993) *Greek Idioms*, Athens: Efstathiadis Group SA.

Emig, J. (1972) 'Children and Metaphor', in *Research in Teaching of English* 6: 163–175.

Filmore, C. J., Kay, P. and O'Connor, M. C. (1988) 'Regularity and idiomaticity in grammatical constructions: the case of *Let Alone*', in *Language* 64, 3: 501–538.

Fleischer, W. (1982) *Phraseologie der deutschen Gegenwartssprache*, Leipzig: VEB Bibliographisches Institut.

Frenzel, H. (1978) *1000 Idiomatische Redensarten Italienisch. Mit Erklärungen und Beispielen*, Berlin.

Glaap, A.-R. (1979) 'Idioms im Englischunterricht – kontextualisiert, sachfeldbezogen, kontrastiv', in *Die neueren Sprachen* 78: 485–498.

Gläser, R. (1986) *Phraseologie der englischen Sprache*, Tübingen: Niemeyer.

Goodale, M. (1995) *Collins Cobuild Idioms Workbook*, London: HarperCollins.

Guenthner, D. (1975) 'On the Semantics of Metaphor', in *Poetica* 4: 199–220.

Häusermann, J. (1977) *Phraseologie. Hauptprobleme der deutschen Phraseologie auf der Basis sowjetischer Forschungsergebnisse*, Tübingen: Niemeyer.

Heesch, M. (1977) 'Zur Übersetzung von Phraseologismen', in *Fremdsprachen* 21: 176–184.

Itoh, M. (1995) 'Bemerkungen zum phraseologischen Wörterbuch für Ausländer', in

Gengobunka Ronshu (Studies in Languages and Cultures), No. 40, ed. Institute of Modern Languages and Cultures, University of Tsukuba (Japan).

Kettridge, J. O. (1980) *Traveller's Foreign Phrase Book. (English French German Italian Spanish Dutch)*, 11th edn, London: Routledge.

Klappenbach, R. (1968) 'Probleme der Phraseologie', in *Wissenschaftliche Zeitschrift der Karl-Marx-Universität Leipzig* 17.

Lister, R. (1993) *English Idioms – A Complete Study Course*, Woodbridge, Suffolk: Hugo.

Littlewood, W. T. (1984) *Foreign and Second Language Learning: Language Acquisition Research and its Implications for the Classroom*, Cambridge: Cambridge University Press.

McLaughlin, B. (1987) *Theories of Second-Language Learning*, London.

Menac, A. (1987) 'Gemeinsame semantische Gruppen in der Phraseologie der europischen Sprachen', in Burger, H. (ed.) *Aktuelle Probleme der Phraseologie: Symposium 27.–29.9.1984 in Zürich*, Paris (Züricher Germanistische Studien Bd. 9).

Morris, T. (1995) *English Idioms – A Fun New Approach*, Oxford: Black Sheep Press of Oxford.

Mrosowski, B. and Coulon, P. (1978) 'Quelque aspects de la phraséologie comparée', in *Fremdsprachen* 22: 125–128.

Palm, Ch. (1995) *Phraseologie. Eine Einführung*, Tübingen: Narr.

Seidl, J. and McMordie, W. (1988) *English Idioms*, Oxford: Oxford University Press.

Taylor, R. and Gottschalk, W. (1973) *A German–English Dictionary of Idioms. Idiomatic and Figurative German Expressions with English Translations*, Munich: Hueber.

Trübner, G. (1970) 'Einige Bemerkungen zu den Redewendungen im Englischen', in *Fremdsprachenunterricht* 14: 497–502.

Werny, P. and Snyckers, A. (1976) *Dictionaire des locutions français-allemand*, Paris.

Witnitzer, M. (1977) *Bildliche Redensarten. Deutsch Englisch Französisch*, Stuttgart: Klett.

Wotjak, B. (1992) *Verbale Phraseolexeme in System und Text*, Tübingen: Niemeyer.

Zutt, H. (ed.) (1968) 'Hartmann von Aue', in *Die Klage – Das* [zweite] *Büchlein* (v. 1613–1625), Berlin: de Gruyter, p. 97.

Further reading

Daniels, K. (1985) '"Idiomatische Kompetenz" in der Zielsprache Deutsch. Voraussetzungen, Möglichkeiten, Folgerungen', in *Wirkendes Wort* 35: 145–156.

Fliegner, J. (1976) 'Laßt den Wörtern Flügel wachsen. Indirekter und bildhafter Sprachgebrauch', in *Praxis Deutsch* 16: 20–23.

Földes, C. and Kühnert, H. (1992) *Hand- und Übungsbuch zur deutschen Phraseologie*, Budapest: Tankönyvkiadó.

Földes, C. (1997) *Idiomatik / Phraseologie* (Studienbibliographien Sprachwissenschaft, Bd. 18), Heidelberg: Julius Groos Verlag.

Gulland, D. M. and Hinds-Howell, D. G. (eds) (1986) *Dictionary of English Idioms*, London: Penguin Books.

Hessky, R. (1992) 'Aspekte der Verwendung von Phraseologismen im Unterricht Deutsch als Fremdsprache', in E. Zöfgen (ed.) *Idiomatik und Phraseologie*, Tübingen: Narr.

Kühnert, H. (1985) 'Die Rolle des Bildverständnisses bei Phraseologismen im Fremdsprachenunterricht für Fortgeschrittene', in *Deutsch als Fremdsprache* 22: 223–227.

Lakoff, G. (1987) *Fire, Woman and Dangerous Things: What Categories Reveal about the Mind*, Chicago: University of Chicago Press.

Luchtenberg, S. (1993) '"Ohne Fleiß kein Preis". Überlegungen zu Sprichwörtern und

Redensarten im interkulturellen Deutschunterricht', in *Lernen in Deutschland* 13: 6–18.

Mieder, W. (1995) *Deutsche Redensarten, Sprichwörter und Zitate. Studien zu ihrer Herkunft, Überlieferung und Verwendung*, Wien: Verlag Edition Praesens.

Petrovic, V. (1988) 'Phraseologie im Fremdsprachenunterricht', in *Deutsche Sprache* 16: 351–361.

Scherer, Th. (1982) *Phraseologie im Schulalter. Untersuchungen zur Phraseologie deutschschweizer Schüler und ihrer Sprachbücher*, Bern: Peter Lang.

Stolze, P. (1995) 'Phraseologismen und Sprichwörter als Gegenstand des Deutschunterrichts', in R. Baur and Ch. Chlosta (eds) *Von der Einwortmetapher zur Satzmetapher. Akten des Westfälischen Arbeitskreises Phraseologie/Präomiologie*, Bochum: Brockmeyer.

Ulbricht, A. (1989) 'Idiomatische Wendungen im Fremdsprachenunterricht Deutsch', in *Deutsch als Fremdsprache* 26: 29–34.

Workman, G. (1995) *Phrasal Verbs and Idioms, Advanced*, Oxford: Oxford University Press.

14

SELECTING IDIOMS TO ENRICH MODERN LANGUAGE TEACHING

Sophia Zevgoli

Introduction

Vocabulary is without doubt one of the most important aspects in foreign language learning; but what elements does the term vocabulary include? Certainly not only single lexical items, but also multi-word units, i.e. recurring fixed expressions. One familiar type of fixed expressions is idioms. While no FL teacher questions the necessity of teaching single words, the majority of teachers consider the teaching of idioms as 'sheer luxury'. Indeed, a student need not learn to say *Tom spilled the beans*. He/she can very well use the literal expression *Tom revealed the secret* instead. However, would these two expressions communicate exactly the same meanings, emotions and evaluations, and which one would a native speaker be more likely to use? Idioms mean a lot more than their literal paraphrases; they communicate a feeling or an attitude towards the event they denote, which is not as readily communicable in the case of literal expressions. Moreover, idioms enliven speech; they are 'the life and soul' of language. It is not surprising, therefore, that native speakers of a language use idioms quite frequently in their everyday speech. This explains the fact that, no matter how well the student learns the meanings and appropriate use of single words, without idioms he/she can neither 'enter the spirit' of the foreign language nor speak it with native fluency.

The purpose of this chapter is to draw FL teachers' attention to idioms and to make suggestions concerning their teaching sequence. Before making these suggestions, however, we will present a short descriptive analysis of idioms, in order to help the teacher realize the different properties of idiomatic expressions which should be taught to FL learners.

Primary properties of idioms

We think of an expression as idiomatic if it is characterized by *conventionality* and *invariability*. The reason why our definition of idioms is based exclusively on these properties of conventionality and invariability is that they apply to all idioms to a greater or lesser extent. They are therefore considered as *primary properties*.

1   *Conventionality of idioms*: Idioms are conventionalized, in the sense that their meaning or conventions of use cannot be entirely predicted. (Nunberg, Sag and Wasow (1994: 493); Fillmore, Kay and O'Connor (1988: 504))
2   *Invariability of idioms*: Idioms are invariable in three different ways: lexically, syntactically and morphologically. Idioms are lexically invariable, i.e. their parts cannot be substituted by other words to a greater or lesser extent (Benson (1985: 66); Cermak (1988: 421, 429); Fotopoulou (1989: 224), (1993: 41–43)). By syntactic invariability or inflexibility we mean that idioms can appear in a limited number of syntactic constructions (Fraser (1970); Cutler (1982); Gibbs and Gonzales (1985); Reagan (1987); Nunberg *et al.* (1994: 492, 499–509, 511–514)). Finally, idioms are morphologically invariable, in the sense that their parts cannot undergo internal changes (e.g. changes in verb tense or noun number). All aspects of invariability are however a matter of degree.

Secondary properties of idioms

Apart from conventionality and invariability, idioms are characterized by some other properties that do not apply to all of them. These properties, which we call secondary properties of idioms, are compositionality or analysability, grammaticality, figurative property, informality and affective property.

Compositionality or analysability of idioms

Compositionality or analysability is defined as the degree to which an idiom meaning can be analysed into different components, each of which is distributed to a different idiom part.[1] The idiom *to break the ice*, for example, is considered to be compositional or analysable, because its parts *to break* and *the ice* can be respectively assigned the interpretations 'to ease' and 'the formality of a social situation'. Idioms of this kind are called *idiomatic combinations*. On the other hand, there are non-compositional or non-analysable idioms, i.e. idioms whose meanings cannot be distributed to their parts, i.e. German *ins Gras beißen* (to die), or *to kick the bucket* (to die). Idioms of this kind are called *idiomatic phrases*.[2]

Careful examination of idiomatic combinations has shown that not all of them have entirely idiomatic meanings. This leads to a distinction of idiomatic combinations into the following three categories:

1   Idiomatic combinations whose constituents have all idiomatic meanings: *to spill the beans* (to reveal secret information), *einer Sache auf den Grund*

219

gehen (to find out the exact cause of something), $\alpha\nu o i\gamma\omega\ \tau\alpha\ \chi\alpha\rho\tau\iota\alpha\ \mu o\upsilon$ (lit.: I open the papers of mine), meaning 'to reveal one's intentions'.

2   Idiomatic combinations in which verbs preserve their literal meanings, while other constituents are assigned idiomatic meanings: *to ask for the moon* (to ask for something that is difficult or impossible to obtain), German: *zu Brei schlagen*, meaning 'to hit hard', $\alpha\lambda\lambda\alpha\zeta\omega\ \mu\nu\alpha\lambda\alpha$ (lit.: I change brains), meaning 'to change one's way of thinking'.

3   Idiomatic combinations in which verbs are assigned idiomatic meanings, while other constituents preserve their literal meanings. This category includes a small number of idiomatic combinations: *to kick the habit* (to give up a habit), German: *sich das Lachen verbeißen* (to keep from laughing), $\beta\gamma\alpha\zeta\omega\ \lambda o\gamma o$ (lit: I take out a speech), meaning 'to make a speech'.

Grammaticality of idioms

The grammatical structure of idioms can serve as a basis for their distinction into two categories (Fillmore *et al.* (1988: 505); Nunberg *et al.* (1994: 515)):

1   Grammatical idioms, i.e. idioms whose grammatical structures conform to the familiar rules of grammar, e.g. $\tau\alpha\ \beta\alpha\varphi\omega\ \mu\alpha\upsilon\rho\alpha$ (lit.: I paint them black), meaning 'to be deeply disappointed or sad', *to spill the beans*, or German: *jemandem aufs Dach steigen* (lit.: to climb on someone's roof), meaning 'to treat someone very roughly'.

2   Extragrammatical idioms, i.e. idioms whose grammatical structures do not conform to the familiar rules of grammar, e.g. $\varepsilon\chi\omega\ (\kappa\alpha\pi o\iota o\nu)\ \sigma\eta\kappa\omega$ $\sigma\eta\kappa\omega\ \kappa\alpha\tau\sigma\varepsilon\ \kappa\alpha\tau\varepsilon$ (I have someone whom I can make stand up and sit down), meaning 'to make someone do everything one wishes' (sit-down-you [*sing.-imper.*]). In this example the verb does not follow its typical combinatory possibilities; instead, it presents an idiosyncratic structure. (Other examples: *to trip the light fantastic, weder aus noch ein wissen*).

Figurative property of idioms

Idiom meanings are often based on metonymies[3] (*to lend a hand*), hyperboles ($\delta\varepsilon\nu\ \alpha\xi\iota\zeta\varepsilon\iota\ \pi\varepsilon\nu\tau\alpha\rho\alpha$ (lit: not is-worth-it penny, meaning 'not worth a damn'), metaphors (*den Stier bei den Hörnern packen*) and other kinds of figuration (Nunberg *et al.*, 1994: 492).

Metaphor is the most common kind of figure in idioms. In fact, idioms themselves are often based on metaphors which provide the foundation for much of our everyday thought and reasoning (Gibbs 1992: 485–486). For example, the interpretation of the Greek idiom $\beta\rho\alpha\zeta\omega\ \alpha\pi'\ \tau o\ \theta\upsilon\mu o\ \mu o\upsilon$ (lit: I boil from my anger, meaning 'to be extremely angry') is motivated by two independently existing metaphors: 'mind is a container' and 'anger is heated fluid in a container' (ibid).

Informality of idioms

Idioms 'are typically associated with relatively informal or colloquial registers and with popular speech and oral culture' (Nunberg *et al.*, 1994: 493). However, there are also formal idioms, which indicate that the speaker or writer has a formal relationship with the person(s) he/she is speaking to. Formal idioms are often used in official letters, public speeches, etc. (*Longman Dictionary of English Idioms*, 1979: xv): *to lift (up) one's heart, seine Hände in Unschuld waschen, αναπαυομαι στις δαφνες μου* (lit: I rest on my laurels, meaning 'to rest on one's laurels').

Moreover, there are formal idioms which include archaic or very unusual words (*Longman Dictionary of English Idioms*, 1979: x–xi): *to cast pearls before swine, to gird up one's loins, ad calendas greacas / bis zu den griechischen Kalenden aufschieben, advocatus diaboli sein* (typically, German idioms of this kind include Latin elements).

In Greek, idioms of this sort are traced back to ancient, Byzantine and learned language tradition and are still frequently used: *νιπτω τας χειρας μου* (lit: I wash my hands, meaning 'to refuse to accept any responsibility for something or someone'); *κρουω τον κωδωνα του κινδυνου* (lit: I sound the bell of the danger, meaning 'to warn of approaching danger'); *πνεω μενεα εναντιον (καποιον)* (lit: I blow furies against someone, meaning 'to be furious with someone').

Affective property of idioms

'Idioms are typically used to imply a certain evaluation or affective stance toward the things they denote' (Nunberg *et al.*, 1994: 493). Furthermore, idiom meanings may vary according to the situational contexts in which idioms are used and according to the speaker's stance. The Greek idiom *ανοιγω την καρδια (καποιον)* (lit: I open someone's heart), for example, may mean either 'to give somebody pleasure' or 'to cause somebody pain' (Dimitriou, 1995: 147); that depends on the social and psychological circumstances in which the idiom in question is used and on the speaker's intentionality.

The secondary properties of idioms have served as a basis for their distinction into several categories. These distinctions provide us with the means for constructing a typology of idiomatic expressions, which is represented in Figure 14.1.

Why idioms should be taught to FL learners

The theoretical discussion about idioms raises the question of whether idioms should be taught to FL learners and if so, why. Our answer to this question is that idioms should be taught to FL learners for the reasons listed below:

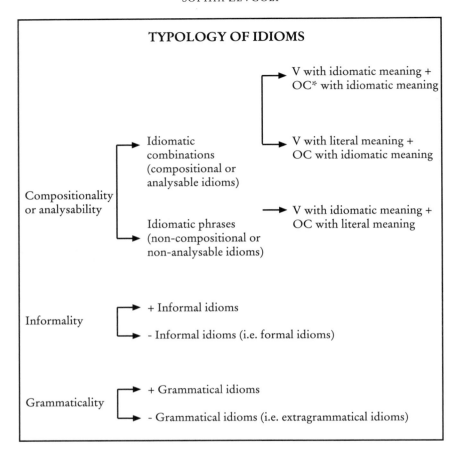

Figure 14.1 Typology of idioms as to their secondary properties
Note: *Other constituents of idioms, i.e. constituents which do not include verbs.

1   Each language possesses a large number of idiomatic expressions, whose frequency of occurrence in everyday speech is quite high. Students learning idioms thus enrich their vocabulary with expressions that form an important part of FL vocabulary.

2   As mentioned above, idioms communicate an attitude towards the things they denote. That is probably the reason why idioms are typically used in a conversational setting (Lattey, 1986: 218). Comprehending the use and meanings of idioms therefore helps learners not only to understand a conversation in FL, but also to participate in it as efficiently as native speakers.[4]

3   Idioms are for the most part expressions peculiar to one language. Consequently, appropriate use of idioms makes FL learners sound knowledgeable

and fluent. Native speakers, moreover, will recognize with approval the fact that by using idiomatic expressions, the FL learner is trying to enter the spirit of the language. This approval provides psychological support for the learner and makes him/her feel more confident about using the foreign language in general (Adam, 1992: 11, 29).

4   Idioms convey concepts which are for the most part particular to one culture and one language. Teaching idioms therefore offers FL learners a unique opportunity for looking into the target culture's notions about the world. In addition, learners become more consciously aware of their own culture by comparing the cultural notions and values expressed in FL idioms with those expressed in idioms of their mother tongue (Adam, 1992: 10–11). For these reasons, it is suggested that idioms play an important role in the foreign language cultural syllabus.

What FL learners need to know about idioms

Teaching idioms involves teaching not only their meaning, but also the conventions which govern their use. Learners should particularly acquire the ability:

1   To recognize the meaning of idioms.
2   To recognize the degree of lexical invariability of each idiom. In other words, students should learn the words with which idiom parts can be substituted.
3   To use idioms according to their syntactic and morphological constraints. Learners should learn the variety of permissible constructions in which an idiom may appear, as well as the variety of permissible morphological changes that idiom parts may undergo (Irujo, 1986: 237; Gibbs, 1987: 583; MacCarthy and Dell, 1994: 148).
4   To use idioms spontaneously and appropriately in order to efficiently communicate their messages. Using idioms appropriately means two different things: choosing the appropriate idioms according to the content of the intended message and the emotions or evaluations to be communicated and using idioms in the appropriate registers and social circumstances (Irujo, 1986: 237; Lattey, 1986: 230; Adam, 1992: 12–13; Itoh, 1995: 113).
5   To recognize the feelings, intentions and emotions expressed in idioms.
6   To recognize the cultural notions and values idioms convey.

Selecting idioms to be taught first to FL learners

In our opinion idioms should be gradually introduced into teaching at all levels of FL learning; but how should they be taught and in which order? Parts of the descriptive analysis of idioms presented in chapters 2 and 3 can serve as a basis in order to make the following suggestions concerning the two issues raised above:

1   Compositionality or analysability is adopted as a criterion for selecting idioms to be taught first to FL learners. In other words, compositional or analysable idioms should be taught to FL learners prior to non-compositional or non-analysable idioms.[5]

What needs to be stressed here is that compositionality should be adopted in combination with other criteria for selecting idioms to be taught to FL learners, which have been proposed in the literature of FL teaching (see e.g. Irujo, 1986: 238–241; 1993: 217). Among these, the criterion of idiom frequency of occurrence and the criterion of equivalency between idioms of FL and idioms of learners' mother tongue appear to be the most common. Such a combination of criteria involves initially choosing the most frequent idioms, as well as idioms having identical or similar first language equivalents. These idioms should be divided into two groups: analysable and non-analysable. The teaching of idioms could begin with the most frequent analysable idioms that have first language equivalents and be continued with the corresponding non-analysable idioms.

2   The teaching of analysable idioms should begin with idioms whose verbs or other constituents preserve their literal meaning. In this way, learners have to relate only one idiom part to an idiomatic meaning at a time, since the other parts of the idiom preserve their literal meanings, which are already known to learners.

Once learners have familiarized themselves with these idioms, the teacher can begin teaching those idioms whose constituents do not have any literal meaning.

3   Our third suggestion concerns a way of teaching analysable idioms. FL teachers should encourage their students to adopt a 'word-by-word' parsing strategy in the process of understanding analysable idioms.[6] FL learners should be encouraged to analyse the meaning of analysable idioms into components and to relate each of these components to a different idiom part.

This process helps the learner not only to understand but also to retain the meaning of analysable idioms. In order for the teacher to demonstrate the compositionality of an idiom, he/she could use examples similar to the one given in Figure 14.2.

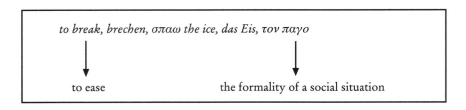

Figure 14.2 A way of representing the compositionality of an idiom in the classroom

4   It is suggested that grammaticality should also be adopted as a criterion for selecting idioms to be taught first to FL learners. According to this criterion, grammatical idioms should be taught prior to extragrammatical ones.

The reason why we make this suggestion is that in the case of grammatical idioms, learners come across familiar structures. In the case of extragrammatical idioms, learners come across structures which are not made intelligible by knowledge of the familiar rules of grammar. They therefore have to make a greater effort in order to understand and remember the latter type of idiom.

5   Our final suggestion concerns idioms of Modern Greek that include elements which are traced back to the ancient, Byzantine and learned tradition. It is advisable that idioms of this sort be taught to beginning MGFL learners who have already studied Ancient Greek, as these expressions include words with which learners are already familiar. In this way, learners can be motivated in learning Modern Greek as a foreign language.

Activities for teaching idioms to FL learners

In this section five activities for teaching idioms in the FL classroom are presented. Although each activity is designed for the teaching of idioms of a specific language (Modern Greek, German or English), it can be used equally for the teaching of idioms of the other two languages.

Activity A

This activity aims to help learners to adopt the 'word-by-word' parsing strategy when trying to understand and retain the meaning of an analysable idiom.

Look for words having the same meaning!

Look for words in the following sentences (taken from the *Longman Dictionary of English Idioms*) that have the same meaning as the words in the box below.

---

find, harm, secret information, reduce, one's duty, reveal, fulfil, the exact cause, the strength, one's own interest

---

1   You can't trust him to keep a secret; he is sure to spill the beans before long.

2   The police are eager to get to the bottom of the mystery.

3   The smaller company was able to cut the claws of its opponents.

4   You try to persuade him now, I talked to him all last night, I've done my part.

5   If he refuses to help his neighbours now, he'll just be fouling his own nest.

Activity B

In this activity, learners practise using idioms according to their syntactic and morphological constraints.

Εντοπισε τους ιδιωματισμους!

Διαβασε τις παρακατω προτασεις και προσπαθησε να βρεις αν οι εκφρασεις με τα πλαγια γραμματα εχουν ιδιωματικη η κυριολεκτικη σημασια

1   (α) Ο Γιαννης μου αναψε μεγαλες φωτιες κι εγω τωρα δεν ξερω τι να κανω.
       (β) Ο Γιαννης δεν εχει καμια σχεση με το *αναμμα των φωτιων*.
       (γ) *Τις φωτιες που μου αναψες* θα τις θυμαμαι σε ολη μου τη ζωη.

2   (α) Δεν μου ειναι ευκολο *να ανοιξω τα χαρτια μου*.
       (β) Ολοι ανοιξαν τα χαρτια τους, μονο εσυ δεν θελεις *να ανοιξεις τα δικα σου*.
       (γ) Μπορεις σε *παρακαλω να ανοιξεις το χαρτι σου*;

3   (α) Αργα η γρηγορα *θα βαλει* κι αυτος *νερο στο κρασι του*.
       (β) *Ποσο νερο θα βαλεις στο κρασι σου*;
       (γ) *Σε αυτο το κρασι δεν χρειαζεται να βαλεις νερο*.

4   (α) Παλι εγω *θα βγαλω τα καστανα απο τη φωτια*.
       (β) *Ποσα καστανα να βγαλω απο τη φωτια*;
       (γ) *Επιτελους τα καστανα βγηκαν απ' τη φωτια*.

Spot idioms!

Read the following sentences and try to find out whether the expressions in italics are idiomatic or literal.

1   Idiom used: light-I fires [*acc.*] to someone [*acc.*] (to cause someone serious troubles)
       (a) the [*nom.*] John [*nom.*] I [*gen.*] lit big [*plural-acc.*] fires [*acc.*] and

now not know-I what [*acc.*] to do-I (John caused me serious troubles and now I don't know what to do) > idiom.

(b) the [*nom.*] John [*nom.*] not has no [*acc.*] relation [*acc.*] with the [*acc.*] lighting [*acc.*] the [*gen.*] fires [*gen.*] (John has nothing to do with the lighting of the fires) > literal expression.

(c) the [*acc.*] fires [*acc.*] that I [*gen.*] you [*sing.*] will them remember-I in all [*acc.*] I [*gen.*] the [*acc.*] life [*acc.*] (I will remember the problems you caused me all my life) > idiom.

2   Idiom used: open-I the [*acc.*] papers [*acc.*] I [*gen.*] (to reveal one's intentions)

(a) not I [*gen.*] is-it easy [*sing.-neutr.*] to open-I the [*acc.*] papers [*acc.*] I [*gen.*] (it's not easy for me to reveal my intentions) > idiom.

(b) all [*plural-nom.*] opened the [*acc.*] papers [*acc.*] they [*gen.*] only you [*sing.*] not want to open-you [*sing.*] the [*plural-acc.*] your [*plural-acc.*] you [*gen.*] (i.e. everybody revealed his intentions, only you don't want to reveal yours) > (idiom).

(c) Can-you [*sing.*] you [*sing.-acc.*] please-I to open-you [*sing.*] the [*sing.-acc.*] paper [*sing.-acc.*] you [*gen.*]? (can you please open your paper?) > literal expression.

3   Idiom used: put-I water [*acc.*] in-the [*acc.*] wine [*acc.*] I [*gen.*] (to moderate one's demands)

(a) slow [*adv.*] or fast [*adv.*] will put-he and he [*nom.*] water [*acc.*] in-the [*acc.*] wine [*acc.*] he [*gen.*] (sooner or later he will moderate his demands too) > idiom.

(b) how-much [*acc.*] water [*acc.*] will put-you [*sing.*] in-the [*acc.*] wine [*acc.*] you [*gen.*]? (how much water will you put in your wine?) > literal expression.

(c) in this [*acc.*] the [*acc.*] wine [*acc.*] not needs-it to put-you [*sing.*] water [*acc.*] (you don't need to put water in this wine) > literal expression.

4   Idiom used: take-out-I the [*acc.*] chestnuts [*acc.*] from the [*acc.*] fire [*acc.*] (to pull the chestnuts out of the fire)

(a) again I will take-out the [*acc.*] chestnuts [*acc.*] from the [*acc.*] fire [*acc.*] (I will pull the chestnuts out of the fire again) > idiom.

(b) how-much [*acc.*] chestnuts [*acc.*] to take-out-I from the [*acc.*] fire [*-acc.*]? (how many chestnuts do you want me to take out of the fire?) > literal expression.

(c) at-last the [*nom.*] chestnuts [*nom.*] took-out [*pass.*] from the [*acc.*] fire [*acc.*] (the chestnuts were at last taken out of the fire) > literal expression.

Activity C

In this activity learners practise recognizing the degree of idiom lexical invariability.

Wählen Sie die passenden Wörter aus!

Ergänzen Sie die idiomatischen Wendungen in den folgenden Sätzen mit einem oder mehreren von den Wörtern, die in Klammern stehen.

1 Er schafft es immer, seinen .... (Kopf/Dick-schädel/Hals) durchzusetzen.
2 Ihre Reaktion hat mich .... (in Fahrt/auf den Baum/auf die Palme) gebracht.
3 Wer böses Blut .... (macht/tut/schafft), macht sich bald mißliebig.
4 Was? Wußte Karl nichts darüber? Deshalb .... (schaute/sah/guckte) er so .... (dumm/blöd/hirn-los/doof) aus der Wäsche.
5 Der Soldat hat leider .... (in den Schlamm/ins Gras/in die Erde) gebissen.

Activity D

In this activity learners practise using idioms in specific communicative situations. Before assigning roles, the teacher should help learners to collect idioms having meanings relevant to the situation described.

Role play!

You have just lost your job. You meet a friend in the street who wants to know why you look so unhappy. Explain to him/her what has happened to you. Your friend should try to encourage you. Before playing the dialogue try to think of idioms whose meanings have to do with 'dismissal' (e.g. *to get/to be given the sack*), 'dissatisfaction' (e.g. *to pull a long face*), 'anger' (e.g. *to hit the roof/ceiling*) and 'encouragement' (e.g. *to stick it out*). When practising the dialogue try to use as many of these idioms as possible.

Activity E

This activity aims at showing learners a way in which idioms are used in real life. Moreover, learners practise using idioms to satisfy a specific communicative need. Idioms used in this activity must already be known to learners.

Εισαι καλος διαφημιστης;

(α) *Ταξιδεψτε με Delsey για να παει μακρια η βαλιτσα!*
(β) *Νεμεα Καμπα : Δεν μενει στο ραφι, γιατι 'παντρευεται' ολες τις γευσεις!*
(γ) *Storemaster : Κανει τα παντα στο Πι και PHILIPS!*
(δ) *Club Med One : Επιτελους η ιδεα πηρε ... καταρτια και οστα!*
(ε) *SEB : Στο ματι της κουζινας!*

Οι διαφημισεις αυτες εμφανιστηκαν σε ελληνικα περιοδικα.

Μια εταιρια σου ανεθεσε να διαφημισεις το προιον της σε γνωστο περιοδικο. Εσυ ετοιμασες ενα απο τα διαφημιστικα κειμενα α εως ε, το οποιο πρεπει τωρα να παρουσιασεις στους εκπροσωπους της εταιριας. Στην παρουσιαση σου πρεπει να εξηγησεις τι ειδους προιον διαφημιζεις και ποιος ειναι ο ιδιωματισμος και το λογοπαιγνιο στα οποια στηριζεται η διαφημιση. Επειδη δεν ειναι βεβαιο οτι η διαφημιση σου θα ικανοποιησει τους εκπροσωπους της εταιριας, πρεπει να ετοιμασεις και μια δευτερη, η οποια θα περιλαμβανει και παλι εναν ιδιωματισμο κι αν ειναι δυνατο, ενα λογοπαιγνιο.

Are you a good advertiser?

1   Idiom used: goes-it away the [*nom.*] suitcase [*nom.*] (something goes on or lasts for too long). Advertised products: travel articles travel-you [*plural-imper.*] with Delsey to goes-it away the [*nom.*] suitcase [*nom.*] (travel with Delsey in order for the suitcase to go far away!).

2   Idiom used: stay-I on-the [*acc.*] shelf [*acc.*] (not to find anyone to get married to). Advertised product: a sort of wine Nemea Camba: not stays-it on-the [*acc.*] shelf [*acc.*] because marries-it all [*acc.*] the [*acc.*] tastes [*acc.*] (Nemea Camba: It doesn't stay on the shelf, because it 'marries' all tastes!).

3   Idiom implied: do-I (something [*acc.*]) in-the [*acc.*] pi and phi (to do something very quickly). Advertised product: a household appliance.
       Storemaster: does-it the [*plural-acc.*] all [*plural-acc.*] in-the [*acc.*] Pi and Philips (Storemaster: It does everything in Pi and PHILIPS!).

4   Idiom implied: take-I flesh [*acc.*] and bones [*acc.*] (to come true). Advertised product: a cruiseship.

Club Med One: at-last the [*nom.*] idea [*nom.*] took masts [*acc.*] and bones [*acc.*]

(Club Med One: At last the idea took . . . masts and bones!).

5　Idiom implied: in-the [*acc.*] eye [*acc.*] the [*gen.*] cyclone [*gen.*] (to be at an extremely dangerous spot). Advertised products: pots and pans SEB: on-the [*acc.*] eye [*acc.*] the [*gen.*] kitchen [*gen.*] (SEB: on the eye of the kitchen, i.e. on the hotplate!). These advertisements appeared in Greek magazines.

A firm has asked you to advertise its product in a well-known magazine. You have come up with one of the advertising texts 1 to 5 (above), which you have to present to the firm representatives. In your presentation you should explain what sort of product is being advertised and which idiom and pun your advertisement is based on. There is a chance that your advertisement won't satisfy the firm representatives; that's why you should prepare an additional one, which should again involve an idiom and, if possible, a pun.

Conclusions

In this chapter we have argued that idioms are expressions characterized by the properties of *conventionality* and *invariability*. These properties have been considered as *primary properties of idioms*, because they apply to all of them to a greater or lesser extent. A distinction has then been drawn between different aspects of invariability, which have all been considered as a matter of degree.

Except for primary properties of idioms, this chapter has also been concerned with *secondary properties of idioms*; that is, properties that do not apply to all them (these are *compositionality* or *analysability, grammaticality, figurative property, informality* and *affective property*). On the basis of most of these properties, idioms have been distinguished into various types. These distinctions have provided us with the means for constructing a typology of idioms. We then went on to argue that idioms need to be taught to FL learners for several reasons, the most important being the fact that by using idioms learners communicate in FL in a native-like manner. We also explained what FL students need to know about idioms (the meaning, appropriate use, values and feelings idioms convey, etc.).

Suggestions have subsequently been made concerning the teaching sequence of idioms. In short, it has been argued that compositionality or analysability and grammaticality are adopted as criteria for the selection of idioms to be taught first to FL learners. Furthermore, it has been suggested that FL teachers encourage their students to adopt a 'word-by-word' parsing strategy in the process of understanding compositional or analysable idioms (i.e. idioms whose parts carry identifiable idiomatic meanings).

230

Finally, five activities for teaching idioms in the FL classroom have been presented. We have tried, among other things, to show a way of applying the results of linguistic theory to language teaching: our teaching suggestions have mainly been based on parts of the descriptive analysis of idioms presented in Chapters 2 and 3. Clearly, there is still much to be learned about idioms and even more to be said about the teaching of idioms in the foreign language classroom.

Notes

1   One should not confuse conventionality with compositionality. Conventionality, which characterizes all idioms, is their property of having meanings that cannot be predicted from the *literal* meanings of their constituents. On the other hand, compositionality, which characterizes some idioms, is their property of having *idiomatic* meanings that can be analysed into different components, each of which is distributed to a different idiom part; see Nunberg *et al.* (1994: 498).

2   For the distinction between idiomatic combinations (or analysable idioms) and idiomatic phrases (or non-analysable idioms) see Gibbs *et al.* (1989) and Nunberg *et al.* (1994).

3   Metonymy is the use of one word to denote another (for example, in the expression *lend a hand*, we use the word *hand* to denote the literal word *help*).

4   See also Gibbs (1987: 569) who claims that 'acquiring conversational competence in a language requires an understanding of the use and meanings of idiomatic expressions'.

5   This suggestion is based: (1) on the findings of an experimental study performed by Gibbs *et al.* (1989), which demonstrated that people comprehend analysable idioms faster than they do non-analysable idioms, and (2) on the findings of an experiment performed by the author, Zevgoli (1996), which demonstrated that MGFL learners learn as a rule analysable idioms prior to non-analysable ones.

6   This suggestion is based: (1) on van der Linden's (1993) assumption that compositional analysis will be preferred (at least at some point) in the learning process; (2) on the findings of an experiment performed by Schraw *et al.* (1988), which demonstrated that in the process of understanding an idiomatic or literal statement, non-natives are more likely to use a 'word-by-word' parsing strategy, and (3) on the findings of an experiment performed by the author, Zevgoli (1996), which demonstrated that MGFL learners who adopt the 'word-by-word' analysis when processing analysable idioms have greater success in learning them.

References

Adam, A. (1992) *The Semantic Categorization of Idiomatic Expressions*, Athens: Seagull Publications.

Benson, M. (1985) 'Collocations and Idioms', in R. Ilson (ed.) *Dictionaries, Lexicography and Language Learning*, Oxford: Pergamon Press and The British Council.

Cuttler, A. (1982) 'Idioms: The Colder the Older', in *Linguistic Inquiry* 13: 317–320.

Dimitriou, A. (1995) *Lexiko Neoellinismon. Idiotismi, stereotipes metafores, paromiosis, lexis ke frasis* [in Greek] [trans. *Dictionary of Neohellenisms. Idioms, Fixed Metaphors, Similes, Words and Phrases*]. Athina: Ekdosis Grigori.

Fillmore, C. J., Kay, P. and O'Connor, M. C. (1988) 'Regularity and Idiomaticity in Grammatical Constructions: The Case of *Let Alone*', *Language* 63/3: 501–538.

Fotopoulou, A. (1989) 'Taxinomisi ton stereotypon protaseon sta Nea Ellinika –

morfosintaktiki analisi ton protaseon me ena antikimeno' [in Greek] [trans. 'Classification of Fixed Sentences in Modern Greek – Morphosyntactic Analysis of Sentences with one Object'], in *Meletes gia tin Elliniki Glossa. {Studies for Greek Language}. Proceedings of the 9th Annual Meeting of the Department of Linguistics, Faculty of Philosophy, Aristotelian University of Thessaloniki*, 18–20 April 1988, 223–241.

Fotopoulou, A. (1993) 'Une classification des phrases à compléments figés en Grec Moderne', Thèse de Doctorat de Linguistique. Université Paris VIII.

Fraser, B. (1970) 'Idioms Within a Transformational Grammar', *Foundations of Language* 6: 22–42.

Gibbs, W. R. (1987) 'Linguistic Factors in Children's Understanding of Idioms', *Journal of Child Language* 14: 569–586.

Gibbs, W. R. (1992) 'What Do Idioms Really Mean?', *Journal of Memory and Language* 31: 485–506.

Gibbs, W. R. and Gonzales, G. (1985) 'Syntactic Frozenness in Processing and Remembering Idioms', *Cognition* 20: 243–259.

Gibbs, W. R., Nayak, N. P. and Cutting, C. (1989) 'How to Kick the Bucket and Not Decompose: Analyzability and Idiom Processing', *Journal of Memory and Language* 28: 576–593.

Irujo, S. (1986) 'Don't Put Your Leg in Your Mouth: Transfer in the Acquisition of Idioms in a Second Language', *TESOL Quarterly* 20: 287–304.

Itoh, M. (1995) 'Bemerkungen zum Phraseologischen Wörterbuch für Ausländer', *Gengobunka Ronshu {Studies in Languages and Cultures}* 40: 109–122.

Lattey, E. (1986) 'Pragmatic Classification of Idioms as an Aid for the Language Learner', *IRAL* XXIV/3: 217–233.

Longman Dictionary of English Idioms (1979) Thomas Hill Long, Editorial Director. Harlow and London: Longman.

MacCarthy, M. and O'Dell, F. (1994) *English Vocabulary in Use*, Cambridge: Cambridge University Press.

Nunberg, G., Sag, I. A. and Wasow, T. (1994) 'Idioms', *Language* 70/3: 491–538.

Reagan, R. T. (1987) 'The Syntax of English Idioms: Can the Dog be Put on?', *Journal of Psycholinguistic Research* 16/5: 417–441.

Schraw, G., Trathen, W., Reynolds, R. E. and Lapan, R. T. (1988) 'Preferences for Idioms: Restrictions Due to Lexicalization and Familiarity', *Journal of Psycholinguistic Research* 17/3: 413–424.

Zevgoli, S. (1996) 'Idioms: A Theoretical and Teaching Approach', unpublished MA thesis, University of Athens.

Further reading

Antoniadou, C. and Kaltsas P. (1994) *Lexikon der idiomatischen Redewendungen. Griechisch-Deutsch/Deutsch-Griechisch*, Köln: Romiosini-Vanias.

Chomsky, N. (1980) *Rules and Representations*, New York: Columbia University Press.

Delicostopoulos, A. (1993) *Greek Idioms*, Athens: Efstathiadis Group.

Demiri-Prodromidou, E., Nikolaidou-Nestora, D. and Trifona-Antonopoulou, N. (1983) *I glossa ton idiotismon ke ton ekfraseon* [in Greek][trans. *The Language of Idioms and Expressions*]. Thessaloniki: University Studio Press.

Irujo, S. (1993) 'Steering Clear: Avoidance in the Production of Idioms', *IRAL* XXXI/3: 205–219.

Markantonatos, G. (1994) *Lexiko archeon, vizantinon kai logion fraseon tis Neas Ellinikis* [in Greek] [trans. *Dictionary of Ancient, Byzantine and Learned Phrases of Modern Greek*]. Athina: Gutenberg.

Sellner, A. (1980) *Latein im Alltag*, Wiesbaden: Vma-Verlag.

van der Linden, E. J. (1993) *A Categorial Computational Theory of Idioms*, Utrecht: OTS Dissertation Series.

INDEX